Marketing Research for Managers

Third edition

Sunny Crouch MA, FCIM, FTS, DipMRS
Matthew Housden DipM, MCIM, MIDM

BUTTERWORTH
HEINEMANN

AMSTERDAM BOSTON HEIDELBERG LONDON NEW YORK OXFORD
PARIS SAN DIEGO SAN FRANCISCO SINGAPORE SYDNEY TOKYO

Butterworth-Heinemann
An imprint of Elsevier
Linacre House, Jordan Hill, Oxford OX2 8DP
200 Wheeler Road, Burlington, MA 01803

First published 1984
Second edition 1996
Reprinted 1998, 1999
Third edition 2003

British Library Cataloguing in Publication Data
Crouch, Sunny
   Marketing research for managers. – 3rd ed.
   1. Marketing research   2. Research – Management
   I. Title   II. Housden, Matthew
   658.8'3

Library of Congress Cataloguing in Publication Data
Crouch, Sunny.
   Marketing research for managers/Sunny Crouch, Matthew Housden. – 3rd ed.
   p. cm
   Includes bibliographical references and index.
   ISBN 0 7506 5453 8 (alk. paper)
   1. Marketing research.   I. Housden, Matthew.   II. Title.

   HF5415.2.C78 2003
   658.8'3–dc21   2003045189

ISBN 0 7506 5453 8

For information on all Butterworth-Heinemann publications
visit our website at www.bh.com

Composition by Genesis Typesetting Limited, Rochester, Kent
Printed and bound in Great Britain by Biddles Limited

Contents

Foreword

Market researchers and managers using market research will be glad to see the publication of a second edition of Sunny Crouch's *Marketing Research for Managers*. This is a very useful handbook for those both with little and great experience in market research.

It is not a book for 'experts', it is a book for managers. Having said that, it runs the qualitative research spectrum from 'thematic apperception tests' to 'psychodrama', and quantitative research from sampling, through questionnaire construction and analysis to its use. This is a practical book, an easy read and very useful for any manager with responsibility for purchasing, conducting, using and getting good value from market research.

Think how much grief for research agencies would be saved by having clients who had read *Marketing Research for Managers*!

Professor Robert M. Worcester
Chairman, MORI

Preface

Preface to the second edition

Many books on marketing research are aimed at developing the technical expertise of the intending or actual research practitioner. This book is aimed at those who are intending or actual managers with a need to *use* research rather than practise it. It owes its existence to managers from many different areas of industry who attended courses on marketing research run by Sunny Crouch. They demonstrated the need for a book aimed squarely at the individual who wishes to use marketing research as an aid to better decision making. Their feedback suggested that the material was both relevant and useful.

These managers attended courses to learn more about marketing research because they believed, as we do, that the more a manager knows about this management tool, then the more effective he or she can be in using it. The book therefore aims to develop a better informed approach to the use of marketing research as an aid to decision making, by giving an insight into how marketing research is carried out. No previous knowledge of the subject by the reader is assumed, and the areas that normally receive a statistical treatment are explained here without the use of statistics.

Our warm good wishes to all readers for their success in improving their managerial ability through applying the techniques of marketing research described in the following pages.

Preface to the third edition

Since this book first appeared in 1984, the marketing research industry has undergone a transformation. The industry has consolidated and concentrated. The turnover of the leading research organizations mirrors that of the largest marketing services organizations. These organizations have internationalized, largely following their client base, so that in almost every country in the world there is access to professional, locally sensitive but internationally aware, research companies.

Progress in computing technology has changed the way the world does business. The cost of processing power and data storage has plummeted. The wholesale introduction of computers and their application in survey design, analysis and reporting has changed the skills required of the researcher. Surveys can be designed, administered, analysed and reported upon using integrated survey management systems that take some of the laborious data processing work out of marketing research.

In addition, the businesses served by marketing research have changed. In the second edition, in 1996, we talked for the first time about the move towards a global economy, and highlighted the skills required to administer pan-national research. We mentioned the word 'online' about five times! Today the global economy is bound together by the Internet and its graphical interface the World Wide Web. Online business, despite the hiccups of the dot-com boom and bust, is now a significant part of the global economy and marketing research has had to develop new techniques to deliver the same quality of intelligence to support the integration of online marketing within business strategy. This edition devotes a whole chapter to research in online businesses, in addition to numerous references throughout the text.

These developments have coincided with introduction of customer relationship management (CRM) systems and the use of databases to store data generated by these systems. The development of interactive relationships with prospects and customers means that organizations have access to more information than ever before. Tesco is now able to produce thousands of viable segmentation models from the vast amount of data that it captures on its customers. If a Clubcard user starts buying nappies, Tesco knows that the customer has undergone a profound, life-changing event. The volume of transactional data gathered by most customer-facing organizations is incredible. It has even been said that marketing research is under threat because of it. Of course, nothing is further from the truth. Data gathered in this way is incomplete, in that it does not record all customer transactions. These systems gather data only from a self-selecting sample. This data simply records what, in a self-selected situation, people have done: not why they behaved in the way they did, nor what the market as a whole may be doing. The transactional data gathered supports (and only in part) the tactical management of the business. It does not contribute fully to corporate strategy and the overall direction of the business.

The codes of conduct that have underpinned the marketing research industry become more and more important. People realize the value of their personal data and are becoming reluctant to give up this data unless they are reassured of the ethical position of the organizations they are talking to. Trust lies at the heart of any relationship and the giving up of personal data demands a great deal of trust on behalf of the respondent and equally a great deal of integrity on behalf of the recipient of this data. Since the second edition this has become enshrined in law as a result of the implementation of the 1998 Data Protection Act.

The knowledge economy cannot be based simply upon data. It must be based upon intelligent and methodologically sound data capture and analysis. These are the skills that marketing research is built upon and that *Marketing Research for Managers* introduces to its readers.

Sunny Crouch
Matthew Housden

Acknowledgements

We acknowledge the support of many readers of the first two editions of this book, whose requests have resulted in this third edition. In presenting the book, our thanks are due to all those who assisted in its preparation, and who will recognize their influence in these pages.

The authors continue to be indebted to Lionel Gordon and Nigel Spackman for their significant contributions to Chapters 9 and 11, respectively. Emma Adams and Simon Coles of the University of Greenwich were largely responsible for updating the secondary desk research section of Chapter 4, Mike Roe of Research International assisted with the International chapter, and Jane Robinson of MORI provided examples of agency questionnaires, checkbacks and other documentation. David Walker, Director of New Media Research at Research International, provided online examples. Thanks are due also to Joyce Moore and Margaret Khan for typing the original manuscript, and to James Burckhardt, now of VNU business publications, who helped with the online sections of the third edition. Combined with his work on the second edition he has made a significant contribution to the book.

Sunny Crouch, author of the first edition, is indebted to Matthew Housden, without whom neither the second nor third edition would have appeared.

We continue to acknowledge with gratitude the constant support and encouragement we received from our respective partners, Bill Crouch and Katherine Housden, and from our families.

We wish our readers well as they use *Marketing Research for Managers* and hope the book will continue to be helpful as an easy-to-read introduction to this fascinating subject.

1 Introducing marketing research

1.1 Introduction

Politicians look anxiously at the results of political polls, as they indicate the standing of the party in the country and the standing of its leader. They show what issues are most significant to the electorate and which seats are most likely to be marginal at the next election. Focus group politics has reached such an extent that politicians react to the results of polls by putting extra effort into areas of the country that are marginal, i.e. where additional effort to market the attractions of the party are more likely to pay off. When the polls say the leader is unpopular, pressure is put on the leader to change stance so as to become more popular; when negative reaction to a leader is strong and sustained, the party thinks of appointing a new one; which issues to push as the main planks of the party's electoral platform are also influenced or even determined by the polls. There is no point in strongly pursuing issues about which the electorate is unconcerned – that is not the most effective way to win votes.

In a rare display of humility one of the world's best known companies admitted to making a big mistake when it unveiled a secret weapon to take on the UK's supermarket chains. McDonald's, the hamburger chain that brought the world the Big Mac, thought it had another winner when it announced the new product to its expectant staff.

Enter the McPloughmans, a cheese, pickle and salad sandwich. A spokesman told the conference that the McPloughmans was designed to compete with supermarkets in the cold sandwich market. Instead of applauding this marketing innovation however, staff were unimpressed. Mr Preston admitted: 'If we had done our homework we would have found that our customers didn't want the product and our staff were embarrassed even to have to say McPloughmans let alone to have to sell it to our customers.'

In a masterly piece of understatement he added that if the company had carried out market research 'We would have found that this was not a highly desirable product.'

When it did a survey of customer attitudes it found even more shocks in store. 'Customers', he said 'told McDonald's they were loud, brash, American, successful, complacent, uncaring, insensitive, disciplinarian, insincere, suspicious and arrogant.' He said, 'We thought we knew about service. Get the order in the customer's hands in 60 seconds – that was service. Not according to our customers. They wanted warmth, helpfulness, time to think, friendliness and advice. What they told us we were giving was horrifying.

What we had failed to see was that our customers were now veterans in the quick service market and their expectations had gone through the roof.' The McPloughmans market test was restricted to central London and short-lived. Only now, more than three years after the sandwich debacle and the first customer survey, has the company felt confident enough to reveal the episode.

The spokesman said the research had been a turning point for McDonald's in the UK, which had led to a radical change in its business approach. Rather than relying on gut feeling that it knew what customers wanted, the company had developed a fact-based approach to planning.

Financial Times

Coke's World Cup tactics

In the 1998 World Cup, Coke produced just one global ad called 'For the fans' by Wieden and Kennedy. Although it is using a re-edited version of that ad this time round, it is augmenting it with around 25 commercials specifically tailored to local markets.

'We simply haven't been this diverse before,' says Nastia Orkina, who as group marketing services manager is responsible for co-ordinating Coca-Cola's pan-European World Cup efforts. 'Previously it's been a big event advertisement and some vertical stuff. McCann–Erickson in the US would probably have done everything. But this time the national ads have been created after researching local attitudes to the World Cup around the world. . . .

Football fans have changed. Compared with just 12 years ago global audiences are far more sophisticated. They are far more likely to include women and children and fans are far more likely to have travelled abroad, appreciating the cross-cultural power of the tournament. Brand advertising must reflect this. . . .

Coca-Cola's management also believes that local marketers, frustrated for so long by Atlanta's "one-size-fits-all" outlook have been liberated by the approach and are becoming much more productive. . . .'

In a world of diversity, and increasing distrust of US cultural hegemony, one suspects the soft drinks giant has finally got its football strategy right.

And whoever brings home the Jules Rimet trophy, it is likely that a certain team in red and white will be celebrating.

Marketing Week

New Brand of the Year winner: Shell UK Oil Products

Fierce price competition between supermarkets and reducing marketing support from the major petroleum corporations have led many motorists to view petrol as a commodity.

In response, Shell made use of market research that identified several different customer segments to create Shell Optimax. Launched last year, it targeted real drivers willing to pay a premium for a fuel offering extra performance and engine protection.

With the technical task of product development, came the need to re-engage customers emotionally. Optimax was given a £5m budget, with the advertising's innovative fish theme rigorously adopted in all through the line communications.

By the end of 2002 Shell Optimax will have been rolled out to all 11,000 Shell service stations. It has met and exceeded all its targets, including winning new customers, upgrading existing customers, and improving margins. The payback period of 15 months was achieved in eight.

The Marketing Society Awards 2002

Customer Insight winner: Walkers Snack Products

Walkers' dilemma was how to meet a 7% sales growth target in a mature and static snacks market.

An extensive segmentation study established that the 'snacking occasion' was the biggest factor in determining what was bought. The biggest was in-home evening snacking where Walkers was underrepresented.

Doritos Dippas was an existing product that had enjoyed only modest success, but seemed to fit this brief perfectly. It was different from daytime snacks, a bit of a treat and adult oriented.

Qualitative research then identified the most motivating positioning as a 'chill out' snack to share with friends after a hard day's work. So was born 'Friendchips'.

Advertising ran from April 26 to May 26. In the immediate aftermath sales of Dippas Big Bags rose 76% year on year. Thanks to the halo effect, total sales of Doritos rose 13.2%, contributing almost 40% of the required uplift in sales across all brands.

The strategy was copied in other markets, including Belgium, Holland and Spain.

The Marketing Society Awards 2002

Shoppers shun shoddy websites

Badly designed websites are damaging the prospects of firms doing business via the web.

Research carried out by Abbey National has revealed that when people have one bad experience online they tend to regard all websites the same way.

It suggests that websites that take too long to load, are hard to navigate, bombard consumers with pop-up adverts and force them to register to get access to services could be stunting the growth of e-commerce in the UK.

Instead customers prefer websites that have a consistent look, are easy to navigate and do not try to cram too much information on one page.

Website woe

A seven month research project by Abbey National and market analysis firm Taylor Nelson Sofres has revealed that companies have only 20 seconds to grab the attention of web shoppers.

During that 20 seconds, consumers must be able to see a page that has almost loaded, that is relevant to their needs and looks easy to navigate. If it does none of these consumers will look elsewhere. . . .

Internal research by Abbey National has shown that web customers are 57% more profitable than the average customer and have 50% more products such as loans, than those who avoid the Internet. Now 20% of the Abbey National's personal loan business comes via the web.

'It's got real critical mass and has a real impact on the cost of the cost base of the whole organisation', . . . Abbey National has rebuilt its website around many of the principles revealed in the research project.

http://news.bbc.co.uk/hi/english/sci/tech/newsid_
1842000/1842142.stm

Victor won't believe it – how young Meldrews are now

Britain's 'grumpy old sods' have got younger, according to a poll of social attitudes which nails the middle-aged as the nation's new champion grumps and complainers.

Years of relentless grind in the country with Europe's longest working hours has soured the 35–54-year-olds into 'premature pensioners', claims the MORI Social Research Institute, which labels them as 'consistently cross and fed up'.

Christening them the 'Meldrews', after Victor in the television series *One Foot in the Grave*, MORI says that the middle-aged have learned to grumble early partly because their seniors are enjoying a relatively good life. Over-55s are generally looking forward to decent pensions, while the middle-aged fear that theirs will be worth less than they had been led to believe.

Rising house prices are also seen as ruling out hopes of a comfortable retirement move, while the media's traditional portrayal of the world as completely disastrous is now accessible and round the clock.

'The 35s–54s are of prime working age in the most over-worked nation in Europe, bearing the brunt of commuting on ever more congested roads or using public transport that is still a byword for failure', says the report. 'There is rising dissatisfaction, made worse by the feeling that things used to be more challenging and interesting when they were younger.'

Some of those in the category are already adopting Meldrew as their icon, including the Rev Chris Morris of Rawdon, Leeds, whose parish magazine describes his 'holiday in hell among fractious, nasty and downright vulgar' younger revellers at Disneyland Paris. 'As I walked round in my Victor Meldrew T-shirt, featuring a mugshot of Victor with the caption Miserable Sod, I was astounded at the rudeness of the crowds.'

The survey finds the Meldrews are undeferential and unwilling to trust 'those in charge'.

The institute's director, Ben Page, said: 'What's interesting about this group is that they seemed to be more rebellious when they were growing up. They witnessed social change in the 1970s and 80s. They are the age group who were most likely to see strikes and demonstrations as signs of a healthy social system. They're not staid, they're just disillusioned about a lot of things.'

The survey's data may be weakened, however, by another characteristic of Meldrews – a dislike of being asked questions by nosey, and probably younger, opinion pollsters. This may account for such bleak responses from former youthful radicals as 95% believing that the NHS will not improve and 90% saying the same about education (compared with 72% of under-34s and 71% of over-55s on both subjects).

Martin Wainwright, 2002, *The Guardian*

1.2 Who needs marketing research?

What these stories have in common is that they illustrate the value of good, up-to-date and detailed market information in making marketing decisions vital to the success of an organization. This holds equally true whether the 'marketing' is concerned with national or local government, fast-moving or durable consumer goods, retail outlets, industrial organizations, dot-com businesses, services or charities and other non-profit-making bodies.

'Marketing' is defined by the Chartered Institute of Marketing as, 'the management process for identifying, anticipating and satisfying customer requirements profitably'. This definition identifies the crucial part marketing research has to play in designing and implementing an effective marketing strategy. Marketing research provides the mechanism for identifying and anticipating customer requirements and for measuring whether customers are satisfied by these product offerings. For non-profit-making organizations the concept of 'profitability', used in the definition, may be translated to 'using resources optimally, i.e. gaining maximum customer satisfaction through the most effective deployment of resources'. The American Marketing Association replaces 'profitably' with the phrase 'to create mutually satisfactory exchanges'. It is in this sense that marketing and marketing research have just as important a contribution to make in the public sector and in non-profit-making organizations as in the private sector.

That customer requirements must be paramount in the thinking of any organization providing goods or services is illustrated by the anecdotes with which this chapter begins and by the demise or declining profitability of companies whose goods do not meet current market requirements. There was no better illustration of this than the failure of dot-com businesses, which failed to ask the simplest question required for success in business: 'where is the customer in all this?'

The problem for many organizations has been their lack of a mechanism for detecting change in the marketplace. Markets have become more competitive and the pace of technology has accelerated change. Gordon Moore at Intel Corporation has speculated that the processing power of computers doubles every 18 months. Organizations can no longer afford to rely simply on making a good product for it to be successful in the long term. It now has to meet a real market need in a very precise way and perhaps for a shorter period than in the past. This book is about the mechanisms available to managers to make organizations more responsive to their markets. This is the province of marketing research and hence the title of this book. It is properly termed 'marketing research' rather than the more colloquial 'market research' because it is research applied not only to measuring and identifying markets and market characteristics, but also to measuring the effectiveness of marketing decision making. Research can be applied in deciding which products or services to offer, what their characteristics should be, the price at which they should be sold, the distribution channels through which the product should be sold, and the selling and advertising messages that are likely to have greatest appeal. Others would argue that there is a separate type of research called 'social research' which is used by those in local and national government in making decisions about the provision of social services. A further debate is concerned with whether research in industrial and service markets differs from research in consumer markets.

This book takes the view that the techniques developed for marketing research in the cause of more effective marketing of fast-moving consumer goods have proved themselves equally effective in contributing to decision making about resource allocation and market response in all consumer markets, in political and social policy decision making, in industrially based markets and in service-based markets. The techniques introduced here are generally applicable in all of those areas, although there may be differences of detail and emphasis in their application.

1.3 Who should read this book?

The belief that the research techniques dealt with in this book can, and indeed should, be used by anyone with responsibility for resource allocation, whether they are in product-based, service-based or public-sector-based organizations, accounts for the fact that its main emphasis is to offer an outline of the process and techniques of research, which the reader can apply to his or her own management situation. The aim is to aid managers in generating reliable research-based information, to enable them to judge the reliability of research produced for them, and to give them a basis for knowing when and when not to use research.

It is assumed that the managers who will find the book most useful are those who wish to use marketing research as one of the tools of a manager's trade and not those whose major responsibility is for the design or conduct of research. For this reason, the emphasis is on the manager's role in commissioning and controlling, rather than conducting, research.

Nevertheless, the manager who must do his or her own research should find considerable guidance to help in that task. It is not suggested that reading this book is all the preparation necessary for carrying out a 'do-it-yourself' research project. In fact, the reaction of most managers learning something about marketing research for the first time is, 'I didn't realize this was such a technical area!' That is not to say, of course, that the manager who is interested will never be able to carry out all or some of the parts of a research project, but simply that the aims of this book are to offer an introduction to and an appreciation of the subject. For the majority of managers this is all they require. Those who wish to take their interest further after reading the book should consider following the suggestions given at the end of the book in Chapter 17, Where do you go from here?

Although this book is aimed primarily at the practising manager with a need to use marketing research, it provides worthwhile reading for those studying business subjects. It is particularly appropriate as background reading on marketing research for those studying general management, or specific areas of it such as marketing or finance. Students following business or management courses will also find the book useful as an introduction to their studies. These include:

- MBA or Masters Degrees in business and marketing
- undergraduate degrees
- HNDs or HNCs
- BTEC awards
- NVQs in business-related areas
- professional courses and the Certificate in E-marketing, Certificate in CRM, Certificate in Direct Marketing and the Interactive and Direct Marketing Diploma run by the Institute of Direct Marketing
- Certificate, Advanced Certificate or Diploma and professional courses of the Chartered Institute of Marketing
- courses run by the Market Research Society, including the Diploma of the Market Research Society and the Certificate in Market Research
- Communications, Advertising and Marketing (CAM) Foundation courses.

1.4 What does the book cover?

Marketing research involves the analysis of marketing problems and techniques for the collection and interpretation of data to assist in developing the most appropriate solutions to them. It is concerned with identifying and anticipating customer requirements and measuring satisfaction with the products and services made available. It also produces data used in assessing and controlling the performance of an organization.

This book aims to assist managers in any organization to become more informed and therefore more effective research users. It introduces marketing research by explaining:

- What marketing research is (Chapter 1)
- Why an organization needs it (Chapter 2)
- What research can be carried out within an organization (Chapter 3)
- What research data is already available (Chapter 4)

- How research surveys are carried out (Chapters 5–10)
- How research services are bought (Chapter 11)
- How research is used (Chapters 12–16)
- How to build on this introduction (Chapter 17).

Four features of the text will be particularly useful for new users of research. First, Chapter 4, on 'off-the-peg' research, guides the reader to sources of readily available information, both online and offline. Two sources not readily identifiable by the new user are listed: syndicated research services and omnibus surveys. These listings form a helpful ready reference for those unfamiliar with the research industry. Second, another highly practical feature of the book is the Research Users' Guides and their accompanying Notes, which form the basis of Chapter 16. The objective here is for the new research user, having read the book, to be able to consult the Guides and say, 'With this problem, I have these research possibilities for finding an answer'. Third, the book reviews two major changes in business. With the increasing internationalization of business, Chapter 15 looks at international marketing research and each chapter, where appropriate, illustrates the overseas' dimension of the area under discussion. Fourth, Chapter 14 looks at marketing research and the Internet, and the role of web-based research and database systems is incorporated where relevant throughout the text.

Any technical terms not already covered in the text are explained in the accompanying notes and all research suggestions are referenced to sections of the text where explanations appear. Because this is an introductory text, it makes no assumptions of background knowledge. Chapter 7, which deals with sampling, and Chapter 10, which deals with statistical analysis of data, deliberately avoid the use of statistical formulae. The aim is to give the research user an understanding of what statistical approaches can do to data, and why they are useful and sometimes essential. Research users do not need to be statistically competent themselves, but they should appreciate the contribution that statisticians can make in the design and analysis of research surveys. It is not the aim of this book to teach basic statistics, so those wishing to carry out the statistical manipulations described will need to have, or to acquire, the appropriate statistical expertise. Chapter 17 suggests some books to assist in this. It also suggests other ways in which those wishing to develop further their interest and expertise in marketing research after reading this introductory text, can do so.

1.5 Using this book

Each chapter is prefaced by a detailed list of contents and ends with a summary. The summary should be consulted for an overview of chapter content and the chapter contents pages will identify where particular topics are dealt with. This format will help those who wish to consult the book on particular topics. For those who want to introduce themselves to marketing research by reading the book right through, it will probably be helpful to read the summary of each chapter before reading the chapter. This will prepare the reader with a framework for what is to be found in the chapter and learning will be further reinforced when the summary is read again at the conclusion of the chapter.

Throughout the book, the word 'product' can be taken as meaning 'product or service'. Services are amenable to research in the same way that products are and can be considered the 'products' of the companies that provide them. Finally, readers are asked to take the words 'him' and 'he' also to mean 'her' and 'she' and vice versa throughout.

2 Getting started

2.1 Introduction

All kinds of organizations use, and need to use, marketing research techniques. The traditional and still the biggest users are the large, fast-moving consumer goods companies. Increasingly, marketing research is being applied by smaller organizations, by manufacturers of consumer-durable products and by suppliers of services. In recent years it has been applied by non-profit-making organizations such as charities, churches, official bodies and government departments at both local and national levels. Despite diversity in the aims and objectives of these widely differing organizations, what they have in common is the need to make decisions about the allocation of resources so as to be as effective and efficient as possible in achieving their goals. Resource allocation decisions can be improved by the acquisition of accurate, relevant and timely data and it is this which market research seeks to produce.

Getting started as a research user begins by answering three questions:

1 What does the organization need research for?
2 What types of research data are there?
3 How can the organization obtain the research it needs?

2.2 What does the organization need research for?

Being able to define precisely what marketing research can and should be doing for the organization is the first step in achieving it. One way of doing this is to reflect on the organization as a whole and decide what are its most pressing problems. The answers below were given by delegates to the Chartered Institute of Marketing's introductory course on market research:

From an insurance company: 'We are a relatively small company in a growing but fiercely competitive business. We need research information to decide how to increase business from our existing customers and attract business from new customers.'

From a whisky manufacturer: 'Whisky sales generally are in decline. We need research to evaluate the potential of new whisky-based drink products. We also need research to select the most effective packaging to maximize product sales in an increasingly self-service market.'

From an integrated communications agency: 'Our clients look to us for advice on internet advertising strategy. How can research help in providing more effective online advertising?'

From a carpet manufacturer: 'The floor-coverings market is in decline and over-supplied. We know that design is an important factor in the market. We need research to help us maintain and improve market share by identifying appealing designs and appropriate target markets for them.'

From a business-to-business IT supplier: 'We are now able to develop an enhanced range of systems integration products. We need research to discover whether a viable market exists for these possible products, who our potential customers might be and whether they know our name and would buy from us.'

From a dot-com business: 'We have never done market research and have no way of evaluating the performance of our site in the market as a whole. Our cash is running out. We need to return to our backers with a solid business plan. We need research to establish our market size and share and the potential in our customer base. What customers should we be attracting and what products will they require and how can we generate revenue from our site?'

Another approach to defining why a particular organization needs marketing research is to consider the range of uses to which it is already put by other organizations. Six main areas are listed here.

2.2.1 Corporate planning

Research is used in corporate planning in order to make decisions about what goals the organization as a whole should have in both the short and long term:

- forecasting the size of future demand and trends for the organization's products
- identifying markets to be served
- assessing the strengths and weaknesses of the organization both absolutely and relative to its competitors
- measuring dissatisfaction and needs in relevant market segments
- industry/market structure and composition
- competitors
- market share and profitability analysis
- highlighting significant marketing problems
- stimulating research for new or exploitation of existing products and markets by planned policies
- evaluating corporate identity and image
- selecting companies for acquisition or divestment.

2.2.2 Market planning

Research is used in market planning to keep the firm in touch with its markets and customers:

- identifying, measuring and describing key market segments' behaviour and attitudes

- assessing relative profitability of markets over time
- analysis and interpretation of general market data
- placing individual customer transactions, perhaps recorded on a database, in the broader market context
- analysing business potential of new market areas
- identifying and evaluating markets for products and new products for markets
- measuring consumer preferences
- identifying changes in competitive activity
- sales forecasting.

2.2.3 Product planning (including packaging and service levels)

Research is used in making and adapting products to fulfil customer wants more accurately and profitably:

- generating and screening new product ideas and modifications
- concept testing
- product testing and retesting for acceptance and improvement
- testing formulation and presentation preferences
- packaging tests
- product name tests
- test marketing
- comparative testing against competitive products
- product elimination or product line simplification
- evaluating perceived service quality.

2.2.4 Promotional planning

Research is concerned with the selection and effectiveness of persuasive communications. Three main areas are identified below.

Communications planning

- developing sustainable brand positioning
- message design and content
- development of the creative proposition
- developing effective multimedia communications strategies
- pre-testing ads
- post-testing ads, e.g. awareness, comprehension, recall, attitude shifts, brand-switching effects
- advertising weight-of-expenditure tests
- media planning: evaluation, selection and scheduling
- advertising effectiveness
- public relations and publicity effects on awareness/attitude
- sponsorship effectiveness
- exhibition effectiveness research

- direct marketing effectiveness research
- assessing the impact of integration
- developing the optimum communications mix.

Sales force planning

- determining sales areas
- testing alternative selling techniques and messages
- setting sales targets
- evaluating sales performance
- evaluating sales compensation system
- making selling operations more productive.

2.2.5 Distribution planning

Research is concerned with the formulation and effectiveness of distribution policy:

- channel selection
- distribution cost analysis
- wholesaler/retailer margin
- incentive policy
- dealer sales levels
- distribution achievement
- penetration levels
- stock checks
- inventory policy.

2.2.6 Price planning

Research may be used as one of the inputs to price selection.

Analysis of what problems the organization has and the uses to which research can be put will establish whether there is a need for research. The next step is to know what types of research information can be acquired.

2.3 What types of research data are there?

The collection of research data may be a *continuous* or an occasional (*ad hoc*) activity of the organization. Usually there is a requirement for both approaches since they serve different purposes. Some information is already available and simply needs organizing if it exists within the organization (*internal*), or tracking down if it is available from elsewhere (*external*). These activities form the basis of *desk* or *secondary research*. Other data needs collecting and organizing before being usable and this is known as *field* or *primary research*. In many markets (mainly for consumers) standardized services carry out primary research on a regular basis and the user simply buys the information produced or the service offered. The term *'off-the-peg'* is used to describe this type of research. Most organizations will also have a need for data more specifically geared to particular problems and this is when *'made-to-measure'* research is required.

These six types of research are introduced briefly in this section and discussed more fully in later chapters.

2.3.1 Continuous research

Any type of research may be organized so as to produce a continuous stream of data. The advantage of doing this is that it indicates trends and measures performance over time. This is particularly valuable in enabling an organization to spot changes in the market before they present themselves as serious problems. Continuous research forms an important element in any management information system and will probably include desk research and off-the-peg services. It is essential for the organization which aspires to being proactive (making things happen) rather than reactive (responding to things that have already happened).

2.3.2 Ad hoc research

One-off research studies meet those information needs that cannot be identified in advance. A new opportunity may suddenly arise or some specific problem may need to be explored. Any type of research data may be used in an ad hoc study, but it is most likely to include made-to-measure research surveys.

2.3.3 Desk research

Desk research is so called because it refers to that type of research data that can be acquired and worked upon mainly by sitting at a desk. That is to say, it is research data that already exists, having been produced for some other purpose and by some other person or body. It is commonly referred to as secondary research because the user is the secondary user of the data and this term reflects the fact that it may not precisely meet the user's need or be sufficiently recent to be wholly useful. Desk research makes a good starting point for any research programme because it is generally quick and cheap to acquire and can be readily assimilated. Whilst a scan of appropriate desk research sources may not produce an answer to the problem, it is extremely useful as a familiarization process and in generating ideas that will help to formulate and refine any subsequent collation of primary data. The range of electronic services that have been developed, including the Internet, extends the ability of the desk researcher to assess a wide range of material.

Internal desk research

This represents the most sensible starting point for any organization and should come before going to great lengths of resource expenditure in acquiring data from outside. Much useful information is generated within all organizations simply in the course of their normal operations. A simple analysis of accounting data should indicate what is being sold, in what sizes, at what prices and to whom in terms of geographical area, type of customer and so on. The key to making use of internal desk research sources is to organize the collection of data in such a way that it is not only useful but also usable. The acquisition, organization and use of internal desk research sources are explored more fully in Chapter 3.

External desk research

The Government is a major producer of all kinds of external research data. Useful external research data is also available from trade organizations, trade publications, banks and many official bodies. The acquisition and use of external desk research data are discussed in Chapter 4.

Both internal and external desk research have limitations for decision makers. Internal desk research by definition is data confined to the organization's own activities. External desk research is characteristically of too general a nature to be applicable to any specific problem. Field research can overcome both of these limitations.

2.3.4 Field research

Field research is so called because it is concerned with the generation and collection of original data from the field of operation or intended operation for the organization. The organization determines exactly what information is necessary and from whom it needs the information and then sets about acquiring it. The data is thus specific to the purpose for which it has been acquired, and this is often called primary research for this reason. There are two kinds of primary research: off-the-peg services and made-to-measure research.

Off-the-peg research services

A considerable amount of original research data is continually being generated by research organizations. Either the data itself or the system for collecting it may be bought off-the-peg. The two types of service referred to are *syndicated research* and *omnibus research*.

Syndicated research

This is research that is of value to a number of organizations, but would be too expensive for any of them to collect individually. The data is therefore collected by a research agency and sold to all the organizations who have a use for it. This system means that effectively the organizations are sharing the costs of generating the kind of original data they require.

Omnibus research

When regular surveys of defined populations are being undertaken, the agency doing the fieldwork may make the service available as an 'omnibus' for other organizations to climb aboard. They may each add a few questions to a questionnaire. Those questions and the answers to them will be entirely confidential to the paying client, but the respondents will find themselves answering a large number of questions about a possibly diverse range of subjects. Omnibus research represents an extremely cost-effective half-way house between carrying out a complete survey and buying the data already available from external desk research or syndicated services. It gives the advantage of being able to specify the questions without having to bear all the costs of fieldwork.

Acquisition of both types of off-the-peg research service is discussed in Chapter 4.

Made-to-measure research surveys

This is the type of research that most often comes to mind when managers think of using research. The organization wishing to acquire information decides what it wants to know and usually briefs a research agency to acquire the information for it. The research agency will design an appropriate questionnaire, organize a team of professional interviewers to collect answers to the questions, process the data when the questionnaires are returned to the office and produce a report for the original client. The whole survey and its findings are guaranteed confidential to the organization that pays for them. This is the most expensive type of research data but should also be the most useful, since, like other custom-built items, it is designed and produced to meet exactly the requirements of the buyer. The design of made-to-measure research surveys is discussed in Chapter 5. Technical aspects of data collection, sampling questionnaire design, fieldwork, and data analysis and interpretation are discussed in Chapters 6–10, respectively.

2.4 How can the organization obtain the research it needs?

2.4.1 Getting started

In getting started as a research user, a logical progression would be to begin with internal and external desk research. Any appropriate syndicated services should be considered for purchase, or a few basic market data questions included on an omnibus survey. These research activities are likely to be followed by made-to-measure field research. This order of research progression reflects the order in which data are most readily acquired. It demands an increasing level of commitment in terms of cost and personnel involved in acquiring the data, and an increasing level of research knowledge in both acquiring and using the data. The quality of information acquired also increases as one moves from one type of research to the next and this may be in step with the ability of the user to handle it.

2.4.2 Resources

An essential point to note for the organization wishing to use research data is that it is equally important to set up an adequate system for using the data when it has been acquired, as it is to set up the information acquisition system in the first place. As with all other services that an organization needs, acquiring useful and usable information costs both time and money. If research is to be used effectively by the organization, then someone within it must be designated as having a primary responsibility for this and be given time to discharge that responsibility properly. The acquisition of market research data costs money and the information product is like most other products, in that the organization seriously wanting to get started on using market research intelligently must be prepared to devote adequate personnel and financial resources to it. Some suggestions follow as to what this might mean in practice.

Internal desk research

Requirements may range from a paper-based filing system, through a local area networked database, to a multinational marketing information system. All will require certain levels of support, ranging from an assistant clipping press reports, through scanning or manual input of data, to a fully integrated systems support department. All of these systems will require managers capable of using the information generated.

External desk research

This requires a research assistant within the organization to identify sources, acquire, organize and report on the data. Increasingly, although not necessarily, this information will be accessed online through various computer-based systems. Alternatively, a specialist desk research organization may be used. In this case, the main resource requirement on the client organization is that of money to pay for it. There is a vast array of specialist desk research agencies whose skills may usefully be bought in. They are often used by industrial organizations for whom desk research usually represents a more important aspect of their overall research programme and by all organizations who wish to operate a cost-effective research programme.

Off-the-peg field research

This requires an executive with a need for such a service, the ability to identify appropriate sources and money to pay for the services available.

Made-to-measure field research

This requires an executive within the organization with responsibility for defining the need for research and briefing and commissioning a research agency to conduct it. Money is needed to pay for the technical expertise of a research agency.

Some research can be carried out by executives within a user organization. Exploratory interviews in industrial or trade research and postal surveys are the most commonly used do-it-yourself research methods because they are possible and practical. However, the fact that they are apparently easy to do means that, as in do-it-yourself in many other areas, a great deal of bad workmanship can result! If an organization does plan to do its own marketing research then the executives concerned will need to know rather more about it than could possibly be covered in a short introductory book such as this. Suggestions for improving personal research expertise are offered in Chapter 17.

Research techniques almost always commissioned from research agencies are those involving large-scale interviewing or telephone research surveys, because these require more routine time and staff than most organizations are likely to wish to handle, or are able to do, cost effectively. Group discussions and consumer depth interviews are normally also commissioned from research agencies since they require specialist expertise for successful application and interpretation.

2.5 Summary

Any organization is likely to have a need to use marketing research in making resource allocation decisions. The first step is to define precisely why the research is needed, and some examples and suggestions about research applications are given. The next step is to realize what types of research data are available, and six types of research are introduced: continuous research, ad hoc research, internal and external desk research, off-the-peg and made-to-measure field research. Finally, the organization needs a method for getting started and appropriate resources for the acquisition of research data, and these are discussed.

3 Marketing research begins at home

3.1 Introduction

Many organizations make judgements, prepare plans and reach decisions with little or no contribution from formal marketing research. This chapter indicates ways in which organization of data readily available from sources within the firm can produce information of great practical relevance. The purpose of an internal information system is to produce a continuous stream of data which can:

- measure current performance
- identify the characteristics of current performance
- establish a baseline for change
- form a basis for comparison: over time, over an industry, etc.
- suggest a basis for resource allocation: geographical, profitability, product, etc.
- indicate trends
- monitor and track performance
- signal change
- provide an early warning detection system
- form a basis for operating control systems
- highlight performance problem areas
- provide information resources
- indicate areas for further research.

The aims of an internal information system are to keep the organization informed about its own performance, to enable the organization to anticipate change in its own competitive and technological environment, and to provide a guideline to focus and monitor company effort.

3.2 What can be done at home?

For all organizations the marketing research budget available is limited. It therefore makes sense to begin by making use of data that is already available. This has the advantage of being quick and relatively cheap to obtain, in addition to being private to the organization and highly relevant and specific to its products, markets and performance.

The following examples illustrate the major categories for research that begins at home.

3.2.1 Data produced in the normal course of running the organization

> A builders' merchant based in a small market town in the south and serving a wide area of the south of England was considering opening a second branch as a result of the success of the established operation. The problem was to decide where to site the new branch so as to increase sales rather than switch them from one branch to the other. Possibilities were five conurbations within 50 miles of the home branch. The decision was made by undertaking a detailed analysis of transactions on the database. Invoice records indicated where current customers were based. Factors were taken into account in order to estimate the potential demand in the areas under review, together with an analysis of the likely impact on the current operation of transferring trade to another location.

This example involved the analysis of sales records. Other data that may be useful in making decisions about the more effective and efficient running of an organization could include production records, distribution statistics or cost data.

3.2.2 Data acquired through personal contacts

> The sales representative of a savoury snacks manufacturer was visiting ANUGA, a major trade fair for the food industry in Cologne. In conversation with a major distributor of grocery products in Germany he was told that there could be an opportunity for the export of his company's unique range of adult-oriented exotic snack products. During the course of the trade fair he explored this idea further with other distributors and retailers and the idea was greeted positively. On return to the UK, he filed his report and met with the international marketing manager. A pan-European research project was commissioned with the support of the DTI. Ten months later the first export orders for the snacks were processed. The company has now carved a profitable European niche for its products.

As this example illustrates, information picked up during the normal course of work by sales representatives, by attendance of executives at conferences and meetings, and by customer suggestions and complaints, made either direct to the firm or via the medium of its retailer and distributor network, can be of value if the organization responds appropriately.

3.2.3 Accumulated research information

> A vinyl manufacturer was planning to launch a new material for covering furnishings. The material had the appearance and feel qualities of cloth combined with the durability and washability of vinyl. The manufacturer felt that there must be a strong market for this material which combined the advantages of both cloth and vinyl. Some years previously the company had launched a floor covering material that had been unsuccessful. Research into the reasons for failure indicated certain areas of pre-market preparation and launch activity which had contributed to the downfall of the product. One of the executives involved in the launch of the new furnishing product remembered to look up the old research report on the floor-covering failure. The information contained in it was extremely useful to the company in ensuring the same mistakes were not repeated and where lessons could be learned they were applied in the approach to launching the new furnishing material.

This example illustrates how a library or database of past research projects and marketing information held by the organization can enable it to learn from past experience and so improve performance.

3.2.4 Decision support systems

> The marketing manager of a charity began to compare monthly giving from the various segments of its market against the forecasts prepared at the beginning of the financial year. Working on the computer she discovered that overall revenue was slightly down against forecasts. Further enquiry showed that while the donations from most segments were holding up against forecast revenue there was a substantial shortfall in the level of giving from the corporate sector. She asked the computer to break down these figures by geographical location and discovered that the major area of shortfall was in the London and South East region. Comparing advertising levels with industry trends she noticed that recently her direct competitors had increased advertising spend and had begun to target this spend towards the corporate sector. A search on other variables showed that there had been little or no change in the dynamics of the market, and other key success factors had remained constant. She resolved to meet with her marketing team the following afternoon to begin to frame a response to this particular problem.

This example shows how the impact of database and statistical software has enabled managers to conduct significant analysis of their market relatively quickly and to frame an appropriate strategic or tactical response. The ability to support hunches or qualitative information with 'hard' evidence is a useful addition to the manager's range of skills. The appropriate software and hardware needed to run relevant analyses are readily available to almost every company in cost-effective form.

3.3 What goes into an internal information system?

Together, the four types of data illustrated can provide an internal desk research information system. This is a system that produces useful and usable information through organized methods for collecting, storing, retrieving, manipulating and reporting on data available from within the firm. The first category of data illustrated is called 'operating data' because it is produced as a result of the operation of the organization. The second data category is called 'market intelligence' because it refers to intelligence information acquired by individuals who work for the organization as a result of the personal contacts they make. Market intelligence differs from marketing research by being less systematic or representative in the selection of sources from which information is acquired. The third category is accumulated research and marketing information, and this forms the basis for setting up an internal 'information library' or database. The last category, decision support systems, enables managers to add meaning to data through the use of computer-generated analysis.

These four aspects of an internal desk research information system are discussed in the following sections.

3.3.1 Operating data

It is perhaps surprising that many companies start by commissioning outside marketing research before organizing an internal desk research system. An entirely human reason is that it is often easier to commission an outside research agency than to persuade heads of functional departments, such as accounting and production, to produce records in a form that is of value in marketing decision making.

An earthenware manufacturer made a range of tableware such as plates, cups and saucers, together with a range of earthenware mugs. Having been very successful it was keen to open a second factory. The decision it had to make was how much of the new capacity should be devoted to the tableware and how much to mugs. The first piece of information required was to know what proportion each of these lines currently contributed to turnover and

profit. Unfortunately the company's accounting system only produced customer invoices indicating a final cash figure. Customers
of different sizes were given different discounts but these were not
shown on invoices. Prices had changed several times during
previous years but goods supplied were not itemized. No records of
production output or breakages were kept. Any goods remaining at
the end of the week were taken away by jobbers, with only a cash
value being recorded. As a result, the company had no internal data
on which to base its decision.

The increased availability and affordability of computer power mean that
basic record-keeping, which would have provided this company with at
least a starting point for its decision-making problem, is easy to undertake.
The first step is for the researcher to co-operate with relevant departments
to ensure that appropriate records are instituted and maintained. The critical
factor in this lies in the design of record-keeping in such a way that the
statistics produced will be useful both to the originating department and to
the management decision maker.

Decisions about the form in which the data is to be produced, its
frequency of production and how it is to be analysed need to be taken before
the system is initiated. No data-collection system should be initiated that
will not or cannot be used; this is the quickest way to ensure that any
research will never be taken seriously by the organization. One factor to be
taken into account may be the period for record-keeping; for example, it is
common to use four-week periods (i.e. 13 'months' per year). These are more
comparable than calendar months, having the same number of working
days in them on a year-on-year basis, which is often not the case when
calendar months are used. Differences in the number of working days can
account for apparent sales fluctuations in year-on-year monthly comparisons. Examples of data useful to the researcher include sales statistics,
expenditure and operations statistics.

Sales statistics

These may be produced in a number of ways, each of which can provide
useful data for management. Analysis may be by:

(a) *Product/product group*: this will indicate the importance of each product
and item in the product range and their effect on overall company
performance. Trend data will indicate which products are growing and
which declining.

(b) *Markets*: this is particularly important in industrial organizations where
analysis of sales data by industrial application of the customer, perhaps
using standard industrial classification (SIC), will indicate the relative
importance of and trends in the company's major markets.

(c) *Outlets*: analysis of sales by different types of outlet will indicate their relative importance, trends and the mix, for demand analysis. The growth of direct selling through mail order and other direct methods, and the changing role of the garage forecourt as an outlet for products from food and drink to audio and video products, indicate a possible need for reorganization of the marketing effort to take account of different outlets for the company's products. Statistics on the regional distribution of outlets may have implications for other marketing activity such as sales and advertising, or for reorganizing the regional outlet pattern.

(d) *Geographical area*: there are several ways in which sales may be analysed with respect to geographical area. The area may be a country for multinational firms, or a sales area or representative territory when selling is an important element of the marketing effort. Television regions are used for analysis of consumer markets in which television advertising is used. Another advantage of using television regions is that much published data, including that on media audiences and readership, is available based on these areas. Using area analysis, performance can be measured and compared, and decreases and increases spotted and dealt with. Implications for regional allocation of marketing effort can be drawn from this analysis.

(e) *Time period*: analysis of sales by time will enable seasonal demand to be plotted and therefore anticipated. Year-on-year or period-on-period performance comparisons can be made.

(f) *Size of orders*: calculation of average orders by size may have a direct bearing on profit per order handled. This could form the basis of calculation of standard delivery charges or standard levels of costs to be applied to small orders. Incentives for order size to be increased may result from this type of analysis.

These examples give some indication of the value in simply analysing sales records in a variety of ways, each of which might have different decision-making implications. But sales statistics are only half the story when the company's real concern is about profit, and so a second set of data records is needed to complete the picture.

Expenditure statistics

Analysis of expenditure statistics can be used to calculate relationships between areas of expenditure and income. This will increase efficiency by leading to optimization of various areas of expenditure against incomes. Expenditures on promotion, sales force, packaging, dispatch or invoicing may be analysed against sales turnover to indicate the relationship between sales and each particular area. This may be used in budget allocation for future years. The same expenditure statistics may be analysed against specific product sales. This forms a basis for the allocation of effort devoted to, or overheads charged against, these products. A more fruitful analysis may be to look at items of expenditure against profit generated. A sales promotion may have produced an increase in sales turnover yet have had no effect at all on profit. The upheaval that sales promotion activity often produces in the production system may be shown to be not worthwhile with this kind of analysis.

Another area of expenditure that can be analysed in a number of ways is advertising expenditure. This may be set against product sales revenue, profit, market type or media. The outcome of any of these analyses will prove useful for planning decisions. Analysis of advertising expenditure by product line may well indicate that most advertising expenditure goes on the biggest product lines. This is particularly likely to be the case when advertising budgets are determined on the basis of sales turnover. Analysis may indicate that greater response could be achieved by diverting advertising expenditure to smaller products with greater potential for growth. This could result in a greater increase in overall profitability.

The value of all these kinds of expenditure analysis lies in the fact that they can increase the organization's perception of what relationships do and do not exist between various types of expenditure and resultant effects in the marketplace.

Operations statistics

Statistical records may be kept on almost any area of an organization's operations and analysis of them can indicate more profitable, more efficient or more effective ways of operating. For example:

(a) **Stock-control statistics:** stock records will indicate stocks being run down or built up, or bottlenecks in the stock system. Calculations can be made of the amount of investment tied up in stock at any particular moment. In these days when additional profits are hard to achieve by increasing sales volume, analysis of stock inefficiencies may make a greater contribution to an overall increase in profitability than any marketing activity. The use of computerized stock control systems has, for example, led to the development of just-in-time delivery, which saves warehousing costs.

(b) **Transport statistics:** maintenance of statistics on mileage, routes covered, vehicle maintenance, and so on, will often lead to more economical handling of a company's distribution and transport system.

All the statistics referred to above should be maintained continuously over time to enable the manager to spot trends or change in the marketplace and deal with it. The danger inherent in producing any continuous set of data is the problem of information overload. This occurs when the system is generating more information than the manager can cope with reading, never mind responding to. Some mechanism needs to be introduced to ensure that the manager's attention is only attracted to continuous sets of statistics when some action may be necessary. This normally involves setting out guidelines that will enable management to identify and deal with only exceptional developments. An instruction may be given that the manager will only see the information personally if the data for any period are outside an operating norm of, say, 10 per cent either way. Statistics based on operations data are also used to calculate operating ratios. These are an input to assessing the efficiencies of different operations and to allocating budgets for those areas.

The data generated from operating data can prove extremely useful in indicating the performance of the company. They are not appropriate for identifying changes in the external environment that do not necessarily show themselves in company sales. It is for this reason that the market intelligence system is particularly useful.

3.3.2 Market intelligence

Sources of information such as personal contacts, feedback from trade and from the sales force, informal store checks and monitoring of competitors' products and publicity efforts can be extremely useful. A problem with market intelligence data lies in the procedures used for its collection. Most sales people would argue, often rightly, that additional paperwork reduces profitable selling time. At the same time, sales people are often keen to be the first to report some new marketplace development to the organization, particularly when they know that the organization will respond to that information.

This indicates two key points in the design of market intelligence systems. First, the reporting system should be as straightforward as possible and organized in such a way as to minimize the work involved in reporting. Second, the response mechanism to market intelligence must be good and known to the individuals making reports. The single most important incentive for members of the organization to participate in a market intelligence system is the feeling that it is of real value to the organization and does feed into its decision-making procedure.

Exactly what type of market intelligence may be of value will depend on the organization, but the most commonly collected areas are those already referred to. In the more rapidly developing industries it may be that the market intelligence system would be extended to include feedback from conferences and meetings at which new technology is discussed. Other avenues for feedback of useful snippets of intelligence gathered through personal contact may suggest themselves.

3.3.3 Information library

When an organization is starting to develop a research facility, it makes sense to ensure that the research undertaken is classified and stored in such a way that it is usable and utilized on future occasions. Reading past research studies can be extremely helpful in indicating ways in which the same problem may be approached again. If it is appropriate to update the piece of research then the earlier work will serve as a benchmark, indicating change. If an earlier piece of research used a method that did not work very well, then the same mistakes can be avoided. There is usually something to learn about where the product is now in the marketplace from an analysis of how it got there.

Sometimes, new executives in the organization will come up with ideas that have been tried before. Although there may be good reasons for believing that something that did not work on some occasion in the past may or may not work now, it is nevertheless of value for the new executive to know when something has been tried before and what the circumstances and outcomes were. With the fairly rapid turnover of both marketing and market research executives, it is useful to have a retrieval system operating so that when a manager intends to carry out some research in a particular area there is ready access to any previous work done. It is still common practice in organizations that copies of research reports are kept only by the managers who have commissioned them and are not readily accessible by, or made available to, other members of the same organization. The establishment of an information library will rectify this. All information can now be computer based, with new information scanned into the company's information database. This can be made accessible to a remote sales force or marketing agents through the company's intranet or extranet.

Another important function for the information library will be to acquire, store and retrieve external desk research information, and this is discussed in Chapter 4.

3.3.4 Customer relationship management systems, data warehouses and data mining

The increased sophistication of computer software and hardware means that managers in even the smallest companies can have reasonably cheap access to high-powered and technical means of managing information generated by the company. An increasingly important area has been in the management of information relating to customer contact so as to improve the relationship between an organization and its customers. This is known as customer relationship management (CRM).

CRM aims to produce a single view of the customer across all potential touchpoints. For example, a car manufacturer may have been contacted by a prospective customer through its website, its call centre and its dealership network. The ability to recognize the reality of customer behaviour is crucial to the successful development and deepening of the relationship between the customer and the organization. If a customer has made an enquiry online they may reasonably expect an organization's retail branches to know this and to recognize the fact.

CRM systems implementation has been one of the major growth areas in the consulting world. Companies have invested huge sums of money in aligning the diverse sources of information and information systems within organizations. For example, General Motors recently was reported to have invested US $1 billion in CRM systems, to manage relationships with its customers more effectively and more efficiently. It is estimated that General Motors removed US $1 billion of costs from its businesses.

In its broader application CRM works to manage customer contacts and the experience that a customer enjoys with the organization.

There are many suppliers of CRM systems and they range from the highly expensive to the relatively inexpensive. Leading players in this market include Oracle, SAP and Siebel. Systems will vary according to the complexity of the task they are designed to manage. A company with multinational operations and multiple product lines and customer groups will need a more complex and generally more expensive system.

A major issue for companies lies in turning the vast amounts of data they hold on their marketplace into actionable intelligence. Data-rich organizations should enjoy a competitive advantage, but in reality this is not always the case. Tesco is an example of a company that has access to a vast warehouse of data about its customers and recently it has made significant strides in its marketplace. Sainsbury's too has developed a loyalty programme which in turn generates a vast amount of data about its customers. This has not stopped their share of the grocery market falling. The ability to interrogate data warehouses for relevant meaning is known as data mining, and it is clear that the ability to mine the data for key customer insight remains the key to success.

Other areas of research can add further value to this raw data and place the information about customers in its broader market context.

Between 1996 and 2001 the call-centre market in the UK grew at 40 per cent per year. If a company's internal records showed growth of 20 per cent, this might have been considered a success. However, in the broader market context this company would have been falling well behind its competitors.

Data has been called 'the raw material of management'. Today's marketing executives have access to an ever greater array of information and the tools with which to analyse this historic data. Analysis software can allow marketers to make relationships between apparently unrelated data to produce valuable approaches to market and customer segmentation. With the development of the Internet the opportunity exists for real-time information gathering, analysis and marketing decisions.

The growth of the knowledge economy and of knowledge management in organizations has had several effects. Perhaps the most obvious of these is information overload. In certain markets there is so much data about the market that it is often hard to analyse the information in such a way as to produce actionable intelligence.

The reliance on data gathered from customers' behaviour is often at the expense of the broader customer or market context.

A small UK-based breakfast cereals company ran a series of tests for a communications programme. The results were excellent and showed that on rollout the company could achieve a 2 per cent uplift in its share of the sector. In reality, rollout achieved a far smaller and temporary uplift in sales. The sector is mature; value growth is negligible. The market is dominated by some of the world's most aggressive food marketers, including Kellogg, Quaker, Nestlé and General Mills, who were not likely to sit back and let this happen. In conjunction with the major retail multiples they launched an aggressive sales promotion campaign that effectively undermined the activity of the smaller company. The research had successfully measured an effective communications programme, but had failed to take the wider market context of aggressive competitors into account.

It should not be forgotten that a database is a sample of the company's customers, not a sample of the market as a whole. Very often this sample itself is a sample only of those who choose to respond to the company's communications. Transactional data about our customers describes what they *have* done, not what they *will* do. It certainly does not explain WHY they behaved in the way they did.

While it is possible to point to the weaknesses of the use of company databases, there is no doubt that careful management and analysis of this type of data has added significantly to the marketer's toolkit. In combination, databases and marketing research techniques provide a powerful planning approach to strategy and its implementation.

3.4 Summary

Organizations are typically rich in information, which would prove extremely useful if it were available in an appropriate form or collected, evaluated and retrievable in some systematic way. This forms the basis of an internal information system to produce continuous data which can be used for measuring, evaluating, monitoring and controlling performance. Four aspects of an information system are discussed: operating data, which flows from normal operating procedures; marketing intelligence, which derives from normal personal contacts; the establishment of an information database, which stores past research data and acquires new information from external desk research sources; and a CRM or other decision-support system which enables the effective and creative analysis of the information held by an organization.

4 'Off-the-peg' research

4.1 Introduction

Much of the data that a company new to marketing research might want to know is probably already in existence; for example, overall market size and structure, basic information about consumer spending patterns, major social and economic trends, financial data about customer firms, competitor firms, supplier firms, markets that are growing and profitable, and markets that are in decline or unprofitable. The purpose of this chapter is to give some indication of the vast amount of 'off-the-peg' data available and an idea about where to locate the appropriate 'pegs'. Once an organization has identified relevant data sources, it will often continue to obtain updating information and, as discussed in the last chapter, this forms an important part of the organization's information system.

There are four main types of 'off-the-peg' research:

- research using the very large body of already published data, usually termed 'secondary desk research'
- research using data available from regular market surveys, often referred to as 'syndicated research'
- research in which the method of data collection is syndicated, but the data is not, called 'omnibus research'
- research making use of specialist expertise available from research agencies, discussed under the heading 'specialist research services'.

This chapter considers each type of research in turn. Inevitably, some of the specific information sources and contact data given in this chapter will become outdated. Nevertheless, the general points made and major sources indicated will prove of value as a guide to off-the-peg research for some years beyond the date of publication.

4.2 Secondary desk research

4.2.1 Introduction

Secondary desk research uses data that has already been published by someone else, at some other time, usually for some other reason than the present researcher has in mind. The researcher is therefore a secondary user of already existing data that can be obtained and worked on at a desk. This accounts for its name. The most characteristic thing about secondary data is the vast amount available. Because it is so overwhelming in its range and sometimes complexity, secondary data is often overlooked as a source of research information. However, much specific data is already in existence on markets and companies operating within those markets. It is therefore worthwhile for any organization to make a determined attempt to identify relevant secondary data sources for its own use.

Secondary data is relatively quick and cheap to obtain. The growth of online services has made the process of accessing secondary data at home and overseas much faster. Once obtained, a regular series of updating information can usually be acquired from the same source. At best, secondary data may provide the complete answer to a problem. At worst, it will save the organization time and money when it comes to carrying out a piece of original field research. Secondary data can define the scope or direction of a field research survey and indicate the type and range of information that may be available. It will suggest possible methods for carrying out field research. If past research surveys are found to be too out of date for the information to be of current relevance, they may at least provide a basis for comparison with a new survey replicating the method. This will give the added insight of market change data to an original piece of research. There are several possible sources of published secondary data.

Online desk research

The amount of information on the Internet, an electronically interconnected network of computers, is incredible. Estimates put the number of pages of information at over 1 billion, but the real figure is almost certainly much higher. Finding a way through this mine of information is perhaps the hardest part. To access the information you need a computer giving access to the Internet (and its graphical interface the World Wide Web); while you are searching you need to be electronically connected, i.e. 'online'.

Surfing, i.e. randomly following links within websites, can generate fruitful information. However, a basic knowledge of online searching techniques can save time, money and a great deal of frustration.

The starting point for any search online if the website address is unknown is to use the search engines or subject directories that are freely available to 'browsers', or people who are searching the web.

There is a difference between a search engine and a directory. Search engines use 'spiders' or 'robots' to go out and search the web and create a database of sites that is then matched against the search terms or keywords entered by the browser in the search engine. There is a great deal of variation in how these search engines work and the same search entered in different engines will generate very different results. It is worth experimenting to find the search engine that suits your needs. Equally, if one engine is not producing the results you require, then try another.

The best search engines from the researcher's point of view are those that are fast, comprehensive and free of undue influence, i.e. sponsors cannot ensure that their site appears in the top ten through the payment of fees to the search engine provider.

Some of the best general search engines are:

Alta Vista: www.altavista.com.
Google: www.google.com
Hotbot: www.hotbot.lycos.com
Infoseek: www.infoseek.go.com
Northern Light: www.northernlight.com

Directories are compiled lists or indexes of websites that are reviewed and often rated by compilers. This can remove the randomness of searches through engines, which may be an advantage in the early stages of exploratory research. It is possible to pay web directory compilers to ensure that a site occurs early in the list of sites presented as the result of a search. Again, care needs to be exercised here.

Examples of subject directories include:

LookSmart: www.looksmart.com
Lycos: www.lycos.com
Yahoo: www.yahoo.com

Searching online

With the vast amount of material available to the online researcher it is clear that any help in clarifying search criteria and reducing the number of sites to be viewed is vital. As with any marketing research problem, online searching is the outcome of a process that involves careful definition of the research problem and the concepts, terms and definitions contained within it.

Work at this stage can save a great deal of time spent searching broad concepts definitions within what is essentially a huge database of information. Search engines will tend to index every word of text, so a search for information on The Post Office on Google produces over three million results and includes results from all those sites that include the word post or office. Some search engines, including Google, have the facility to search specific elements of a site, for example on just the web address, known in the industry as the URL (uniform resource locator). This clearly cuts down on the number of search results but equally may exclude the company or product the browser is searching for. For example, at the time of writing the URL for I Can't Believe It's Not Butter in the USA is www.tasteyoulove.com and Cif bathroom cleaner in the UK is www.blokeinabath.com

Many search engines allow what are known as Boolean logic operators to help the browser to search the web. The simplest of these operators are the words 'and', 'not' and 'or'. Others may allow the use of proximity operators, such as 'followed by' or 'near'. These can help to refine search terms and produce more relevant results. For example, Procter and Gamble and UK not USA would refine search terms on this global company.

Others may have advanced search facilities which employ Boolean operators in a more user-friendly format. The use of Google's advanced search feature reduces the number of results for The Post Office to under 200,000. This works by filtering out all results for the separate words Post and Office and all references to the combined terms in other countries.

Most engines and directories have online help and browsers should familiarize themselves with the complexities of the software to take full advantage of their services.

4.2.2 Sources

Government published data

The Government publishes a great deal of information regularly on almost every aspect of British economic, social, commercial and financial life. It is always worth checking what government information is available for any research problem under review, since this will probably be the cheapest way of obtaining the information. Only the costs of publication are covered by the price of the various reports produced. Much information is available online. The European Union (EU) also provides a statistical service, Eurostat, which is useful in that it compares data from the member countries. The United Nations (UN) also has a statistical service organized around its departments.

Information can be obtained through the following websites:

www.ukonline.gov.uk
www.statistics.gov.uk
www.europe.org.uk
www.europa.eu.int/comm/eurostat/
www.cec.org.uk
www.un.org

Trade published data

When information is required about a particular trade or industry there are five sources likely to have appropriate information available in published form.

(a) *Trade associations.* These exist in almost every industry, e.g. the Brewers' Society, the Road Dressers' Association and the British Audio Dealers' Association. These associations often carry an information library staffed by appropriate information specialists.

CBD (Tel: 020 8650 7745, Fax: 020 8650 0768, E-mail: cbdresearch@cbdresearch.freeserve.co.uk) in Beckenham publishes directories of British and European trade associations which identify those associations providing a statistical or information service.

Web address: www.cbdresearch.com

(b) *Trade press*. Any trade of sufficient size will have newspapers and journals relevant to that industry. These will maintain a database of past items of news and information that can be consulted to provide a background picture for any particular aspect under consideration. Access to archives online is often free of charge or at low cost.

The Advertisers' Annual, published by Hollis Publishing Limited, Harlequinn House, High Street, Teddington, Middlesex TW11 8EL (Tel: 020 8977 7711, Fax: 020 8977 1133, E-mail: orders@hollis-pr.co.uk), is a useful source of information on the trade (and general) press in the UK with a less comprehensive world-wide cover.

Web address: www.hollis-pr.co.uk

For the international press, *Willings Press Guide* is an alternative source both online and offline (Tel: 0870 736 0015).

Web address: www.willings press.com

(c) *Professional institutes*. Most professions have an institute, e.g. the Chartered Institute of Marketing, the Market Research Society (MRS), the Law Society and the Chartered Management Institute. These organizations are equipped with libraries and online information services available to members. They also provide a service to non-members of those professions, usually for a small charge.

Web addresses:

www.cim.co.uk
www.mrs.org.uk
www.lawsoc.org.uk
www.managers.org.uk

For exporters, a starting point may be the Institute of Export, Export House, 64 Clifton Street, London (Tel: 020 7247 9812, Fax: 020 7377 5343, E-mail: institute@export.co.uk) or the British Exporters' Association, London (Tel: 020 7222 5419, Fax: 020 7799 2468, E-mail: bexamail@aol.com).

Institute of Export website: www.export.co.uk

British Exporters' Association website: www.bexa.co.uk

Other Institutes are listed in the CBD directory.

(d) *Chambers of Commerce*. If the problem under consideration refers to a particular regional location, contact with the local chamber of commerce for the area may prove particularly useful. The quality of information available from chambers of commerce varies, but the larger chambers provide quite comprehensive and relevant information on many aspects of business in their areas. International chambers of commerce may be of use in overseas research. Information can be obtained from the Association of British Chambers of Commerce, London (Tel: 020 7565 2000).

British Chambers of Commerce website: www.chamberonline.co.uk

The World Chambers Federation is based at 38 Cours Albert 1er, Paris 75008, France (Tel: +33 49 53 29 44, Fax: +33 1 49 53 30 79)

Web address: www.iccwbo.org

(e) *Regulatory bodies and pressure groups.* Certain sectors are subject to the attention of regulatory bodies, e.g. the telecommunications industry in the UK is monitored by OFTEL. Other industries are the focus of pressure group interest, e.g. the tobacco industry and Action on Smoking and Health (ASH), and those industries with broader environmental impact may be monitored by, for example, Friends of the Earth or Greenpeace. These organizations may be able to help with information on certain subjects and many operate world-wide.

Financial institutions' published data

Regular reports on various industries, their performance, their financial record, trends and potential are produced by the major banks, consultancies, accountancy practices and financial and industry analysts within brokerages. These should always be checked to see whether a relevant report has recently been published. If the company is international then the report will generally cover performance in all its markets. Industry analysts are very useful sources of information and the information departments of the major trading banks are extremely well resourced.

Press published data

The 'quality' press and the financial and economic press regularly produce industrial and commercial reports on various aspects of business, companies and products. Information services of the relevant press can be contacted to discover whether a report is available. Searches are available online for most quality newspapers. This may involve registering and paying a fee. Many libraries hold back copies of newspapers on CD-ROM and this can help the free search for relevant articles.

Some of the best press websites include:

- *The Financial Times*: www.FT.com
- *The Guardian*: www.guardian.co.uk
- *Wall Street Journal*: www.wsj.com
- *The Economist*: www.economist.com
- *Far Eastern Economic Review*: www.feer.com

Most of these sites allow a limited search of the archive but may charge for this service.

Foreign and international organizations' published data

All the data referred to as being available for the UK are available for most well-developed economies through a variety of foreign and international data-producing organizations. The Trade Partners Information Centre in London maintains a library of world statistics and this provides an excellent starting point for any investigation into overseas markets. This is a free service.

Trade Partners UK Information Centre, Kingsgate House, 66–74 Victoria Street, London SE1E 6SW (Tel: 020 7215 5444, Fax: 020 7215 4231)
Web address: www.tradepartners.gov.uk

Specialist organizations

A number of specialized organizations exists to provide the type of desk research information obtainable through published sources. These organizations act as 'information brokers' and produce relevant abstracts and digests of statistics and news items to subscribers. An example would be the London Business School Information Service (Tel: 020 7723 3404, Fax: 020 7706 1897, E-mail infoserve@london.edu)
Web address: www.bestofbiz.com/bis/

Online aggregators

Online databases enable enquiries to be made of multiple data sources via the Internet. The best online services are those of information aggregators. Aggregators obtain 'content' from a number of different suppliers and make it accessible through a single website. These include general databases, e.g. Profound, Hoovers and Lexis Nexis, and specialist services, e.g. the World Advertising Research Centre (WARC). These often contain translations from a range of international publications. They generally charge for the most useful information and library access may be more appropriate for the researcher working on a small budget.

Web addresses:

www.profound.com
www.hoovers.com
www.lexis-nexis.com
www.warc.com

Other useful sites are listed below.

http://www.oecd.org

The Organization for Economic Co-operation and Development (OECD) has active relationships with over 70 countries, of which 30 are members, all assisting in supplying information on macroeconomics, statistics, trade, education, development, innovation and country reviews. There is a limited range of links to other useful websites.

http://www.business.com

A comprehensive business search engine covering over 25,000 industry, product and service subcategories. Partners include FT.com and Business

Week. This site has excellent links to other websites and relevant information.

http://www.asia-pacific.com

An extremely comprehensive website containing strategic business information on Asia and Pacific Rim countries, including book and journal listings coupled with expert critique from area specialists. This site has an excellent level of links to other useful websites.

http://www.businessdaily.com.au

A good-quality business news website with an Australasian predominance, giving in-depth coverage of key business news globally. It also has good links to other websites covering featured reviews and business news stories and to sites such as the *New York Times*.

http://www.europeanbusinessforum.com

An excellent online magazine that has critique from consultants, academics and industry leaders all focused on global management issues within a European context. This site has limited links to other websites owing to the forum nature of the site.

http://www.feer.com

The Far Eastern Economic Review is a website specific to Asia that covers mainly business news for the Asia region. This site has fairly limited additional links to other sites.

http://www.ilo.org

The International Labour Organization website, as part of the UN, seeks to promote international human and labour rights. This is a very extensive and informative site on all issues concerning human rights. It also has some excellent links to other relevant websites.

http://www.jetro.go.jp/top

The Japan External Trade Organization's website is wholly focused on providing information on the business climates of Japan and Asia, including advice on how to do business with Japanese companies. This site has excellent links to other relevant sites, including government ministries.

http://www.bubl.ac.uk/soc.html

The British Universities' Business Libraries site offers a comprehensive listing of books, authors and other research information on many topics, ranging from business theory to medicine. This site has extensive links to other relevant sites.

http://www.rba.co.uk/sources

This site is specific to business information sources on the web. It is a useful starting point for business research and has extensive links to other key relevant sites on the web.

http://news.ft.com

The Financial Times site is excellent for research and holds up-to-date critiques on all areas of business. It also has excellent links to other relevant business websites. This site is a must for any business information required.

http://www.meansbusiness.com

This site is a database of business text passages that have been stored and can then be grouped together by topic area so as to gain a variety of views from differing authors on the same subject area. This site does not offer many other links to other relevant sites.

http://www.ioma.com

The Institute of Management and Administration provides a subscription service for business and management information of all descriptions. It also offers some free research information and an online forum facility. This site has a number of good links to other sites.

http://harvardbusinessonline.hbsp.harvard.edu

The Harvard Business Online site offers a huge array of services based on the global business management arena. It includes the *Harvard Business Review* archive, and has a search facility that searches by article, journal and author of the publication or topic area. This site has limited links to other relevant sites.

http://www.fedworld.gov

This is a specialist site for American Government information; it is a comprehensive guide to most federal information required and offers excellent links to other relevant websites, including governmental bodies.

http://www.ceoexpress.com

An extremely comprehensive website with a massive business listings directory. Although it has an American bias it is still very useful and covers every area of commerce possible. The links to other relevant sites are excellent.

http://www.ukonline.gov.uk

This extensive site is a comprehensive guide to UK government information from citizenship to local authorities. This site also has an extensive list of other sites for further information, including all areas of government.

http://www.clickmt.com

The *Management Today* magazine's website offers some good critiques on current management issues and also offers a useful search-by-issue feature. The site has a reasonable number of links to other relevant sites.

http://www.managementfirst.com

This site is very extensive and covers all management areas, mainly on a pay-to-view basis. It has an extensive journal database that can be searched; however, only a limited number of other useful website links is given.

http://online.wsj.com

The news website of the *Wall Street Journal* is extensive and covers the global business remit, although in some areas a paid subscription mechanism is used. The site also has some useful links to other sites.

4.2.3 Finding the pegs

Generally speaking, for the beginner, the most difficult part of a desk research survey using secondary sources is actually beginning. This section will therefore concentrate on indicating some of the more general starting points for a desk research survey. Once the research survey is under way each source uncovered, or contact made, will generally lead on to the next. Following up these leads will provide the depth of information the researcher may need for any particular area of interest.

This is particularly the case with online searches. Online access has changed this area significantly and access to a vast range of sources is possible. The skill for the desk researcher is knowing where to look and being able to interrogate the data for accuracy, relevance and methodological competence. Data searches online may be frustrating as the most valuable data is often available only on a paid-for basis. It is still possible to use paper-based sources at libraries and government information centres to produce excellent desk research cheaply or free of charge.

The section that follows suggests various leads. It begins by indicating some of the sources available that list information sources and classify them. It goes on to suggest sources for some of the more commonly required types of information: about companies, about industries and about markets. It then comments on and identifies some government statistics. The section concludes with a list of some of the information services available to give help on data collection using secondary sources. The section includes information on international sources.

Where to start looking

This section includes lists of information sources and directories. Where available, telephone numbers, websites and e-mail addresses are included rather than postal addresses.

1 *Euromonitor*, London (Tel: 020 7251 8024, Fax: 020 7608 3149, E-mail: info@euromonitor.com). This is a useful starting point as a major publisher of guides to information sources. These include:

   • *China: A Directory and Source Book*
   • *Eastern Europe: A Directory and Source Book*
   • *International Marketing Data and Statistics*

- *Latin America: A Directory and Source Book*
- *World Database of Business Information Sources on the Internet*
- *World Directory of Business Information Libraries*
- *World Directory of Business Information Websites*
- *World Directory of Marketing Information Sources*
- *World Directory of Non Official Statistical Sources*
- *World Marketing Data and Statistics on the Internet*
- *Findex 2002: The World Wide Directory of Market Research, Reports, Studies and Survey* (a classified list of over 8400 market research studies covering 12 product sectors including a broad description of contents, price and contact details).

Web address: www.euromonitor.com

Other companies publish lists of market research reports, for example:

2 *Market Search Directory,* Marketsearch (Tel: 020 7495 1940, Fax: 020 7409 2557, E-mail: marketsearch@Execuplace.co.uk), is a list of 20,000 market research reports from 700 research companies world-wide.

Web address: www.marketsearch-dir.com

3 *Croners Executive Companion, Croners Office Companion*, London (Tel: 020 8547 3333, Fax: 020 8547 2638, E-mail: info@croner.cch.co.uk). This incorporates the A–Z of business information services and is a comprehensive and international listing of sources of business informa-tion which is regularly updated. This service is available online and offline. Online product subscriptions include a range of other services and a help-desk service.

Web address: www.croner.co.uk

4 www.web.idirect.com is a listing of online sources of business information.

5 www.europa.eu.int is an EU listing of information sources including links through to national newspapers and a range of other information sources.

6 *The Chartered Institute of Marketing*, Cookham (Tel: 01628 427500, Fax: 01628 427 499, E-mail: membership@cim.co.uk), has an extensive library and can help members with requests for information by e-mail and post. The website is a useful starting point.

Web address: www.cim.co.uk

7 *The Research Buyer's Guide* (annual), Market Research Society, London (Tel: 020 7490 4911, Fax: 020 7490 0608, E-mail: info@mrs.org.uk), provides a comprehensive list of organizations providing market research services in Great Britain and other useful information. The MRS website has a searchable directory of research organizations and comprehensive information on other aspects of the industry.

Web address: www.mrs.org.uk

8 *ESOMAR* (Tel: 00 31 20 664 21 41, Fax: 00 31 20 664 29 22, E-mail: e. mail@esomar.nl). For international market research organizations, the European Society for Marketing Research (ESOMAR) website is a useful resource. It has a fully searchable database of 1500 organizations world-wide, which subscribe to the ESOMAR ICC Code Of Marketing and Social Research. The site also has a range of other information, including a significant catalogue of publications and conference proceedings

Web address: www.esomar.nl

9 www.researchinfo.com lists research suppliers and has a range of research discussion groups and online tutorials to enhance skills in areas such as online surveys and palm pilot applications.

10 *The World Association for Public Opinion Research* (WAPOR) (Tel: 00 1 402 458 2030, Fax: 00 1 402 458 2038, E-mail: renaereis@gallup.com) is an American-based membership organization that looks at the individual within the profession. It has 400 members in 50 countries. Its website has a directory of members.

Web address: www.unl.edu/WAPOR/

Information about companies

This section includes sources of data about companies: their existence, location, type of business, ownership, performance, financial and commer-cial statistics.

1 *Companies House*, Cardiff (headquarters), and regional centres in Edin-burgh, Leeds, Manchester, Birmingham and London (Tel: 0870 333 3636, Fax: 029 203 0900, E-mail: enquiries possible via the website). Companies House is a vital resource. It provides financial and other related information on all limited companies in the UK. It holds information on 1.5 million companies and receives over 5 million documents a year. The service is available online for a reasonable fee or documents can be sent to regional centres or by post, fax or document package. The Companies House website also has a range of links to international disclosure of company data and links through to the relevant sites.

Web address: www.companies-house.gov.uk

2 *Kompass United Kingdom*, Reed Business Information, East Grinstead (Tel: 01342 3335 864, Fax: 01342 335 745, E-mail: in the UK Justine.gillen@ree-dinfo.co.uk). A key source of information on companies in several formats, Kompass covers a wide range of countries. Products include *Kompass UK Register*, a CD or paper directory of UK companies, and Kompass.com, an online service covering 1.7 million companies world-wide in over 70 countries. Kompass.com also covers:

● *Kompass Products and Services*: lists suppliers of most products
● *Company Information*: lists company names and locations and web addresses with information about each company and its products

- *Kompass Financial Information*: provides the last three years' accounts on listed companies
- *Parents and Subsidiaries*: identifies who owns which companies. Lists 85,000 subsidiaries of 15,000 parent companies
- *Industrial Trade Names*: lists who owns over 100,000 brand names in diverse sectors, excluding food.

Web address: www.kompass.co.uk
www.britishexports.co.uk
www.kompass.com

3 *Kelly's* (contact via the website) is an online database for UK industry. Searches may be made by product/service, trade-name, town, street or postcode. Kelly's holds data on 150,000 companies and 110,000 product categories.

Web address: www.kellys.co.uk

4 *Dun & Bradstreet* (Tel: 01494 422000, Fax: 01494 422260, E-mail: customerhelp@dnb.com). Dun & Bradstreet (D&B) maintains a global database of 70 million companies, from 214 countries, in 95 languages or dialects, covering 181 currencies. D&B is an established source of data on companies in the business-to-business (B2B) market. D&B DUNS numbers are a recognized way of classifying businesses. D&B can help to identify, locate and credit score companies. It offers a broad range of products in areas including Who Owns Whom, the D&B Small Business Centre, D&B monitoring service, D&B Business Information Report among many others; contact D&B for a full product list.

Web address: www.dnb.co.uk

The international site opens up a range of international data:

Web address: www.dnb.com

5 *Euromonitor* (Euromonitor International Plc. Tel: 020 7251 1105, Fax: 020 7251 0985, E-mail: info@euromonitor.com) is a significant provider of syndicated reports on companies. Reports feature national and multi-national companies with industry rankings based on Euromonitor's opinion. Analysis includes Business overview, Strategic overview, Markets and products, and Company performance.

Web address: www.euromonitor.com

6 *Hemscott* (Tel: 020 7496 0055, Fax: 020 7847 1716, E-mail: marketing@hemscott.co.uk) Hemscott provides a range of company information from the perspective of investment analysis. It is one of the fastest growing providers of information on UK stockmarket-listed companies. Company Insight is a service provided by Hemscott, giving detailed and updated information daily on all London Stock Exchange listed companies.

Web address: www.hemscott.net

7 *Thomson Financial* (Tel: 020 7369 7000). Thomson Financial is located in more than 40 countries; the website provides detailed contact and product listings. Thomson Financial provides a huge array of data about industries and companies through many different product lines. Services target the financial community.

Web address: www.tfn.com

8 *Hoover's* (Tel: 00 1 512 374 4500, Fax: 00 1 512 374 4505, E-mail enquiries through the website). An online aggregator with useful company and industry profiles.

Web address: www.hoovers.com/uk/

8 Several companies provide a search for annual reports online. These are available free of charge from companies, but a subscription to a retrieval service may save time. Corporate Reports is one example of this type of service. It offers online company reports, with free summary information.

Web address: www.corpreports.co.uk

9 *UK Business Park* provides comprehensive coverage of UK business activity. It is a subscription site, but with a free trial. Information is provided on acquisitions, new projects, expansion plans, strategy and major new projects by sector. It also provides a database of sales leads and company contact details.

Web address: www.ukbusinesspark.co.uk

10 *Primark/Thomson Financial Global Access* (Tel: 020 7369, Fax: 020 7369 7634) provides a range of information on companies, including Company Briefs and Extel Cards, offering information on business description, finances, acquisitions and disposals, etc., on over 15,000 quoted companies in 55 countries. Peer group analysis enables comparison with similar companies. Information can be downloaded in PDF or HTML format.

Web address: www.primark.com

11 FT.com provides access to a range of company data, much of which is free of charge.

Web address: www.ft.com

12 www.economist.com is a comprehensive site with links to the Economist Intelligence Unit.

Information about industries

As well as the relevant government data sources, trade associations and online aggregators, the following may be helpful.

1 *ICC Information Group Ltd* (Tel: 020 7426 8506, Fax: 020 7426 8551, E-mail: helpdesk@icc.co.uk) provides information via a range of databases, including Juniper and Plum, offering information on industries and companies internationally.

Web address: www.icc.uk

2 *Euromonitor* (Euromonitor International Plc. Tel: 020 7251 1105, Fax: 020 7251 0985, E-mail: info@euromonitor.com) provides reports on a range of industry sectors internationally.

Web address: www.euromonitor.com

3 *The Marketing Pocket Book*. The Advertising Association in association with WARC, Henley-on-Thames (Tel: 01491 574 671, Fax: 01491 571 188). One in a series of very useful little books supporting marketing and business activity in the UK. A compilation of consumer marketing data from published sources, *The Marketing Pocket Book* includes social and economic, marketplace, media and advertising data, and it has a small international section. A list of publications is available from the Advertising Association's website or the World Advertising Research Centre.

Web addresses:
www.adassoc.org.uk
www.warc.com

4 *The Economist Intelligence Unit* (Tel: 020 7830 1007, Fax: 020 7830 1023, E-mail: london@eiu.com) provides research on a range of industries internationally.

Web address: www.eiu.com

Information about markets

Subscription services. These are designed to provide the latest information regularly. An annual charge is made for the service. Individual reports and back copies are usually available.

Many companies provide regular reports on markets. Their data collection methods are largely the same. These reports are produced through secondary research supported by some primary interviews with key industry personnel. Researchers within these companies are often respected experts in their field and may have far greater access to material and personnel than will be available generally. Users should check the methodology carefully and try to verify data through several sources. Many of these companies will also carry out ad hoc or consultancy work, for a fee.

1 *Mintel International Group Ltd* (Tel: 020 77606 4533, Fax: 0202 7606 5932, E-mail: info@mintel.com). Mintel publishes a range of reports on

markets, companies and industries. Increasingly, these are international in scope. The Mintel website gives full details of the range of reports published and also gives details of a number of searchable databases. Many academic libraries carry copies of Mintel reports and these can be accessed online for a fee. All Mintel reports are available electronically, grouped under the following headings.

- Clothing, footwear and accessories
- Consumer lifestyle
- Drink
- Food and food service
- Health and well being
- Holidays and travel
- Household/house and home
- Industrial
- Leisure time
- Media and electrical goods
- Miscellaneous
- Personal finances
- Personal goods and toiletries
- Retail
- Technology.

Mintel: examples of recent reports
Internet Quarterly Report, September 2002
Analgesics, September 2002
Canned Meat, September 2002
Organic Alcoholic Drinks, September 2002
Pies and Pasties, September 2002
Baby Food and Drink Market (The): US Report, September 2002
Call Centres (Industrial Report), September 2002
Disposable Baby Products Market (The): US Report, September 2002
Hotels Market (The): US Report, September 2002
House Building (Industrial Report), September 2002
Out-of-Town vs In-Town Retailing, September 2002
Red Meat Market (The): US Report, September 2002
Women's Hosiery Market (The): US Report, September 2002
Deposit and Savings Accounts, September 2002
Private Medical Insurance, September 2002
Sub-prime Lending: Entering the Mainstream, September 2002
Petfood & Petcare Retailing, September 2002
Womenswear Retailing, September 2002
European Retail Briefings, September 2002
Independent Holidays, September 2002
Roadside Catering, September 2002
Snowsports, September 2002
Video and Computer Games, September 2002

Retailing in the Middle East, September 2002
Occupational Health (Industrial Report), August 2002
Industrial Gases (Industrial Report), August 2002
Asia Pacific Hotel Industry (The), August 2002
Austria Outbound, August 2002
Batteries, August 2002
Christmas Foods, August 2002
Deep Vein Thrombosis (DVT) and the Future of Long-Haul Air Travel, August 2002
European Leisure Groups, August 2002
European Meetings and Incentives Industry (The), August 2002
Food Safety, August 2002
Home Baking, August 2002
Hotels in France, August 2002
Hotels in Germany, August 2002
Hotels in Ireland, August 2002
Hotels in Italy, August 2002
Hotels in Spain, August 2002
Hotels in the UK, August 2002
Household Fresheners, August 2002
Make-up, August 2002
Nursery Equipment: Transport, August 2002
Poultry, August 2002
Teenage Magazines, August 2002
Whiskies, August 2002
Menswear Retailing, August 2002
Wine Retailing, August 2002

Market Intelligence (monthly). Each issue contains a detailed market report on about five markets. As Mintel operates on a two year publishing cycle it is always worth checking to see whether relevant reports are available. Other Mintel services include:

- *Retail Intelligence* (six per year): similar to *Market Intelligence* but about retailing rather than products
- *Leisure Intelligence*
- *Personal Finance Intelligence*
- *International Information Services*
- *Daily Digest:* daily information on subject profile specified
- *Monthly Digests* on 12 different market areas
- Special subject reports also available, e.g. the gardening market, the kitchen report
- *International New Product* report
- Market reports compiled from a variety of published sources
- Consultancy.

Report prices range from £495 to £1295 per report.

2 *Keynote Publications Ltd*, London (Tel: 020 8481 8750, Fax: 020 8783 0049, E-mail: sales@keynote.co.uk). Market and other reports compiled from a variety of published sources, priced from £345

Web address: www.keynote.co.uk

3 *Datamonitor* (Tel: 020 7675 7000, Fax: 020 7675 7500, E-mail: eur-info@datamonitor.com). Reports on automotives, consumer, energy, financial services, healthcare and technology sectors, covering market and company analysis. Online or CD-ROM databases are available. Reports are priced at $1000–$5000.

Web address: www.datamonitor.com

4 *Frost and Sullivan* (Tel: 020 7730 3438, Fax: 020 7873 9942). An international company producing often highly specialized research and consultancy covering a range of markets including business-to-business and industrial markets. Prices reflect the complexity of the research task in these markets.

Web address: www.frost.com

5 *The Economist Intelligence Unit* (Tel: 020 7830 1007, Fax: 020 7830 1023, E-mail: london@eiu.com) provides research on a range of industries internationally.

Web address: www: eiu.com

6 *Euromonitor* (Euromonitor International Plc. Tel: 020 7251 1105, Fax: 020 7251 0985) publishes directories, journals and various market reports focusing on Europe but with an increasingly broad international perspective.

Web address: www.euromonitor.com

7 *Newsletter subscription services*. Most online information services have a newsletter subscription service which may be free of charge. These are designed to provide the latest information regularly. Back copies are usually available through archive searching. Most of the services listed will provide a newsletter service free but will charge for the main content of the website

8 *ACNielsen Co. Ltd*, Oxford (Tel: 01865 742 742, Fax: 01865 742 222, E-mail: marketing@acnielsen.co.uk). ACNielsen is a key provider of information to the fast-moving consumer goods (FMCG) sector. It offers a range of subscription and other services, including a retail measurement service using electronic point of sale (EPOS) data and store visits, and a range of scanning-based consumer panels including homescan. Through its ACNielsen MMS (Media Monitoring Service) subsidiary it can also provide data on advertising spend and media spend. Nielsen/NetRatings provides data on Internet business and browser behaviour. ACNielsen is a global provider of marketing services and should be

contacted for a list of its services by anyone operating in consumer markets.

Web address www.acnielsen.co.uk

9 *Taylor Nelson Sofres* (Tel: 020 8967 0007, Fax: 020 8967 4060). Like Nielsen, TNSofres produces a range of syndicated and ad hoc research. Super panel is a panel of 15,000 households and produces data on consumer purchasing. Data is gathered twice weekly.

Web address: www.tnsofre.com/uk

10 *BMRB International* (Tel: 020 8566 5000, Fax: 020 8579 9208, E-mail: web@bmrb.co.uk). TGI (Target Group Index), a service provided by BMRB, is a comprehensive source of customer information for a broad spectrum of consumer goods and services. It is based on a sample size of 25,000 comprehensive interviews. Questions cover product consumption and usage, media buying behaviour and attitudinal data. Data is available demographically by age, gender, income and family size, etc., and is presented as a series of indices.

Web address: www.bmrb.co.uk

Information about media

1 Cinema and Video Audience Research (CAVIAR), Pearl and Dean Cinemas Ltd, 3 Waterhouse Square, 138–142 Holborn, London EC1N 2NY (Tel: 020 7882 1100, Fax: 020 7882 1111)

www.pearlanddean.com/

2 Outdoor Advertising, POSTAR Ltd, Summit House, 27 Sale Place, London W2 1YR (Tel: 20 7479 9700, Fax: 20 7706 7143, E-mail: mail@postar.co.uk)

www.postar.co.uk/

3 Radio RAJAR Ltd, Gainsborough House, 81 Oxford Street, London W1D 2EU (Tel: 020 7903 5350, Fax: 020 7903 5351, E-mail: info@rajar.co.uk)

www.rajar.co.uk

or Radio Advertising Bureau, 77 Shaftesbury Avenue, London W1V 7AD (Tel: 020 7306 2580, Fax: 020 7306 2505)

www.rab.co.uk

4 Television: BARB

www.barb.co.ukj
enquiries@barb.co.uk

5 Press and magazines
NRS Ltd, 42 Drury Lane, London WC2B 5RT (Tel: 020 7632 2915, Fax: 020 7632 2916)

www.nrs.co.uk

Joint Industry Committee for Regional Press Research (JICREG), c/o The Newspaper Society, Bloomsbury House, 74–77 Great Russell Street, London WC1B 3DA (Tel: 020 7636 7014, Fax: 020 7436 3873)

www.jicreg.co.uk

Audit Bureau of Circulations Ltd, Saxon House, 211 High Street, Berkhamsted, Hertfordshire HP4 1AD (Tel: 01442 870800, Fax: 01442 200700, E-mail: marketing@abc.org.uk)

www.abc.org.uk

British Business Survey
Ipsos UK Ltd, Middlesex (Tel: 020 8861 8000, Fax: 020 8861 5515)

www.ipsos-uk.co.uk

6 The Internet
Interactive Advertisers' Bureau

www.iabuk.net

7 General Media

www.carat.co.uk
www.zenithmedia.co.uk/
www.totalmedia.co.uk/
www.acnielsenmms.com/

Government statistics

1 *National Statistics* (Tel: 0845 601 3034, Fax: 01633 652747, E-mail: info@statistics.gov.uk) is the official Statistical Service of the UK. It produces 'up to date comprehensive and meaningful description of the UK's economy and society'. As such, it is an invaluable resource for marketing researchers. The National Statistics website also has a wealth of data on a huge range of topics. The website is an excellent starting point. Data sets are organized under the following headings:

- Agriculture, fishing and forestry
- Commerce energy and industry
- Crime and justice
- Economy
- Education and training
- Health and Care
- Labour Market
- Natural and built environment
- Population and migration
- Public sector and other
- Social and welfare
- Transport travel and tourism.

Following links within these lists generates the full range of data. For example, clicking on the Social and welfare link reveals the following list of options:

- Culture leisure and social participation
- Income expenditure and wealth
- Social Justice
- Households families and individuals
- Quality of life and welfare

Clicking on Income expenditure and wealth reveals:

- Income and wealth of households and individuals

Clicking here reveals another list of options which includes:

- Types of income
- Consumer durables owned
- Income distribution of households, etc.

If the title of the data set is known then a search option may be used. In addition, www.ukonline.gov.uk is a quick-find option which lists over 1000 government websites.

Other publications are grouped under the following headings:

- Agriculture
- Commerce and industry
- Compendia and reference
- Crime and justice
- Economy
- Education
- Health and care
- Labour market
- Natural and built environment
- Population and migration
- Social and welfare
- Transport and tourism
- Other.

Key statistics services include:

2 *Economic Trends* (monthly). Provides a broad background to trends in the UK economy, supported by a detailed annual supplement.
3 *Financial Statistics* (monthly). Key financial and monetary statistics of the UK.
4 *UK Balance of Payments*. Balance of payment statistics including information on visible and invisible trade, investment and other capital transactions.
5 *Size Analyses of United Kingdom Businesses* (PA 1003). Analysis of company size by sector, by turnover size for service industries and turnover and employment size for manufacturing industry.

6 *Social Trends* (annual). The life of Britain through statistics. A statistical series about people relating to social policies and conditions that provides a picture of some significant ways in which our society is changing, and background information on society.

7 *Family Expenditure Survey* (annual since 1967). Data on characteristics, incomes and expenditure of private households in the UK. Trend data useful for indicating change in patterns of expenditure. Presented in report format in *Family Spending*.

8 *New Earnings Survey* (annual). Indicates earnings of employees by industry, occupation, region, age and gender.

9 For specific topics of interest, consult the subject list on the website.

Web address: www.statistics.gov.uk

www.ukonline.gov.uk is also a useful starting point for exploring government data.

10 European statistical information is available via Eurostat.

Web address: www.europa.eu.int/comm/eurostat/

11 The UN also has a statistical service.

Web address: www.un.org

Information services

1 *Trade Partners.* Headquarters: Kingsgate House, 66–74 Victoria Street, London SW1E 6SW (Tel: 020 7215 5444/5, Fax: 020 7215 4231, E-mail: via the website). Trade Partners is the UK national reference service for public use of world-wide statistics and is of particular use to exporters. The centre holds a significant amount of information on UK and overseas markets. Economic, social, industry and market data is held for all countries of the world. It includes telephone, fax and trade directories (except UK), market surveys, development plans and mail order catalogues. It has online databases and CD-ROM-based information on a number of countries, which may be searched by country, sector or subject. The website is an invaluable starting point with a full index of the site's services.

Visits may be made to the headquarters office or enquiries can be made by telephone or online.

The website contains links to information on key services such as the Export Market Research scheme and the Export Credit Guarantees Scheme.

Web address: www.tradepartners.gov.uk

2 *Export Marketing Research Scheme.* British Chambers of Commerce (Tel: 024 76 694484, Fax 024 76 694690, E-mail: enquiry@britishchambers.org.uk). Free professional advice and, in approved cases, financial support, to help UK firms and trade associations to undertake marketing research overseas for exports.

Web address: www.britishchambers.org.uk/exportzone.

3 Other specialist business libraries may be worth contacting, particularly if easily accessible, e.g. the City Business Library or the Science Reference Library in London. Equally useful are university libraries, particularly those with a significant business offer, e.g. London Business School, Manchester Business School, the University of Warwick, and Strathclyde University.

Business Link is a UK nation-wide organization offering support services to business. Local Business Link offices will help with international marketing enquiries. There are links to local Business Link offices at the Trade Partners website.

Where relevant international information is not available, commercial staff based at embassies abroad may be commissioned to carry out basic marketing research at a reasonable fee.

Trade Partners: list of services

A
About Trade Partners UK
Action Single Market
Aid Funded Business
Annual Review
Area Advisory Groups
Ask Us by E-Mail
Awards: Queen's Awards for Enterprise

B
Bribery
British Chambers of Commerce
British Embassies
British Overseas Industrial Placement (BOND) Scheme
British Standards Institute (BSI)
British Trade International
Business Languages Information Service (BLIS)
Business Libraries
Business Links
Business Links: International Trade Teams
Business Performance
Business Secondees

C
Central Office of Information (COI)
Checklist: Are You Ready to Export?
Commercial Publicity
Commonwealth Games Business Club
Contact Us
Copyright
Corporate Plan of British Trade International

Corporate Brochure of Trade Partners UK
Corruption Overseas
Countertrade
Currency Converter
Currency: The Euro
Customs & Excise

D
Defence Export Sales Organization (DESO)
Department for Environment, Food & Rural Affairs (DEFRA)
Department of Trade & Industry
Development Business Team
Disclaimer
Duke of York's BTI Programme 2001/2002

E
E-Business Strategy of British Trade International
Economic and Monetary Union
Email Us
Euro
Euro Zone
Events Database
Exhibitions Supported by Trade Partners UK
Export Awards for Small Business
Export Canada
Export Clubs
Export Communications Review
Export Control Organization
Export Credit Guarantee Department
Export Explorer
Export Finance and Insurance
Export Licences
Export Marketing Research Scheme (EMRS)
Export Opportunities
Export Promoter Initiative
Export Success Newsfile
Export USA
Exporting and Business Performance

F
Feedback
Finance
First Time Visit Packages
Foreign & Commonwealth Office
Frequently Asked Questions for Potential Exporters

G
Getting Paid
Global Partnerships Initiative

H
Help

I
ICT Investment Strategy of British Trade International
In Depth Research
Information Centre
Information Centre: Online Catalogue
Insurance
International Business Awards
International Buyers
International Trade Teams
Investment Overseas
Invest Northern Ireland
Invest UK
Inward Missions

J
Joint Environmental Market Unit

K
Key Partners of Trade Partners UK

L
Language & Culture
Language Training for Exporters
Law on Corruption Overseas
Licences
Local Trade Partners UK International Trade Teams

M
Market Explorer
Market Research
Minister of State for International Trade & Investment
Missions: Outward
Multilateral Development Aid

N
National Languages for Export Campaign
National Strategy for Trade Partners UK
New Products From Britain
Newsroom
Nottingham University Research

O
OECD Guidelines for Multinational Enterprises
Offset
On Line Information Market Service (OMIS)
Outward Missions Scheme
Overseas Buyers (Non UK)
Overseas Events
Overseas Investment
Overseas Project Fund
Overseas Trade Magazine

P
Partners of Trade Partners UK
Passport to Export Success
Payment
Press Releases
Privacy Policy
Publicity Services for Overseas Markets
Public Private Partnerships

Q
Queen's Awards for Enterprise

R
Reports by Country
Reports by Sector
Research Overseas Markets

S
Sales Leads Online
Scottish Development International
Search Our Site
Sector Partnership Report
Sector Reports listed by Country
Security Briefing for Business
Service Delivery Agreements
Simplification of Trade Procedures (SITPRO)
Small Business Service
Standards & Quality Expected from Trade Partners UK
Standards (Technical Help for Exporters: THE)
Success Stories
Support for Exhibitions and Seminars Abroad (SESA)
Support for Export Marketing Research

T
Tailored Market Information Reports (TMIRs)
Technical Help for Exporters (THE)
Tour Our Site

Trade Advisors
Trade Associations: Sector Partnership Report
Trade Associations: Support
Trade Barriers
Trade Fair Explorer
Trade Fairs Supported by Trade Partners UK
Trade Missions
Trade Procedures
Travel Advice

U
UK Suppliers Database

V
Visiting the Market
Visit Trade Partners UK

W
Wales Trade International
Websites for Exporters Database
Western Europe: Visits
What's New This Month
Who We Are
Works of Art
World Trade Organization: 4th Ministerial Conference
World Trade Organization: General Information

Source www.tradepartners.gov.uk

4.2.4 Using secondary data

Whenever secondary data sources are being used a number of points need to be checked.

(a) Who is producing the data? This is a relevant question because, particularly with information from trade associations, the possibility of bias is present. An association which exists on members' subscriptions, with the objective of furthering members' interests, is unlikely to publish data that is against those members' interests. This is not to say that they will publish false data, but simply that they may not publish data that gives both sides of every question relevant to members' interests.

(b) Why was the information collected in the first place? Answering this question will give greater insight into the nature, and therefore value, of the data that has been collected.

(c) How was the information collected? From the chapters in this book on methods of data collection (Chapters 6–10) it will be apparent that the value of information for use in making a decision is partly determined by the method used in collecting data. In deciding how useful a particular item of secondary information is, it is therefore necessary to consult the technical appendix of the report to see how the data was collected.

(d) When was the information collected? A particular problem with government statistics is that they may not be published until 18 months or even longer after the period in which the data was collected. Depending on the nature of the data and the market to which it refers, this may be a serious limitation in using the statistics.

(e) Is the data comparable? In multicountry research this is a major problem. It is important to realize that classification of data varies from country to country, as do definitions of product sectors. For example, data on the sugar confectionery industry in south-east Asia may include information on candied fruits, and the definition of what constitutes a low alcohol beer varies substantially even within Europe. The answer is to check the methodology and if in doubt to contact the producer of the data.

Sources of secondary data will vary widely in terms of reliability of the data, how specific it is to a particular problem, how recent the information is, the amount of bias or vested interest in the data source and, particularly when using press report services, the amount of useful information hidden in the verbiage. Nevertheless, the desk researcher can almost always produce an extremely useful background report on any industry, in a relatively short space of time and at a relatively low cost. It is recommended that a desk research survey of secondary sources be carried out before any major field research survey is undertaken.

4.3 Syndicated research services

Syndicated research services originated when a group of manufacturers all interested in data on a particular market formed a syndicate to buy a research survey jointly providing that data on a continuous basis. Alternatively, a research agency might suggest the idea to a number of companies with common data needs. No single manufacturer could afford the costs of the research survey, but by clubbing together, research costs are shared and information is available to all members of the syndicate. Over time, the original services have proved useful to a wider number of manufacturers than those forming the original syndicate and, because the surveys have been continuous, they have become the property of the research agencies that provide them. In this sense, the term 'syndicated' is a hangover from the origins of these services, rather than a description of their current ownership.

In practice nowadays, most syndicated research services are owned by the research companies that run them. An association of users of a service may meet to ensure that user interests are expressed in the method of collection and presentation of the data. Most syndicated research surveys are continuous panels and the advantages of these as a method of data collection are discussed in Chapter 6. (Where this is not the method used, then this is indicated for the services listed below.)

The main problem for the intending user of syndicated research services is to identify what services are available and which companies provide them. The MRS website contains a searchable directory of organizations providing marketing research services in Great Britain. This is also available in *The Research Buyer's Guide*. Not all marketing research organizations supply syndicated services and so the following index and list of suppliers of syndicated research services was compiled from *The Research Buyer's Guide* and other sources to give an idea of the range available. The index lists sectors covered. Full details of the services offered, the method by which data is collected and costs of the services can be obtained from the organizations named, for which telephone numbers are given.

BMRB TGI: an example of syndicated data

TGI is a leading provider of single-source media and marketing surveys. Its family of research products covers an ever-widening spectrum of population specifications and geographies, all using a self-completion data collection technique to gather respondent information.

TGI is segmented into several subproducts, which include the following:

- *Premier.* A continuous survey that is designed to gather information on the social grades 'AB'. This survey offers insight into a group of consumers who are difficult to target yet considered highly attractive to marketers and advertisers on the basis of their disposable income.
- *Youth TGI:* A survey of 7–19-year-olds with data released twice a year (spring and autumn). Sample size is approximately 6000, and survey samples are split equally across three age bands, 7–10, 11–14 and 15–19 years.
- *TGI Gold:* A survey of 50+-year-olds conducted every two years. The survey is based on a sample size of over 4000 and focuses on issues relevant to this target market, e.g. holidays, motoring and health
- *TGI Wavelength:* Wavelength measures approximately 90 commercial radio stations and is able to add to the basic demographic profile information that can be obtained through RAJAR (Radio Joint Audience Research Limited), the officially commissioned data on behalf of the radio industry.

● *Republic of Ireland/Northern Ireland*: The TGI in the Republic of Ireland and Northern Ireland is specifically tailored to the Irish markets, although it follows a similar format to the main TGI in Great Britain.

BMRB offers an online example of TGI and its website contains information about the range of other products this key supplier of research services offers to the market.

		TOTAL	Budweiser – most often – canned lager	Grolsch – most often – canned lager	Heineken – most often – canned lager	Heineken Export – most often – canned lager
TOTAL	000s	**45,350**	**1326**	**396**	**3263**	**328**
	Resps	25,296	649	203	1724	157
	%Vert/Row	100	2.9	0.9	7.2	0.7
ADULTS	000s	45,350	1326	396	3263	328
	Resps	25,296	649	203	1724	157
	%Horz/Col	100.0	100.0	100.0	100.0	100.0
	% Vert/Row	**100.0**	**2.9**	**0.9**	**7.2**	**0.7**
	Index	100	100	100	100	100
MEN	000s	**21,899**	**847**	**294**	**1815**	**210**
	Resps	11,678	395	144	936	104
	% Horz/Col	**48.8**	**63.9**	**74.2**	**55.0**	**64.0**
	% Vert/Row	100.0	3.9	1.3	8.3	1.0
	Index	100	132.3	153.7	115.2	132.6
WOMEN	000s	**23,451**	**479**	**102**	**1448**	**118**
	Resps	13,623	254	59	788	53
	% Horz/Col	51.7	36.1	25.8	45.0	36.0
	%Vert/Row	100.0	2.0	0.4	6.2	0.5
	Index	100	69.9	49.8	85.8	69.6

The presentation of TGI data is complex but once it is understood it is very easy to interpret.

In the above example four lager brands are shown:

45,350 represents the total UK lager market
25,296 represents number of responses

21,899 represents adult male lager drinkers
11,678 is the number of male responders

This represents 48.3 per cent of the population and 100 per cent of responders.

23,451 is the adult female population
13,623 is the number of female responders

This represents 51.7 per cent of the population and 100 per cent of responders.

The index for both males and females is 100.

Taking the Budweiser column only:

1326 represents the product universe

649 represents the response

2.9 is the product universe as a percentage of the total population.

847 is the male customer universe

395 is the number of male responders

63.9 is the male Budweiser universe as a percentage of the total Budweiser universe response

3.9 is the Budweiser male universe as a percentage of the total universe.

The index figures show that men are 32.3 per cent more likely to consume Budweiser than the population as a whole and that women are 30.1 per cent less likely to consume Budweiser than the population as a whole.

Comparative data across the brands represented shows that significantly more men than women drink Grolsch and there is a more even distribution in the consumption of Heineken.

4.3.1 Index to syndicated research surveys

The index gives the specialist areas of companies offering syndicated services. Following this index is the numbered list of companies. They should be contacted for further details.

Advertising, 1, 2, 3, 5, 6, 7, 10, 11, 13, 15, 16, 17, 19, 20, 21, 22, 23, 24, 26, 27, 29, 31, 32, 33, 34, 35, 37, 38, 39, 42, 43, 45, 46, 47, 48, 49, 50, 52, 54, 56, 57, 58, 59, 61, 62, 63, 64, 65, 67, 68, 71, 72, 73, 75, 76, 78, 79, 80, 81, 84, 85, 87, 88, 89, 90, 93, 95, 96, 97, 98, 99, 103, 104, 105, 106, 107, 108, 109, 112, 113, 114, 116, 118

Agriculture, 27, 39 49, 50, 71, 81, 87, 88

Automotives, 4, 5, 11, 18, 19, 21, 22, 24, 30, 31, 32, 33, 34, 37, 41, 42, 46, 49, 50, 54, 55, 57, 66, 68, 71, 72, 75, 76, 79, 84, 88, 89, 93, 94, 102, 103, 106, 107, 113, 114, 116, 117

Branding, 8, 11, 26, 37, 44, 46, 47, 48, 52, 57, 71, 72, 76, 79, 85, 89, 93, 98, 99, 104, 109

Business-to-business, 2, 3, 4, 5, 7, 9, 10, 18, 19, 20, 21, 22, 23, 26, 27, 30, 31, 32, 33, 34, 39, 41, 42, 45, 49, 50, 53, 54, 55, 57, 58, 59, 60, 61, 63, 64, 65, 66, 67, 68, 71, 72, 73, 75, 76, 77, 78, 79, 80, 81, 83, 84, 86, 87, 88, 93, 94, 96, 97, 102, 104, 105, 106, 107, 108, 110, 112, 113, 114, 115, 117, 118

Children/youth, 4, 5, 6, 11, 13, 15, 16, 19, 20, 21, 27, 29, 31, 32, 43, 44, 47, 50, 52, 57, 58, 62, 64, 65, 68, 72, 79, 82, 84, 88, 98, 99, 104, 106, 107, 114

Consumer, 2, 3, 5, 6, 7, 8, 10, 11, 13, 14, 17, 18, 21, 22, 25, 26, 27, 29, 30, 31, 32, 33, 34, 35, 36, 42, 44, 45, 47, 49, 50, 57, 59, 61, 62, 63, 66, 68, 69, 70, 71, 72, 74, 75, 76, 77, 79, 80, 82, 86, 87, 88, 90, 93, 94, 96, 98, 103, 104, 105, 107, 109, 113, 116, 118

Media, 1, 2, 3, 4, 5, 10, 11, 15, 16, 19, 20, 21, 27, 31, 32, 33, 34, 37, 39, 42, 47, 49, 50, 52, 54, 56, 57, 58, 60, 63, 64, 68, 71, 72, 73, 75, 76, 77, 78, 79, 81, 84, 85, 88, 93, 94, 95, 96, 98, 100, 104, 106, 107, 113, 114, 115, 117, 118

Pharmaceuticals, 2, 3, 11, 21, 23, 25, 27, 31, 33, 42, 44, 46, 49, 50, 51, 54, 57, 58, 59, 61, 62, 68, 71, 72, 79, 81, 88, 93, 94, 102, 107, 114, 116

Pricing, 11, 26, 37, 44, 71, 72, 81, 101, 104

Print/packaging, 5, 14, 16, 21, 27, 33, 43, 44, 45, 64, 68, 71, 72, 81, 88, 93, 103, 104, 107

Product development/testing, 2, 3, 5, 6, 7, 11, 13, 14, 16, 17, 21, 22, 24, 27, 29, 30, 33, 34, 35, 36, 43, 44, 45, 50, 54, 56, 59, 61, 62, 63, 64, 65, 68, 71, 72, 77, 78, 79, 80, 81, 82, 83, 84, 85, 87, 88, 93, 99, 102, 103, 104, 105, 107, 113, 118

Property/construction/housing, 27, 53, 57, 58, 62, 66, 72, 89, 103, 118

Public services/utilities, 4, 5, 7, 8, 9, 11, 14, 17, 18, 19, 22, 23, 26, 27, 33, 34, 36, 39, 40, 41, 45, 50, 53, 54, 55, 57, 58, 59, 60, 61, 63, 66, 68, 71, 72, 74, 76, 77, 79, 81, 82, 84, 86, 88, 93, 94, 96, 102, 103, 107, 109, 114, 118

Retail/wholesale, 1, 2, 3, 5, 7, 10, 11, 12, 13, 14, 16, 17, 18, 19, 21, 22, 27, 29, 31, 33, 34, 35, 40, 42, 45, 46, 47, 50, 53, 57, 59, 61, 62, 63, 64, 65, 66, 68, 69, 70, 71, 72, 73, 76, 77, 78, 79, 80, 84, 88, 90, 91, 93, 94, 97, 98, 105, 106, 107, 114, 115

Social research, 5, 8, 9, 10, 11, 19, 21, 26, 27, 32, 33, 36, 39, 43, 45, 50, 57, 58, 60, 63, 65, 71, 72, 74, 77, 82, 86, 92, 93, 99, 107

Sports/leisure/arts, 5, 11, 15, 18, 19, 21, 26, 27, 29, 37, 38, 50, 57, 58, 60, 63, 64, 68, 71, 72, 74, 75, 77, 79, 82, 85, 87, 88, 89, 91, 94, 100, 103, 107, 113, 118

Telecommunications, 4, 5, 10, 11, 16, 19, 20, 21, 22, 25, 26, 27, 31, 32, 33, 34, 37, 40, 42, 45, 46, 47, 49, 50, 57, 58, 61, 64, 65, 67, 68, 70, 71, 72, 76, 77, 78, 79, 84, 85, 88, 93, 94, 95, 98, 101, 104, 105, 106, 107, 108, 111, 114

Tobacco, 1, 6, 34, 65, 71, 88, 106, 107

Training/education, 5, 6, 9, 11, 21, 27, 29, 38, 45, 57, 58, 60, 61, 63, 72, 74, 77, 80, 92, 105, 115, 118

Transport/distribution, 5, 17, 21, 22, 23, 26, 27, 33, 34, 42, 50, 53, 57, 60, 61, 64, 66, 68, 71, 72, 76, 77, 78, 88, 89, 93, 101, 103, 106, 107, 110, 112, 118

Travel/tourism, 1, 5, 7, 9, 11, 12, 16, 17, 19, 21, 22, 23, 26, 27, 29, 33, 35, 37, 42, 50, 57, 58, 60, 63, 64, 65, 67, 68, 71, 72, 76, 77, 79, 81, 84, 87, 81, 88, 89, 93, 94, 95, 97, 99, 101, 102, 103, 106, 107, 108, 112, 113, 115, 117, 118

4.3.2 Guide to syndicated research services

The following list is compiled from the MRS *Research Buyer's Guide* (UK & Ireland) 2002, and provides an indication of which companies provide syndicated research services and in which market sector they specialize. The index in the preceding section gives the specialist areas of companies offering syndicated services. They should be contacted direct for further information.

1 ACNielsen, Oxford (Tel: 01865 742742, Fax: 01865 742222). Advertising, Drinks (alcoholic), Food, Health/beauty/toiletries, Media: TV/radio/ press, Retail/wholesale, Tobacco, Travel/tourism.

Website: www.acnielsen.co.uk

2 ASE, London (Tel: 020 7935 7979, Fax: 020 7935 3395). Advertising, Business-to-business, Consumer, Customer satisfaction, Drinks (alcoholic), Drinks (non-alcoholic), Employment/human resources, Energy, Environment, Finance/investment, Food, Health/beauty/toiletries, Healthcare, Industrial, Information technology, Media: TV/radio/press, Pharmaceutical, Product development/testing, Retail/wholesale.

Website: www.aselondon.co.uk

3 ASE Dublin, Dublin (Tel: +353 1 678 5000, Fax: +353 1 678 5566). Advertising, Business-to-business, Consumer, Customer satisfaction, Drinks (alcoholic), Drinks (non-alcoholic), Employment/human resources, Energy, Environment, Finance/investment, Food, Health/beauty/ toiletries, Healthcare, Industrial, Information technology, Media: TV/ radio/press, Pharmaceutical, Product development/testing, Retail/wholesale.

Website: www.asedublin.ie

4 Abacus Research, Sussex (Tel: 01825 761788, Fax: 01825 765755). Automotive, Business-to-business, Children/youth, Customer satisfaction, Energy, Finance/investment, Food, Government/politics, Media: TV/radio/press, Public Services/utilities, Telecommunications.

Website: www.abacus.uk.com

5 Ace Fieldwork Ltd, London (Tel: 020 7263 9696, Fax: 020 7263 5202). Advertising, Automotive, Business-to-business, Children/youth, Consumer, Customer satisfaction, Drinks (alcoholic), Drinks (non-alcoholic), Employment/human resources, Energy, Fashion/textiles, Finance/investment, Food, Government/politics, health/beauty/toiletries, Healthcare, Home/garden/DIY Information technology, Media: TV/radio/press, Printing/packaging, Product development/testing, Public services/utilities, Retail/wholesale, Social research, Sport/ leisure/arts, Telecommunications, Training/education, Transport/distribution, Travel/tourism.

Website: www.acefieldwork.co.uk

6 Albemarle Marketing Research, London (Tel: 020 7462 7272, Fax: 020 7462 7561). Advertising, Children/youth, Consumer, Drinks (alcoholic), Drinks (non-alcoholic), Finance/investment, Food, health/beauty/ toiletries, Healthcare, Product development/testing, Tobacco, Training/ education.

Website: www.a-m-r.co.uk

7 Alchemy Research Associates Ltd, West Yorkshire (Tel: 01924 382863, Fax: 01924 382864). Advertising, Business-to-business, Consumer, FMCG, Food, Home/garden/DIY, Product development/testing, Public services/utilities, Retail/wholesale, Travel/tourism.

   Website: www.alchemyresearch.co.uk

8 Anne Bowden Research Solutions, Warwickshire (Tel: 01926 815106, Fax: 01926 815106). Branding, Consumer, Customer satisfaction, Employment/human resources, Public services/utilities, Social research.

9 BMG, Birmingham (Tel: 0121 333 6006, Fax: 0121 333 6800). Business-to-business, Customer satisfaction, Employment/human resources, Government/politics, Public services/utilities, Social research, Training/education, Travel/tourism.

   Website: www.bostock.co.uk

10 BMRB Direct, London (Tel: 020 8566 5000, Fax: 020 8579 9208). Advertising, Business-to-business, Consumer, Customer satisfaction, Finance/investment, Healthcare, Information technology, Media: TV/radio/press, Retail/wholesale, Social research, Telecommunications.

    Website: www.bmrb-direct.co.uk

11 BMRB International, London (Tel: 020 8566 5000, Fax: 020 8579 9208). Advertising, Automotive, Branding, Business-to-business, Children/youth, Consumer, Customer satisfaction, Drinks (alcoholic), Drinks (non-alcoholic), Employment/human resources, Energy, Environment, Finance/investment, FMCG, Food, Government/politics, health/beauty/toiletries, Healthcare, Home/garden/DIY, Information technology, Insurance, International, Internet/e-commerce, Media: TV/radio/press, Pharmaceutical, Pricing, Product development/testing, Public services/utilities, Retail/wholesale, Social research, Sport/leisure/arts, Telecommunications, Training/education, Travel/tourism.

    Website: www.bmrb.co.uk

12 CADS: Coding and Data Services, Kent (Tel: 020 8650 1187, Fax: 020 8663 3897). Retail, Travel, Complex medical subjects.

13 CFS International, Berkshire (Tel: 01628 668888, Fax: 01628 668546). Advertising, Children/youth, Consumer, Customer satisfaction, Food, Product development/testing, Retail/wholesale.

    Website: www.cfsinternational.co.uk

14 Cambridge Market Research Ltd, Essex (Tel: 01799 524625, Fax: 01799 521726). Consumer, Drinks (non-alcoholic), Drinks (alcoholic), FMCG, Food, health/beauty/toiletries, Healthcare, Home/garden/DIY, Printing/packaging, Product development/testing, Public services/utilities, Retail/wholesale.

    Website: www.cambridge-market-research.co.uk

15 Carrick James Market Research, London (Tel: 020 7724 3836, Fax: 020 7224 8257). Advertising, Children/youth, Customer satisfaction, Food, Government/politics, Media: TV/radio/press, Sport/leisure/arts.

Website: www.cjmr.co.uk

16 Cognition, London (Tel: 020 7909 0925, Fax: 020 7909 0921). Advertising, Children/youth, Customer satisfaction, Drinks (alcoholic), Drinks (non-alcoholic), Fashion/textiles, Finance/investment, Food, health/beauty/toiletries, Media: TV/radio/press, Printing/packaging, Product development/testing, Retail/wholesale, Telecommunications, Travel/tourism.

Website: www.cognitionresearch.com

17 Conquest Research Ltd, Surrey (Tel: 020 8481 3999, Fax: 020 8547 1788). Advertising, Consumer, Drinks (alcoholic), Drinks (non-alcoholic), Energy, Finance/investment, Food, health/beauty/toiletries, Insurance, Internet/e-commerce, Product development/testing, Public services/utilities, Retail/wholesale, Transport/distribution, Travel/tourism.

Website: www.conquestuk.com

18 Consumer Link, Wiltshire (Tel: 01793 514055, Fax: 01793 512477). Automotive, Business-to-business, Consumer, Energy, Government/politics, Home/garden/DIY, Public services/utilities, Retail/wholesale, Sport/leisure/arts.

Website: www.consumerlink.org.uk

19 Continental Research, London (Tel: 020 7490 5944, Fax: 020 7490 1174). Advertising, Automotive, Business-to-business, Children/youth, Customer satisfaction, Finance/investment, Government/politics, Information technology, Media: TV/radio/press, Public services/utilities, Retail/wholesale, Sport/leisure/arts, Telecommunications, Travel/tourism.

Website: www.continentalresearch.com

20 Counterpoint Research, London (Tel: 020 7224 2622). Advertising, Business-to-business, Children/youth, Finance/investment, Government/politics, Information technology, Media: TV/radio/press, Telecommunications.

Website: www.counterpoint-research.co.uk

21 CRAM International Ltd, London (Tel: 020 7836 0727, Fax: 0207 240 6697). Advertising, Automotive, Business-to-business, Children/youth, Consumer, Drinks (alcoholic), Drinks (non-alcoholic), Employment/human resources, Environment, Fashion/textiles, Finance/investment, Food, Government/politics, health/beauty/toiletries, Healthcare, Home/garden/DIY, Information technology, Media: TV/radio/press, Pharmaceut-

ical, Printing/packaging, Product development/testing, Retail/whole-sale, Social research, Sport/leisure/arts, Telecommunications, Tobacco, Training/education, Transport/distribution, Travel/tourism.

22 Croydon Market Research Centre, Surrey (Tel: 020 8760 0776, Fax: 020 8688 3343). Advertising, Automotive, Business-to-business, Consumer, Customer satisfaction, Drinks (alcoholic), Drinks (non-alcoholic), FMCG, Food, health/beauty/toiletries, Industrial, Information technology, Insurance, International, Product development/testing, Public services/utilities, Retail/wholesale, Telecommunications, Transport/distribution, Travel/tourism.

23 Customer Care Research, Hertfordshire (Tel: 01279 718900, Fax: 01279 718901). Advertising, Business-to-business, Customer satisfaction, Employment/human resources, Finance/investment, Government/politics, health/beauty/toiletries, Industrial, Pharmaceutical, Public services/utilities, Transport/distribution, Travel/tourism.

Website: www.customer-care-research.com

24 Direct Dialogue, Suffolk (Tel: 01379 855340, Fax: 01379 855414). Advertising, Automotive, Drinks (alcoholic), Drinks (non-alcoholic), health/beauty/toiletries, Internet/e-commerce, Product development/testing.

Website: www.directdialogue.net

25 Echo Research, Surrey (Tel: 01483 413600, Fax: 01483 413601). Consumer, Employment/human resources, Finance/investment, Healthcare, Information technology, International, Pharmaceutical, Telecommunications.

Website: www.echoresearch.com

26 Enteleca Research and Consultancy, Surrey (Tel: 020 8948 8866, Fax: 020 8948 8899). Advertising, Branding, Business-to-business, Consumer, Customer satisfaction, Environment, Exhibitions/events, Finance/investment, Information technology, Pricing, Public services/utilities, Social research, Sport/leisure/arts, Telecommunications, Transport/distribution, Travel/tourism.

Website: www.enteleca.co.uk

27 FDS International Ltd, London (Tel: 020 7272 7766, Fax: 020 7272 4468). Advertising, Agriculture, Business-to-business, Children/youth, Consumer, Customer satisfaction, Drinks (alcoholic), Drinks (non-alcoholic), Employment/human resources, Energy, Environment, Fashion/textiles, Finance/investment, FMCG, Food, Government/politics, health/beauty/toiletries, Healthcare, Insurance, International, Media: TV/radio/press, Pharmaceutical, Printing/packaging, Product development/testing, Property/construction/housing, Public services/utilities, Retail/wholesale, Social research, Sport/leisure/arts, Telecommunications, Training/education, Transport/distribution, Travel/tourism.

Website: www.fds.co.uk

28 FML (Field Management Ltd), London (Tel: 020 7553 6777, Fax: 020 7553 6771).

   Website: www.fm-ltd.co.uk

29 Family Research Dynamics, London (Tel: 020 8444 5595, Fax: 020 8444 2753). Advertising, Children/youth, Consumer, Drinks (non-alcoholic), Food, health/beauty/toiletries, Product development/testing, Retail/ wholesale, social research, Sport/leisure/arts, Training/education, Travel/tourism.

30 Field Connection Ltd, Middlesex (Tel: 020 8423 3925, Fax: 020 7423 3940). Automotive, Business-to-business, Consumer, Customer satisfaction, Food International, Product development/testing.

   Website: www.fieldconnection.com

31 Field Initiatives, Hertfordshire (Tel: 020 8449 6404, Fax: 020 8449 8132). Advertising, Automotive, Business-to-business, Children/youth, Consumer, Finance/investment, Information technology, Internet/ e-commerce, Media: TV/radio/press, Pharmaceutical, Retail/whole-sale, Telecommunications.

   Website: www.fieldinitiatives.co.uk

32 Field and Research Matters, Surrey (Tel: 01372 279779, Fax: 01372 270861). Advertising, Automotive, Business-to-business, Children/ youth, Consumer, Finance/investment, Healthcare, Information technology, Media: TV/radio/press, Social research, Telecommunications.

   Website: www.fieldmatters.com

33 Field2Data, Kent (Tel: 0870 870 1450, Fax: 0870 870 1451). Advertising, Automotive, Business-to-business, Consumer, Customer satisfaction, employment/human resources, Finance/investment, FMCG, Food, Government/politics, health/beauty/toiletries, International, Internet/ e-commerce, Media: TV/radio/press, Pharmaceutical, Printing/packaging, Product development/testing, Public services/utilities, Retail/ wholesale, Social research, Telecommunications, Transport/ distribution, Travel/tourism.

   Website: www.ssrg.co.uk

34 Fieldforce: The Fieldwork Facility Ltd, Middlesex (Tel: 020 8979 3199, Fax: 020 8783 0701). Advertising, Automotive, Business-to-business, Consumer, Customer satisfaction, Drinks (non-alcoholic), Energy, Finance/investment, Food, Healthcare, Home/garden/DIY, Media: TV/radio/press, Product development/testing, Public services/utilities, Retail/wholesale, Telecommunications, Tobacco, Transport/distribution, Travel/tourism.

   Website: www.Fieldforce.co.uk

35 FieldQuest, Surrey (Tel: 020 8481 3888, Fax: 020 8547 1814). Advertising, Consumer, Finance/investment, Food, Product development/testing, Retail/wholesale, Travel/tourism.

Website: www.fieldquestuk.com

36 First Surveys, Lancashire (Tel: 01253 893480, Fax: 01253 893051). Consumer, Customer satisfaction, Government/politics, Media: TV/radio/press, Product development/testing, Public services/utilities, Social research.

Website: www.first-surveys.com

37 First T, London (Tel: 020 8832 9300, Fax: 020 8832 9301). Advertising, Automotive, Branding, Customer satisfaction, Direct marketing, Drinks (alcoholic), Fashion/textiles, Finance/investment, FMCG, health/beauty/toiletries, Media: TV/radio/press, Pricing, Sport/Leisure/arts, Telecommunications, Travel/tourism.

Website: www.firstt.co.uk

38 Genesis Consulting, West Sussex (Tel: 01403 785057, Fax: 07836 627749). Advertising, Drinks (non-alcoholic), Employment/human resources, Sport/leisure/arts, Training/education.

Website: www.genesisconsulting.eu.com

39 George Street Research Ltd, Edinburgh (Tel: 0131 478 7505, Fax: 0131 478 7504). Advertising, Agriculture, Business-to-business, Customer satisfaction, Employment/human resources, Energy, Finance/investment, Government/politics, Information technology, Internet/e-commerce, Media: TV/radio/press, Public services/utilities, Social research.

Website: www.george-street-research.co.uk

40 GFK Marketing Services Ltd, Surrey (Tel: 0870 603 8100, Fax: 0870 603 8200). Fashion/textiles, Home/garden/DIY, Information technology, Public services/utilities, Retail/wholesale, Telecommunications.

Website: www.gfkms.com

41 Group Sigma Ltd, Kent (Tel: 020 8460 9191, Fax: 020 8460 3969). Automotive, Business-to-business, Customer satisfaction, Employment/human resources, Finance/investment, Public services/utilities.

42 Hall and Partners Europe Ltd, London (Tel: 020 7534 4500, Fax: 020 7534 4501). Advertising, Automotive, Business-to-business, Consumer, Drinks (alcoholic), Drinks (non-alcoholic), Energy, Fashion/textiles, Finance/investment, Food, health/beauty/toiletries, Healthcare, Information technology, Internet/e-commerce, Media: TV/radio/press, Pharmaceutical, Retail/wholesale, Telecommunications, Transport/distribution, Travel/tourism.

Website: www.hall-and-partners.co.uk

43 Headworks: Child-Centred Research, Surrey (Tel: 01428 651982, Fax: 01428 641629). Advertising, Children/youth, Drinks (non-alcoholic), Food, Printing/packaging, Product development/testing, Social research.

44 Healthcare Research Worldwide Ltd, Oxfordshire (Tel: 01491 822515, Fax: 01491 824666). Branding, Children/youth, Consumer, FMCG, health/beauty/toiletries, Healthcare, International Pharmaceutical, Pricing, Printing/packaging, Product development/testing.

Website: www.hrwhealthcare.com

45 IFF Research Ltd, London (Tel: 020 7837 6363, Fax: 020 7278 9823). Advertising, Business-to-business, Consumer, Customer satisfaction, Direct marketing, Employ-ment/human resources, Energy, Finance/investment, Government/politics, Indus-trial, Insurance, Internet/e-commerce, Printing/packaging, Product development/testing, Public services/utilities, Retail/wholesale, Social research, Telecom-munications, Training/education.

Website: www.iffresearch.com

46 Icon Brand Navigation (UK) Ltd, Buckinghamshire (Tel: 01628 642900, Fax: 01628 642909). Advertising, Automotive, Branding, Direct marketing, FMCG, Food, International, Pharmaceutical, Retail/wholesale, Telecommunications.

Website: www.icon-brand-navigation.com

47 Informer Brand Development, London (Tel: 020 7734 2331, Fax: 020 7734 4350). Advertising, Branding, Children/youth, Consumer, Drinks (alcoholic), Drinks (non-alcoholic), Fashion/textiles, FMCG, E-commerce, Media: TV/radio/press, Retail/wholesale, Telecommunications.

Website: www.informer.com

48 Ipsos-ASI, Middlesex (Tel: 020 8861 8000, Fax: 020 8861 5515). Advertising, Branding.

Website: www.ipsos-asi.com

49 Ipsos-International CatiCentre, Middlesex (Tel: 020 8861 8641, Fax: 020 8427 5228). Advertising, Agriculture, Automotive, Business-to-business, Consumer, Customer satisfaction, Food, Information technology, Media: TV/radio/press, Pharmaceutical, Telecommunications.

Website: www.ipsos.com

50 Ipsos UK Ltd, Middlesex (Tel: 0208861 8000, Fax: 020 8861 5515). Advertising, Agriculture, Automotive, Business-to-business, Children/youth, Consumer, Cus-tomer satisfaction, Drinks (alcoholic), Finance/investment, FMCG, health/beauty/toiletries, Healthcare, Home/garden/DIY, Information technology, Internet/e-commerce, Media: TV/radio/press, Pharmaceutical, Product development/testing, Public services/utilities, Retail/wholesale, Social research, Sport/Leisure/arts, Tele-communications, Transport/distribution, Travel/tourism.

Website: www.ipsos-uk.co.uk

51 Isis Research Plc, London (Tel: 020 8788 8819, Fax: 0208 789 6876). Healthcare, Pharmaceutical.

Website: www.isisresearch.com

52 KMR (Kantar Media Research), London (Tel: 020 8566 5000, Fax: 020 8579 9208). Advertising, Branding, Children/youth, Information technology, International, Internet/e-commerce, Media: TV/radio/press.

Website: www.kantarmedia.com

53 Keith Gorton Services, East Yorkshire (Tel: 01964 535181, Fax: 01964 532823). Business-to-business, Customer satisfaction, Property/construction/housing, Public services/utilities, Retail/wholesale, Transport/distribution.

Website: www.kgs.co.uk

54 Kudos Research Ltd, London (Tel: 020 7490 7888, Fax: 020 7894 4123). Advertising, Automotive, Business-to-business, Customer satisfaction, Employment/human resources, Energy, Finance/investment, Government/politics, Industrial, Information technology, Internet/e-commerce, Media: TV/radio/press, Pharmaceutical, Product development/testing, Public services/utilities.

Website: www.kudosresearch.com

55 Lorien Customer Management, Surrey (Tel: 01932 577800, Fax: 01932 577877). Automotive, Business-to-business, Customer satisfaction, Employment/human resources, Government/politics, Public services/utilities.

Website: www.lorien.co.uk

56 MORI Financial Services (MFS), London (Tel: 020 7222 0232, Fax: 020 7222 1653). Advertising, Customer satisfaction, Direct marketing, Finance/investment, Media: TV/radio/press, Product development/testing.

Website: www.mori.com

57 MORI, London (Tel: 020 7347 3000, Fax: 020 7347 3800). Advertising, Automotive, Branding, Business-to-business, Children/youth, Consumer, Customer satisfaction, Employment/human resources, Energy, Environment, Finance/investment, Government/politics, Healthcare, Information technology, Insurance, International, Internet/e-commerce, Media: TV/radio/press, Pharmaceutical, Property/construction/housing, Public services/utilities, Retail/wholesale, Social research, Sport/leisure/arts, Telecommunications, Training/education, Transport/distribution, Travel/tourism.

Website: www.mori.com

58 MORI Scotland, Edinburgh (Tel: 0131 558 1515, Fax: 0131 558 1717). Advertising, Business-to-business, Children/youth, Customer satisfaction, Employment/human resources, Environment, Finance/investment, Government/politics, Healthcare, International, Internet/e-commerce, Media: TV/radio/press, Pharmaceutical, Property/construction/housing, Public services/utilities, Social research, Sport/leisure/arts, Telecommunications, Training/education, Travel/tourism.

Website: www.mori.com

59 MRSL Group, Oxford (Tel: 01865 788000, Fax: 01865 788001). Advertising, Business-to-business, Consumer, Customer satisfaction, Drinks (alcoholic), Finance/invest-

ment, Food, health/beauty/toiletries, Home/garden/DIY, Information technology, Insurance, Internet/e-commerce, Pharmaceutical, Product development/testing, Public services/utilities, Retail/wholesale.

Website: www.mrsl.co.uk

60 MVA, Surrey (Tel: 01483 728051, Fax: 01483 755207). Business-to-business, Customer satisfaction, Employment/human resources, Government/politics, Media: TV/radio/press, Public services/utilities, Social research, Sport/leisure/arts, Training/education, Transport/distribution, Travel/tourism.

Website: www.mva-research.com

61 Magenta, Oxford (Tel: 01865 788000, Fax: 01865 788001). Advertising, Business-to-business, Consumer, Customer satisfaction, Drinks (alcoholic), Finance/investment, Food, health/beauty/toiletries, Home/garden/DIY, Information technology, Insurance, Internet/e-commerce, Pharmaceutical, Product development/testing, Public services/utilities, Retail/wholesale, Telecommunications, Training/education, Transport/distribution, Travel/tourism.

Website: www.magenta.uk.net

62 Magpie Research Services Ltd, Hertfordshire (Tel: 01462 632220, Fax: 01462 632221). Advertising, Children/youth, Consumer, Customer satisfaction, Drinks (alcoholic), Finance/investment, Food, Pharmaceutical, Product development/testing, Property/construction/housing, Retail/wholesale.

Website: www.mrsgroup.co.uk

63 Market Research Wales Ltd, Cardiff (Tel: 029 2025 0740, Fax: 029 2025 0745). Advertising, Business-to-business, Consumer, Customer satisfaction, Drinks (alcoholic), Finance/investment, Food, Government/politics, Media: TV/radio/press, Product development/testing, Public services/utilities, Retail/wholesale, Social research, Sport/leisure/arts, Training/education, Travel/tourism.

Website: www.mrwales.co.uk

64 Marketing Direction, Surrey (Tel: 020 8979 8111, Fax: 020 8979 8111). Advertising, Business-to-business, Children/youth, Customer satisfaction, Drinks (alcoholic), Employment/human resources, Finance/investment, Food, Home/garden/DIY, Information technology, Media: TV/radio/press, Printing/packaging, Product development/testing, Retail/wholesale, Sport/leisure/arts, Telecommunications, transport/distribution, Travel/tourism.

Website: www.mdlresearch.com

65 Marketing Sciences Ltd, Hampshire (Tel: 01962 842211, Fax: 01962 840486). Advertising, Business-to-business, Children/youth, Customer satisfaction, Drinks (alcoholic), Drinks (non-alcoholic), Employment/human resources, Energy, Finance/investment, Food, health/beauty/toiletries, Healthcare, Product development/Testing, Retail/wholesale, Social research, Telecommunications, Tobacco, Travel/tourism.

Website: www.Marketing-sciences.com

66 Maven Management Ltd, Buckinghamshire (Tel: 01494 688400, Fax: 01494 527739). Automotive, Business-to-business, Consumer, Customer satisfaction, Drinks (alcoholic), Energy, Finance/investment, Industrial, Information technology, Property/construction/housing, Public services/utilities, Retail/wholesale, Transport/distribution.

Website: www.Maven.co.uk

67 Michael Herbert Associates, London (Tel: 020 8749 7001, Fax: 020 8749 8566). Advertising, Business-to-business, Direct marketing, Finance/investment, Internet/e-commerce, Telecommunications, Travel/tourism.

Website: www.mhamr.com

68 Millward Brown, Warwickshire (Tel: 01926 452233, Fax: 01926 833600). Advertising, Automotive, Business-to-business, Children/youth, Consumer, Customer satisfaction, Drinks (alcoholic), Drinks (non-alcoholic), Employment/human resources, Energy, Fashion/textiles, Finance/investment, Food, Information technology, Internet/e-commerce, Media: TV/radio/press, Pharmaceutical, Printing/packaging, Product development/testing, Public services/utilities, Retail/wholesale, Sport/leisure/arts, Telecommunications, Transport/distribution, Travel/tourism.

Website: www.millwardbrown.com

69 Minatec Research Ltd, Hampshire (Tel: 01420 590174, Fax: 01420 590175). Consumer, Drinks (alcoholic), Drinks (non-alcoholic), Food, Health/beauty/toiletries, Retail/wholesale.

70 The Mystery Shopping Company, Hertfordshire (Tel: 01531 635310, Fax: 01531 635967). Consumer, Customer satisfaction, Finance/investment, Government/politics, Retail/wholesale, Telecommunications.

Website: www.mysteryshopping.co.uk

71 NFO WorldGroup, Middlesex (Tel: 020 8782 3000, Fax: 020 8900 1500). Advertising, Agriculture, Automotive, Branding, Business-to-business, Consumer, Customer satisfaction, Direct marketing, Drinks (alcoholic), Drinks (non-alcoholic), Energy, Finance/investment, FMCG, Food, Government/politics, health/beauty/toiletries, Healthcare, Home/garden/DIY, Information technology, Insurance, International, Internet/e-commerce, Media: TV/radio/press, Pharmaceutical, Pricing, Printing/packaging, Product development/testing, Public services/utilities, Retail/wholesale, Social research, Sport/leisure/arts, Telecommunications, Tobacco, transport/distribution, Travel/tourism.

Website: www.nfoeurope.com

72 NOP Research Group, London (Tel: 020 7890 9000, Fax: 020 7890 9001). Advertising, Automotive, Branding, Business-to-business, Catering/hospitality, Children/youth, Consumer, Customer satisfaction, Direct marketing, Drinks (alcoholic), Drinks (non-alcoholic), Employment/human resource, Energy, Environment, Exhibitions/events, Fashion/textiles, Finance/investment, FMCG, Food, Government/politics, Health/beauty/toiletries, Healthcare, Home/garden/DIY, Industrial, Information technology, Insurance, International, Internet/e-commerce, Media: TV/radio/press, Phar-

maceutical, Pricing, Printing/packaging, Product development/testing, Property/construction/housing, Public services/utilities, Retail/wholesale, Social research, Sport/leisure/arts, Telecommunications, Training/education, Transport/distribution, Travel/tourism.

Website: www.nopworld.com

73 NTC Research Ltd, Oxfordshire (Tel: 01491 418700, Fax: 01491 571188). Advertising, Business-to-business, employment/human resources, Finance/investment, Government/politics, Media: TV/radio/press, Retail/wholesale.

Website: www.ntc-research.com

74 NWA Social and Market Research, Stockton-on-Tees (Tel: 01642 360982, Fax: 01642 534894). Consumer, Customer satisfaction, Government/politics, Public services/utilities, Social research, Sport/leisure/arts, Training/education.

75 Netpoll Ltd, London (Tel: 020 7710 2800, Fax: 020 7710 2828). Advertising, Automotive, Business-to-business, Consumer, Customer satisfaction, Finance/investment, Healthcare, Information technology, Internet/e-commerce, Media: TV/radio/press, Sport/leisure/arts.

Website: www.netpoll.net

76 Network Research and Marketing Ltd, London (Tel: 020 7233 933, Fax: 020 7233 9955). Advertising, Automotive, Branding, Business-to-business, Consumer, Customer satisfaction, Drinks (alcoholic), Drinks (non-alcoholic), Employment/human resources, Finance/investment, FMCG, Home/garden/DIY, Information technology, Insurance, International, Internet/e-commerce, Media: TV/radio/press, Public services/utilities, Retail/wholesale, Telecommunications, Transport/distribution, Travel/tourism.

Website: www.networkresearch.co.uk

77 ORC International Ltd, London (Tel: 020 7675 1000, Fax: 020 7675 1900). Business-to-business, Consumer, Customer satisfaction, Drinks (alcoholic), Drinks (non-alcoholic), Employment/human resources, Energy, Finance/investment, Food, Government/politics, Information technology, Insurance, Internet/e-commerce, Media, TV/radio/press, Product development/testing, Public Service/Utilities, Retail/wholesale, Social research, Sport/leisure/arts, Telecommunications, Training/education, Transport/distribution, Travel/tourism.

Website: www.orc.co.uk

78 Outlook Research Ltd, London (Tel: 020 7482 2424, Fax: 020 7482 2427). Advertising, Business-to-business, Energy, Finance/investment, Internet/e-commerce, Media: TV/radio/press, Product development/testing, Public services/utilities, Retail/wholesale, Telecommunications, Transport/distribution.

Website: www.outlookresearch.co.uk

79 Pegram Walters, London (Tel: 020 7689 5000, Fax: 020 7689 5600). Advertising, Automotive, Branding, Business-to-business, Children/youth, Consumer, Customer satisfaction, Drinks (alcoholic), Fashion/textiles, Finance/investment, Food, health/beauty/toiletries, Healthcare, Information technology, Internet/e-commerce, Media:

TV/radio/press, Pharmaceutical, Product development/testing, Public Services/ utilities, Retail/wholesale, Sport/leisure/arts, Telecommunications, Travel/ tourism.

Website: www.pegramwalters.com

80 Phoenix Market Research and Consultancy, Gloucestershire (Tel: 01242 256816, Fax: 01242 256817). Advertising, Business-to-business, Consumer, Customer satisfaction, Direct marketing, Employment/human resources, Finance/investment, Food, Information technology, Product development/testing, Retail/wholesale, Training/ education.

Website: www.phoenixmrc.co.uk

81 Produce Studies Research, Berkshire (Tel: 01635 46112, Fax: 01635 43945). Advertising, Agriculture, Business-to-business, Consumer drinks (alcoholic), Drinks (non-alcoholic), Environment, FMCG, Food, Government/politics, health/beauty/toiletries, Healthcare, Home/garden/DIY, Industrial, Information technology, International, Internet/e-commerce, Media: TV/radio/press, Pharmaceutical, Pricing, Printing/ packaging, Product development/testing, Public services/utilities, Travel/tourism.

Website: www.produce-studies.com

82 RBA Research, West Yorkshire (Tel: 0113 285 6300, Fax: 0113 246 8719). Children/ youth, Consumer, Customer satisfaction, Employment/human resources, Government/politics, Healthcare, Product development/testing, Public services/utilities, Social research, Sport/leisure/arts.

Website: www.rba-research.co.uk

83 RDA Marketing and Change Facilitation, London (Tel: 020 8672 3166, Fax: 020 8767 2617). Business-to-business, Customer satisfaction, Finance/investment, Healthcare, Insurance, International, Product development/testing.

84 RDSI, London (Tel: 020 7837 7700, Fax: 020 7837 7823). Advertising, Automotive, Business-to-business, Children/youth, Drinks (alcoholic), Drinks (non-alcoholic), Environment, Fashion/textiles, Finance/investment, Food, Government/politics, health/beauty/toiletries, Healthcare, Home/garden/DIY, Information technology, Media: TV/radio/press, Product development/testing, Public services/utilities, Retail/wholesale, Social research, Telecommunications, Travel/tourism.

Website: www.rdsiresearch.com

85 Recom Research in Communications, Middlesex (Tel: 020 8560 0808, Fax: 020 8560 0890). Advertising, Branding, Business-to-business, Customer satisfaction, FMCG, Information technology, International, Internet/e-commerce, Media: TV/radio/ press, Product development/testing, Sport/leisure/arts, Telecommunications.

Website: www.recomresearch.com

86 Research By Design Ltd, West Midlands (Tel: 0121 711 1495, Fax: 0121 711 4944). Business-to-business, Consumer, Finance/investment, Industrial, Public services/ utilities, Social research.

87 Research In Focus Ltd, Berkshire (Tel: 01344 894894, Fax: 01344 894800). Advertising, Agriculture, Business-to-business, Consumer, Customer satisfaction, Drinks (alcoholic), Finance/investment, Food, Product development/testing, Sport/leisure/arts, Travel/tourism.

Website: www.focus-group.co.uk

88 Research International Group Ltd, London (Tel: 020 7656 5500, Fax: 020 7201 0701). Advertising, Agriculture, Automotive, Business-to-business, Children/youth, Consumer, Customer satisfaction, Drinks (alcoholic), Employment/human resources, Energy, Finance/investment, Food, health/beauty/toiletries, Healthcare, Industrial, Information technology, Media: TV/radio/press, Pharmaceutical, Printing/packaging, Product development/testing, Public services/utilities, Retail/wholesale, Sport/ leisure/arts, Telecommunications, Tobacco, Transport/distribution, Travel/tourism.

Website: www.research-int.com

89 Research and Marketing Associates Ltd, West Midlands (Tel: 01564 770095, Fax: 01564 770307). Advertising, Automotive, Branding, Customer satisfaction, Drinks (alcoholic), Home/garden/DIY, Property/construction/housing, Sport/leisure/arts, Transport/distribution, Travel/tourism.

Website: www.rama-research.co.uk

90 Researchcraft Ltd, Warwickshire (Tel: 01926 424518, Fax: 01926 336669). Advertising, Consumer, Customer satisfaction, Finance/investment, FMCG, Retail/wholesale.

Website: www.researchcraft.com

91 RHMR, Derbyshire (Tel: 01283 704475, Fax: 01283 704485). Drinks (alcoholic), Finance/investment, FMCG, Home/garden/DIY, Retail/wholesale, Sport/leisure/ arts.

Website: www.rhmr.co.uk

92 SMSR: Social and Market Strategic Research Ltd, Yorkshire (Tel: 01482 211200, Fax: 01482 211201). Customer satisfaction, Government/politics, Healthcare, Social research, Training/education.

Website: www.smsr.co.uk

93 The Sample Surveys Research Group, Kent (Tel: 01732 874450, Fax: 01732 875100). Advertising, Automotive, Branding, Business-to-business, Consumer, Customer satisfaction, Employment/human resources, Exhibitions/events, Finance/investment, FMCG, Food, health/beauty/toiletries, Information technology, Insurance, International, Internet/e-commerce, Media: TV/radio/press, Pharmaceutical, Printing/packaging, Product development/testing, Public services/utilities, Retail/ wholesale, Social research, Telecommunications, Transport/distribution, Travel/ tourism.

Website: www.ssrg.co.uk

94 Sample Surveys Telephone, London (Tel: 0870 870 7010, Fax: 0870 870 7020). Automotive, Business-to-business, Consumer, Customer satisfaction, Employment/

human resources, Energy, Finance/investment, Healthcare, Information technology, International, Media: TV/radio/press, Pharmaceutical, Public services/utilities, Retail/wholesale, Sport/leisure/arts, Telecommunications, Travel/tourism.

Website: www.ssrg.co.uk

95 Saville Rossiter-Base, Bedfordshire (Tel: 01582 483043, Fax: 01582 419276). Advertising, Customer satisfaction, Finance/investment, Media: TV/radio/press, Telecommunications, Travel/tourism.

Website: www.sr-b.co.uk

96 Scottish Opinion Ltd, Edinburgh (Tel: 0131 332 7799, Fax: 0131 332 9129). Advertising, Business-to-business, Consumer, Government/politics, Internet/e-commerce, Media: TV/radio/press, Public services/utilities.

Website: www.scottishopinion.com

97 Select Research Ltd, Worcester (Tel: 01886 884009, Fax: 01886 884141). Advertising, Business-to-business, Food, Home/garden/DIY, Retail/wholesale, Travel/tourism.

Website: www.select-research.com

98 Simons Priest and Associates, London (Tel: 020 7253 0123, Fax: 020 7336 6500). Advertising, Branding, Children/youth, Consumer, Customer satisfaction, Drinks (alcoholic), Drinks (non-alcoholic), FMCG, International, Internet/e-commerce, Media: TV/radio/press, Retail/wholesale, telecommunications.

Website: www.simonspriest.com

99 Solutions Strategy, Research, Facilitation Ltd, London (Tel: 020 7700 5500, Fax: 020 7700 5123). Advertising, Branding, Children/youth, Drinks (alcoholic), FMCG, Government/politics, Healthcare, International, Internet/e-commerce, Product development/testing, Social research, Travel/tourism.

Website: www.solutions-research.co.uk

100 Sports Marketing Surveys Ltd, Surrey (Tel: 01932 350600, Fax: 01932 350375). Catering/Hospitality, Exhibitions/events, International, Internet/e-commerce, Media: TV/radio/press, Sport/leisure/arts.

Website: www.sportsmarketingsurveys.com

101 Steer Davies Gleave, London (Tel: 020 7919 8500, Fax: 020 7827 9850). Government/politics, Pricing, telecommunications, Transport/distribution, Travel/tourism.

Website: www.sdgworld.net

102 Sunrise Tabulations, Kent (Tel: 01622 618763, Fax: 01622 618764). Automotive, Business-to-business, Finance/investment, Industrial, Pharmaceutical, Product development/testing, Public services/utilities, Travel/tourism.

Website: www.sunrisetabulations.co.uk

103 Survey and Marketing Services Ltd, Newcastle upon Tyne (Tel: 0191 270 0596, Fax: 0191 266 6291). Advertising, Automotive, Consumer, Customer satisfaction, Drinks

(alcoholic), Drinks (non-alcoholic), environment, Finance/investment, Food, health/ beauty/toiletries, Healthcare, Printing/packaging, Product development/testing, Property/construction/housing, Public services/utilities, Sport/leisure/arts, Transport/distribution, Travel/tourism.

Website: www.surveymarketing.co.uk

104 Sweeney Pinedo, London (Tel: 020 7704 0410, Fax: 020 7359 7365). Advertising, Branding, Business-to-business, Children/youth, Consumer, Customer satisfaction, Direct marketing, health/beauty/toiletries, Information technology, International, Internet/e-commerce, Media: TV/radio/press, Pricing, Printing/packaging, Product development/testing, Telecommunications.

105 Swift Research, West Yorkshire (Tel: 01937 543600, Fax: 01937 543610). Advertising, Business-to-business, Consumer, Customer satisfaction, Employment, Human resources, Finance/investment, Food, Information technology, Product development/testing, Retail/wholesale, Telecommunications, Training/education.

Website: www.swift-research.co.uk

106 Taylor Nelson Sofres Ireland incorporating Market Research Bureau of Ireland (MRBI), Republic of Ireland (Tel: +353 1 278 1011, Fax: +353 1 278 1022). Advertising, Automotive, Business-to-business, Children/youth, Customer satisfaction, Drinks (alcoholic), Drinks (non-alcoholic), Employment/human resources, Energy, Finance/ investment/Food, Government/politics, health/beauty/toiletries, Media: TV/ radio/press, Retail/wholesale, Telecommunications, Tobacco, Transport/distribution, Travel/tourism.

Website: www.tnsofres.com

107 Taylor Nelson Sofres Plc, London (Tel: 020 8967 0007, Fax: 020 8967 4060). Advertising, Automotive, Business-to-business, Children/youth, Consumer, Customer satisfaction, Direct marketing, Drinks (alcoholic), Drinks (non-alcoholic), Employment/human resources, Energy, Fashion/textiles, Finance/investment, Food, Government/politics, health/beauty/toiletries, Healthcare, Home/garden/DIY, Industrial, Information technology, Insurance, Internet/e-commerce, Media: TV/ radio/press, Pharmaceutical, Printing/packaging, Product development/testing, Public services/utilities, Retail/wholesale, Social research, Sport/leisure/arts, Telecommunications, Tobacco, Transport/distribution, Travel/tourism.

Website: www.tnsofres.com

108 Telephone Surveys Ltd, Northamptonshire (Tel: 01604 230123, Fax: 01604 231003). Advertising, Business-to-business, Customer satisfaction, Information technology, Telecommunications, Travel/tourism.

109 Test Research, London (Tel: 020 7689 8484, Fax: 020 7689 8499). Advertising, Branding, Consumer, Direct marketing, Finance/investment, Government/politics, Public services/utilities.

Website: www.testresearch.co.uk

110 Topflight Research Ltd, Surrey (Tel: 020 8941 8887, Fax: 020 8941 8020). Business-to-business, Transport/distribution.

111 Total Romtec, Berkshire (Tel: 01628 770077, Fax: 01628 785433). Information technology, Internet/e-commerce, Telecommunications.

Website: www.total-romtec.com

112 Travel Research Centre Ltd, London (Tel: 020 7224 4747, Fax: 020 7224 3747). Advertising, Business-to-business, Customer satisfaction, Transport/distribution, Travel/tourism.

113 VAR International Ltd, London (Tel: 020 8994 9177, Fax: 020 8994 2115). Advertising, Automotive, Business-to-business, Consumer, Customer satisfaction, Food, Industrial, Information technology, Media: TV/radio/press, Product development/testing, Sport/leisure/arts, Travel/tourism.

Website: www.varinternational.com

114 Viewpoint, Surrey (Tel: 020 8783 2700, Fax: 020 8783 2710). Advertising, Automotive, Business-to-business, Children/youth, Consumer, Drinks (alcoholic), Drinks (non-alcoholic), Finance/investment, health/beauty/toiletries, Healthcare, Information technology, Insurance, Internet/e-commerce, Media: TV/radio/press, Pharmaceutical, Public services/utilities, Retail/wholesale, Telecommunications.

Website: www.viewpointservices.com

115 Virtual Surveys Ltd, Hampshire (Tel: 01256 767576, Fax: 01256 760894). Business-to-business, Customer satisfaction, Drinks (alcoholic), Finance/investment, Information technology, Internet/e-commerce, Media: TV/radio/press, Retail/wholesale, Training/education, Travel/tourism.

Website: www.virtualsurveys.com

116 Weeks Computing Services, London (Tel: 020 7379 3548, Fax: 020 7240 8870). Advertising, Automotive, Consumer, Customer satisfaction, Insurance, Pharmaceutical.

Website: www.weekscomputing.com

117 Catherine M Whitehead, East Sussex (Tel: 01892 783384, Fax: 01892 784557). Automotive, Business-to-business, Food, Home/garden/DIY, Media: TV/radio/press, Travel/tourism.

118 Woodholmes-ksa, Newcastle upon Tyne (Tel: 0191 213 0788, Fax: 0191 213 0214). Advertising, Business-to-business, Consumer, Customer satisfaction, Employment/human resources, Environment, Finance/investment, Food, Industrial, Media: TV/radio/press, Product development/testing, Property/construction/housing, Public services/utilities, Sport/leisure/arts, Training/education, Transport/distribution, Travel/tourism.

Website: www.woodholmesksa.com

4.4 Omnibus research surveys

Omnibus research represents a middle ground between off-the-peg research services, where the data has already been collected and the researcher simply buys what is available, and primary research, where the researcher has to collect the information personally. Omnibus research describes regular research surveys that are being undertaken with a stated frequency and a decided method, using a set number of respondents and sampling points. The fieldwork 'omnibus' is running and the client is invited to 'board the bus' by adding a few personal questions to the questionnaire. The omnibus user has the advantages of original question design, privacy of information and representativeness of sample, without having to bear all the fieldwork costs alone. The user pays only for the number of questions included and this is a very cheap form of original survey research. Omnibus research is particularly suitable for fairly robust data, e.g. the usage and purchase of products. It is less reliable for attitudinal and opinion data. This is because an omnibus survey might last for 40 minutes or even more. During that time the respondent might be asked about six or more entirely different topics, which could range from voting intentions through bank account ownership and holiday-taking, to the purchase of hair-care products. This miscellaneous mix of bedfellows, who may come together in a single questionnaire, means that if more than superficial data is required the respondent is unlikely to be in a frame of mind to give sufficient concentration to any single topic for reliable attitudinal data to be produced. For straightforward questions, for example, 'When did you last buy . . .?', 'Do you own . . .?' or 'Have you ever . . .?', where top-of-the-head answers are perfectly acceptable, omnibus surveys can provide good original data at a fraction of the cost of a 'made-to-measure' survey.

A list of organizations providing omnibus research services is published each month as an advertising feature in the MRS newsletter *Research*. A copy of this can be obtained from the Market Research Society (Tel: 020 7490 4911) and will identify companies currently offering services.

A *User's and Buyer's Guide* to omnibus surveys is published annually in *ADMAP* magazine (Tel: 01491 411 000, Fax: 01491 571 188). This provides an objective comparison of the available services based on data provided by the respective companies. The following listing is compiled from *ADMAP* and ad hoc information from the MRS.

4.4.1 Omnibus research services and suppliers

The providers of omnibus research can be separated into two categories. First, there are general omnibus surveys which represent the entire adult population. Second, there is a wide range of specialist survey providers covering most major business sectors.

4.4.2 General population omnibus surveys

1 Phonebus. Taylor Nelson Sofres Plc, Westgate, London W5 1UA (Tel: 020 8967 0007, Fax: 020 8967 4060). A consumer omnibus, running twice-weekly, providing data from sample sizes of 1000–2000, with a 4-day turnaround. Methodology: computer-assisted telephone interviews (CATI) and RDD.

Website:
http://www.tnsofres.com/consumeromnibus/phonebus/index.cfm

2 Access by Telephone. BMRB International, Hadley House, 78–81 Uxbridge Road, Ealing, London W5 5SU (Tel: 020 8579 9208, Fax: 020 8579 9208). The survey is conducted every week. Sample size of 2000 adults (aged 16+), who are representative of the British population in terms of age, gender and class.

Website: http://www.bmrb-access.co.uk/

3 Access Face-to-Face. BMRB International, Hadley House, 78–81 Uxbridge Road, Ealing, London W5 5SU (Tel: 020 8579 9208, Fax: 020 8579 9208). The survey is conducted every week. Sample size of 2000 adults (aged 15+), who are representative of the British population in terms of age, gender and class.

Website: http://www.bmrb-access.co.uk/

4 Access to Internet. BMRB International, Hadley House, 78–81 Uxbridge Road, Ealing, London W5 5SU (Tel: 020 8579 9208, Fax: 020 8579 9208). Every week 750 respondents with access to the Internet are contacted at home or work. Methodology: respondents are selected either face-to-face or by telephone.

Website: http://www.bmrb-access.co.uk/

5 Access Online. BMRB International, Hadley House, 78–81 Uxbridge Road, Ealing, London W5 5SU (Tel: 020 8579 9208, Fax: 020 8579 9208). The survey is conducted with a nationally representative sample of 2000 people.

Website: http://www.bmrb-access.co.uk/

6 Telefacts. Facts International Led, Facts Centre, 3 Henwood, Ashford, Kent TN24 8FL (Tel: 01233 637000, Fax: 01233 626950). TeleFACTS is a telephone omnibus covering the whole of the UK, using next-number digit dialling to ensure a complete representative sample of all telephone subscribers/householders. Information is collected by a computerized telephone interviewing package. Questions by Thursday, results on the following Monday. Sample size of 500 or 1000 adults.

Website: http://www.facts.uk.com

7 Omnibus. CID Gallup, Apartado 5413–1000 San Jose, Costa Rica (Tel: +506 2204101, Fax: +506 2312145). CID Gallup carries out omnibus-type surveys every three months.

Website: http://www.cidgallup.com/en/

8 Ncompass. Taylor Nelson Sofres Plc, Westgate, London W5 1UA (Tel: 020 8967 0007, Fax: 020 8967 4060). An international omnibus, with access to cost-effective world-wide consumer behaviour and opinions. The following key consumer markets can be researched within 6 days: France, Germany, Italy, Spain, Great Britain and the USA. Sample size of 1000

adults per country. Questions by Wednesday, results ready by the following Wednesday.

Website:
http://www.tnsofres.com/consumeromnibus/ncompass/index.cfm

9 ICM Omnibus. ICM Research, ICM Research, Knighton House, 56 Mortimer Street, London W1W 7RT (Tel: 020 7436 3114, Fax: 020 7436 3179). Telephone omnibus service, twice weekly. Sample size of 1000 adults aged 16/18+ years. Methodology is random digit dialling. Quotas are set on age, gender, standard geographical regions and housing tenure.

Website: http://www.icmresearch.co.uk/specialist_areas/omnibus.htm

10 MORI Omnibus. MORI House, 79–81 Borough Road, London SE1 1FY (Tel: 020 7347 3000, Fax: 020 7347 3800). Face-to-face interviews on the general public aged 15+ years. Sample design: 210 of the 641 parliamentary constituencies in Great Britain have been selected, on the basis that they are representative of the whole country for region, class, voting patterns, etc. Within each constituency, two mapped areas each containing 5000 addresses are selected. The two areas are rotated so that interviewers approach a different set of addresses each time, within the mapped area.

Website: http://www.mori.com/omnibus/index.shtml

11 Random Location Omnibus. NOP Research Group, Ludgate House, London SE1 9UL (Tel: 020 7890 9000). Interviews are contacted in-home using CAPI laptop computers, three or four times a month. Each face-to-face omnibus survey is conducted with a sample of 2000 adults (aged 15+ years).

Website: http://www.nop.co.uk/

12 Telebus. NOP Research Group, Ludgate House, London SE1 9UL (Tel: 020 7890 9000). A twice-weekly telephone omnibus service, with a turnaround of 2.5 days. Sample size of 1000 adults (aged 15+ years).

Website: http://www.nop.co.uk/

13 NOP E-Omnibus Service. NOP Research Group, Ludgate House, London SE1 9UL (Tel: 020 7890 9000). Representative survey of the Great British public of weekly Internet usage. Sample Size: 1000 weekly users of the Internet aged 16+ years. (A response rate of 50 per cent is expected and therefore 2000 leads are carefully selected from the panel and e-mailed). Survey is intended to run once a month.

Website: http://www.nop.co.uk

14 Omnimas. Taylor Nelson Sofres Plc, Westgate, London W5 1UA (Tel: 020 8967 0007, Fax: 020 8967 4060). The largest weekly consumer omnibus survey in Great Britain. Interviews 2100 adults aged 16+ years per week.

Methodology: a random locations sample, visiting respondents' homes using CAPI.

Website:
http://www.tnsofres.com/consumeromnibus/omnimas/index.cfm

15 Capibus GB. Kings House, Kymberley Road, Harrow, Middlesex HA1 1PT. A weekly omnibus survey that samples 2000 adults, aged 15+ years each week. Collects extensive background information on the respondent and the household, including demographics.

Website: www.ipsos-uk.co.uk

16 CAPIBUS Europe, France (Tel: +33 1 53 68 28 28, Fax: +33 1 53 6801 82). 5000 face-to-face CAPI-based interviews conducted weekly in France, the UK, Germany, Italy and Spain.

Website: http://www.ipsos.com/sitemap/fsite_map.htm

17 NETCAPI Europe, France (Tel: +33 1 53 68 28 28, Fax: +33 1 53 6801 82). 1000 face-to-face CAPI-based interviews conducted weekly with Internet users in France, the UK, Germany, Italy and Spain.

Website: http://www.ipsos.com/sitemap/fsite_map.htm

18 National Flexibus/Superbus. Pegram Walters, International Research and Consulting, 242–233 St. John Street, London EC1V 2PG (Tel: 020 7689 5000, Fax: 020 7689 5600). Four times a year, questionnaires are sent out to between 1000 and 10,000 households. National Superbus is also quarterly and can screen up to 50,000 panel households to identify users of low-incidence products and services.

Website: http://www.marketfacts.ca/products/omnibus.shtml

19 MRUK Omnibus. Every month an omnibus survey is carried out in Scotland. Sample size of 1000 adults, added 16+ years. Methodology: in-home interviews, conducted on a random basis within sampling areas.

Website: http://www.mrscotland.co.uk/omnibus.html

20 Exage Omnibus Surveys. Surveys every three months, seeking information regarding markets and opinions. Sample size of 1000 interviews. A private company that will cater for individual needs.

Website: http://www.exage.com/whatisexage/omnibus.asp

21 Lansdowne Omnibus, Republic of Ireland (Tel: +353 1 661 3483, Fax: +353 1 661 3479). The Lansdowne Omnibus survey covers a variety of topics. Questions can be directed to all adults or to specific groups.

Website: www.lansdownemarketresearch.ie

22 RSGB Omnibus, London (Tel: 020 8967 4224, Fax: 020 8967 4330). The RSGB Omnibus is a weekly survey of 2000 adults (aged 16+ years) in the UK, conducted via face-to-face in-home interviews.

Website: www.rsgbomnibus.com

4.4.3 Specialist omnibus surveys

Age specific

1 Access to Youth. BMRB International, London (Tel: 020 8566 5000, Fax: 020 8579 9208). A tailored omnibus for younger respondents, aged 7–19 years. 1000 interviews conducted monthly.

Website: www.bmrb.co.uk

2 Child, Youth and Parent Research. Carrick James Market Research, London (Tel: 020 7724 3836, Fax: 020 7224 8257). Large-scale quantitative and qualitative research available. Monthly omnibus services carried out.

Website: www.cjmr.co.uk

3 European Child Omnibus. Carrick James Market Research, London (Tel: 020 7724 3836, Fax: 020 7224 8257). Survey conducted in major European countries, including France, Germany, Italy and Spain.

Website: www.cjmr.co.uk

4 Young Generation Omnibus. NOP Research Group, London (Tel: 020 7890 9000, Fax: 020 7890 9001). The collection of attitudes and preferences of the children and youth of today. Reaches a new sample of some 1000 children aged 7–16 years, on a monthly basis.

Website: www.nop.co.uk

5 Survey of Secondary School Pupils in England and Wales. MORI, London (Tel: 020 7347 3000, Fax: 020 7347 3800). Every year MORI runs the only school-based omnibus study devoted exclusively to exploring the views, experiences and aspirations of a large and representative sample of between 2500 and 3000 young people, aged 11–16 years.

Website: www.mori.com

Agriculture

6 Produce Studies Research. Berkshire (Tel: 01635 46112, Fax: 01635 43945). Provides omnibus surveys as one of its research services. Experience includes agricultural inputs and crop protection products, machinery, veterinary, animal health and nutrition and pet products, biotechnology, seed and e-commerce.

Website: www.produce-studies.com

7 FlexiFarm. Ipsos UK, Middlesex (Tel: 020 8861 8000, Fax: 020 8861 5515). Omnibus surveys consisting of farmer panels for the continual monitoring of on-farm usership of key animal health products.

Website: www.ipsos-uk.co.uk

8 Agribus. JT Research Ltd (Tel: 01306 713132, Fax: 01306 713135). A monthly farmers' omnibus survey.

Business

9 Small Business Omnibus. NOP Research Group, London (Tel: 020 7890 9000, Fax: 020 7890 9001). NOP runs a bi-monthly Small Business Omnibus. 500 interviews are conducted with the key financial decision makers of businesses in England and Wales.

Website: www.nop.co.uk

Country specific

10 IMS Omnibus Survey. Irish Marketing Surveys Ltd, Republic of Ireland (Tel: +353 1 676 1196, Fax: +353 1 676 0877). Representative of the adult population aged 15+ years living in the Republic of Ireland. Sample size of 1200 adults, quota controlled by gender, marital status, age, social class, region and area. Data collected through interviews.

Website: www.imsl.ie

11 IMS Catibus. Irish Marketing Surveys Ltd, Republic of Ireland (Tel: +353 1 676 1196, Fax: +353 1 676 0877). Designed to track changes in consumer buying behaviour and opinions. Based on the responses of 1000 adults, aged 15+ years, conducted on a monthly basis.

Website: www.imsl.ie

12 UMS Omnibus. Ulster Marketing Surveys Ltd (Tel: 028 9023 1060, Fax: 028 9024 3887). The Northern Ireland Omnibus Survey is based on adults aged 16+ years.

Website: www.ums-research.com

13 Welsh Omnibus Survey. Beaufort Research Ltd, Cardiff (Tel: 029 2037 8565, Fax: 029 2037 0600). Conducted four times per year, in March, June, September and November. Results are based on a minimum of 1000 adults aged 16+ years who are residents of Wales.

Website: www.beaufortresearch.co.uk

14 Omnibus of Welsh Speakers. Beaufort Research Ltd, Cardiff (Tel: 029 2037 8565, Fax: 029 2037 0600). Surveys are undertaken in March and September each year, with a sample size of 1000 adults (minimum), aged 16+ years, who are resident in Wales and able to speak Welsh.

Website: www.beaufortresearch.co.uk

15 CWMNIBUS. Beaufort Research Ltd, Cardiff (Tel: 029 2037 8565, Fax: 029 2037 0600). A survey that is designed to be representative of all SME business establishments in Wales. 500 interviews are undertaken twice a year, using research techniques such as CATI.

Website: www.beaufortresearch.co.uk

16 Market Research Wales Ltd, Cardiff (Tel: 029 2025 0740, Fax: 029 2025 0745). An omnibus service providing a low-cost alternative to ad hoc research.

Website: www.mrwales.co.uk

17 Scottish Opinion, Edinburgh (Tel: 0131 332 7799, Fax: 0131 332 9129). An omnibus survey that is carried out 7 days a week, interviewing 150 people across Scotland, recruiting a minimum of 1000 new respondents each week.

Website: www.scottishopinion.com

18 MORI Scotland, Edinburgh (Tel: 0131 558 1515, Fax: 0131 588 1717). Established in 1995, provides research services to clients in Scotland and the north-east of England. MORI incorporates the omnibus survey in its research and is able to offer skills and expertise to the public and private sectors.

Website: www.mori.com

19 MORI MRC. Republic of Ireland (Tel: +353 1 676 8651, Fax: +353 1 676 6683). MORI MRC provides a unique combination of the experience and knowledge of the Irish market with the expertise of the UK's largest independent research agency. Research services include a monthly independent omnibus.

Website: www.morimrc.ie

20 MRC Field Ireland. Belfast (Tel: 028 9050 0810, Fax: 028 9050 0811). Research services include an omnibus survey facility.

21 MotoBus Europe. Ultex Group, Kent (Tel: 01732 838155, Fax: 01732 838156). Ultex conducts a single syndicated motorists' omnibus survey covering the whole of Europe. The research is carried out simultaneously in each country, interviewing 1000 people per country.

Website: www.ultexmr.com

22 National Ethnic Omnibus. Ethnic Focus/STRC, Middlesex (Tel: 020 8863 0958). Tracks the opinions of a diverse range of ethnic groups.

Website: www.ethnicfocus.com

23 International Omnibus. International Field and Tab Solutions, Surrey (Tel: 020 8401 1390, Fax: 020 8401 1391). Uses an omnibus survey to provide research in the main European countries.

Website: www.iftsl.com

Leisure

24 Sports Marketing Surveys, Surrey (Tel: 01932 350 600, Fax: 01932 350 375). A full-service market research agency that specializes in sports research.

Website: www.sportsmarketingsurveys.com

Medical

25 Isis Research Plc, London (Tel: 020 8788 8819, Fax: 020 8789 6876). Conducts omnibus surveys on the healthcare and pharmaceutical markets.

Website: www.isisresearch.com

26 PMIS Medical Research Factors Ltd, Buckinghamshire (Tel: 01494 893600, Fax: 01494 893655). Conducts omnibus surveys on the healthcare and pharmaceutical markets.

27 Omnimed International. Taylor Nelson Sofres Plc, London (Tel: 020 8967 0007, Fax: 020 8967 4060). A weekly service that provides online access to a range of doctors' opinions and behaviours within the healthcare market. Sample size is a minimum of 200 general practitioners (GPs) in the USA and each of the major European markets.

Website: www.tnsofres.com

28 Omnimed. Taylor Nelson Sofres Plc, London (Tel: 020 8967 0007, Fax: 020 8967 4060). A weekly service of face-to-face interviews that can be individually tailored to suit a company's objectives.

Website: www.tnsofres.com

29 Pharmacy Omnibus. Taylor Nelson Sofres Plc, London (Tel: 020 8967 0007, Fax: 020 8967 4060). An omnibus that runs every six weeks to a representative field of 200 retail pharmacists, which measures pharmacy information at the point of sale.

Website: www.tnsofres.com

30 GP ROS. NOP Research Group, London (Tel: 020 7890 9000, Fax: 020 7890 9001). A nationally representative random sample of 200 GPs based in practices in Great Britain. Research is carried out nine times per year, using face-to-face interviews.

Website: www.nop.co.uk

31 GP Net. NOP Research Group, London (Tel: 020 7890 9000, Fax: 020 7890 9001). A twice-monthly, nationally representative, online quota-based UK omnibus service among 100 or 200 GPs.

Website: www.nop.co.uk

32 Quest. NOP Research Group, London (Tel: 020 7890 9000, Fax: 020 7890 9001). A monthly programme of omnibus services among nationally representative, random samples of hospital specialists and community-based healthcare professionals in the UK: six hospitals and four community Quest omnibus surveys are offered each month, using both personal and telephone interviewing methodologies.

Website: www.nop.co.uk

33 InterQuest. NOP Research Group, London (Tel: 020 7890 9000, Fax: 020 7890 9001). A monthly programme of (principally telephone) omnibus surveys among random samples of hospital specialists, GPs and retail pharmacists, covering Europe, Japan and the USA.

Website: www.nop.co.uk

Motoring

34 Automotive. NOP Research Group, London (Tel: 020 7890 9000, Fax: 020 7890 9001). NOP carries out a number of continuous studies which track changes in brand image and customer opinion, improvements in vehicle quality, advertising awareness and effectiveness, and owner experience with dealers' sales and service departments.

Website: www.nop.co.uk

4.5 Specialist research services

4.5.1 Types of research offered via the Market Research Society

In addition to the syndicated data and omnibus research services that can be bought off-the-peg, marketing research organizations provide a wide range of specialist research facilities. In this case the client is buying off-the-peg expertise in a particular area of research. The kinds of specialist technique that have been developed and are available for purchase are shown in detail in the MRS publication *The Research Buyer's Guide*. An indication of the range of off-the-peg expertise available is shown in Table 4.1.

More detailed reading of the entries for the many firms listed indicates that there is an organization offering specialist expertise in almost every market of any size: consumer, trade, industrial or service, for both public and private organizations. Special research techniques are also available for a wide variety of applications such as company acquisitions, telephone research, postal research, business research, name testing, market modelling, sales forecasting, colour and design research, transport studies, retail location, and so on.

As this section indicates, a wide range of specialist research services exists and information about them is contained in the MRS publications, *The Research Buyer's Guide* and *Research* (monthly). Both can be obtained on request to: The Market Research Society, 15 Northburgh Street, London EC1 0AH (Tel: 020 7490 4911). The MRS also publishes a series of guides and notes on research in many European and other countries. Some of these can be accessed via the website at www.mrs.org.uk

Information about organizations providing research services can also be obtained from the Management Consultancies Association, which publishes a directory of member firms and their services to clients (Tel: 020 7321 3990, Fax: 020 7321 3991).

Table 4.1   Services offered by members of the Market Research Society

Data collection methods	Areas of expertise
Computer-aided personal interviewing	Business-to-business/industrial
Computer-aided telephone interviewing	Children
Computer aided web interviewing	Consumers
Continuous consumer panel	Customer satisfaction
Executive interviewing	Employee research
Face-to-face	Government/local authority
Hall tests	Investor relations
Observation	New product development
Group discussions	Trade retail
Depth interviewing	Social research
Postal panel surveys	Retail audit
Telephone interviewing	

Market sectors	Market sectors
Advertising	Home furnishing
Agricultural	Information technology
Automotive	Media
Catering	Medical
Chemicals	Office equipment
Clothing and footwear	Packaging and paper
Confectionery	Pharmaceutical
Construction	Product testing
Detergents/household cleaners	Public opinion polling
DIY	Publishing
Drinks	Retail
Energy: fuel gas and oil	Sport and leisure
Engineering	Telecommunications
Environment	Tobacco
Exhibitions	Toiletries
Financial	Transport
Food	Travel
Gardening	Tourism
Home entertainment	

Source: Market Research Society: *The Research Buyer's Guide.*

4.5.2 Consumer classification systems

Regular attempts are made to improve on basic classification data, and advertising agencies and market research companies regularly release the latest panacea to the problem of putting individuals into boxes, a process necessary to allow the effective use of marketing budgets. Direct marketing and database marketing are going some way towards making individual consumers viable 'sectors' for business activity. In some cases this is being combined with enhanced production technology to enable the marketing of customized products at similar cost to mass-produced items. However, in most industries the process of segmentation lies at the heart of successful business activity. Segmentation systems can be divided into three broad categories:

- social grading or social class
- demographic
- geographic and geodemographic.

Social grading or social class

Social grading (used by Joint Industry Classification for the National Readership Survey, JICNARS) is a system of classifying the UK population according to the occupation of the head of the household, allocating people to one of six social grades; these are also referred to as 'social classes' and are shown in Table 4.2. The system was used before the Second World War and is still the major classification system used today. The reason for its widespread use is that members of each social group or class show broadly similar patterns of behaviour, consumption, lifestyle, attitudes and media use in many situations. This can help to explain differences in use of, or response to, all kinds of products and services, and therefore gives a basis for comparison. It is also relatively easy to apply in research surveys and so is used in most surveys and marketing activity. However, the very fact that it is a pre-war classification system highlights its current social grading

Table 4.2

% population 15+*	Social grade	Social status	Chief income earner's occupation
3	A	Upper middle class	Higher managerial, administrative or professional
19	B	Middle class	Intermediate managerial, administrative or professional
27	C1	Lower middle class	Supervisory or clerical, and junior managerial, administrative or professional
23	C2	Skilled working class	Skilled manual workers
16	D	Working class	Semiskilled and unskilled manual workers
12	E	Those at lowest levels of subsistence	State pensioners or widows (no other earner), casual or lowest grade workers

Source: JICNARS National Readership Survey.

deficiencies. Although the process of social change is slow (hence the system still has broad relevance in many situations), since the Second World War there has been considerable social change resulting in more social diversity. For many situations the system of social grading is no longer relevant and so cannot help in explaining or understanding consumer behaviour. The increasing number of single-parent families and the increase in the number of women in paid employment mean that the conventional classification of the male breadwinner is no longer appropriate. In addition, social grading does not reflect propensity to spend or save. In 1990 the MRS published an updated guide to socioeconomic status, but this has still proved problematic. One major area of difficulty is the classification of individuals by interviewers: there are many new occupations that do not fit neatly into the JICNARS system. This explains the recent decision to look again at the social grading system to reflect more accurately contemporary social grading.

Demographic

Sagacity

This is a system of classification pioneered by IPSOS RSL (Tel: 020 8861 6000). Its basic thesis is that in addition to differences between groups of people accounted for by social grading, other important differences in aspirations and behaviour patterns are accounted for by general income level and by the stage of life individuals are at in the 'family life cycle'. Figure 4.1 describes them briefly and indicates their size as a percentage of the total adult population.

Geodemographics

Geodemographics reflects the fact that people living in particular types of neighbourhood tend to exhibit broadly similar patterns of behaviour. Each neighbourhood has its own special characteristics, which become self-perpetuating. People who identify with neighbourhood types are more likely to move in and those who do not are likely to move out. The result is the world we see around us, consisting of 'good', 'bad', 'young', 'trendy', 'dormitory' and 'retired' areas, and so on. These areas can be described by using a mix of variables measured by the census of population. Geodemographic systems relate the characteristics described in the census to postcodes, and these characteristics are then used to describe average households. The postcode groupings can then be linked to behaviour-specific data held on other databases, thus further refining the ability to describe and target specific groups.

ACORN

The first major research service to use geodemographics was ACORN, developed in the early 1980s. ACORN is an off-the-peg service offered by CACI Information Services, London (Tel: 020 7602 6000, Fax: 020 7603 5862). Its title is an acronym for 'A Classification of Residential Neighbourhoods'

The basic thesis of the SAGACITY grouping is that people have different aspirations and behaviour patterns as they go through their life-cycle. Four main stages of life-cycles are defined which are sub-divided by income and occupation groups.

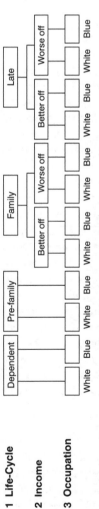

1 Life-Cycle | Dependent | Pre-family | Family | Late

2 Income | | | Better off | Worse off | Better off | Worse off

3 Occupation | White Blue White Blue | White Blue White Blue | White Blue White Blue | White Blue White Blue

Descriptive notations for each of the twelve groups are described below together with their size as a percentage of total adult population.

Dependent, White (DW) 6%
Mainly under 24s living at home or full-time student, where head of household is an ABC1 occupation group.

Dependent, Blue (DB) 10%
Mainly under 24s living at home or full-time student, where head of household is in a C2DE occupation group.

Pre-family, White (PFW) 4%
Under 35s who have established their own household but have no children and where the head of household is in an ABC1 occupation group.

Pre-family, Blue (PFB) 4%
Under 35s who have established their own household but have no children and where the head of household is in a C2DE occupation group.

Family, Better off, White (FW+) 6%
Housewives and heads of household, under 65, with one or more children in the household in the 'better off' income group and where the head of household is in an ABC1 occupation group (63% are AB).

Family, Better off, Blue (FB+) 8%
Housewives and heads of household, under 65, with one or more children in the household in the 'better off' income group and where the head of household is in a C2DE occupation group (80% are C2).

Family, Worse off, White (FW−) 8%
Housewives and heads of household, under 65, with one or more children

in the household in the 'worse off' income group and where the head of household is in an ABC1 occupation group (70% are C1).

Family, Worse off, Blue (FB−) 14%
Housewives and heads of household, under 65, with one or more children in the household in the 'worse off' income group and where the head of household is in a C2DE occupation group (53% are DE).

Late, Better off, White (LW+) 5%
Includes all adults whose children have left home or who are over 35 and childless, are in the 'better off' income group and where the head of household is in an ABC1 occupation group (61% are AB).

Late, Better off, Blue (LB+) 6%
Includes all adults whose children have left home or who are over 35 and childless, are in the 'better off' income group and where the head of household is in a C2DE occupation group (72% are C2).

Late, Worse off, White (LW−) 9%
Includes all adults whose children have left home or who are over 35 and childless, are in the 'worse off' income group and where the head of household is in an ABC1 occupation group (67% are C1).

Late, Worse off, Blue (LB−) 20%
Includes all adults whose children have left home or who are over 35 and childless, are in the 'worse off' income group and where the head of household is in a C2DE occupation group (72% are DE).

Source: Research Services Ltd, 1981.

Figure 4.1 Sagacity groupings

Table 4.3   The ACORN classification

ACORN categories			% Households
A		Thriving	19.0
B		Expanding	10.4
C		Rising	9.0
D		Settling	24.5
E		Aspiring	13.9
F		Striving	23.2

ACORN groups			%
A	1	Wealthy achievers, suburban areas	14.0
A	2	Affluent greys, rural communities	2.2
A	3	Prosperous pensioners, retirement areas	2.8
B	4	Affluent executives, family areas	3.4
B	5	Well off workers, family areas	7.0
C	6	Affluent urbanites, town and city areas	2.5
C	7	Prosperous professionals, metropolitan areas	2.5
C	8	Better off executives, inner city areas	4.0
D	9	Comfortable middle agers, mature home owning areas	13.7
D	10	Skilled workers, home owning areas	10.8
E	11	New home owners, mature communities	9.9
E	12	White collar workers, better-off multi-ethnic areas	4.0
F	13	Older people, less prosperous areas	4.4
F	14	Council estate residents, better off homes	10.9
F	15	Council estate residents, high unemployment	3.6
F	16	Council estate residents, greatest hardship	2.4
F	17	People in multi ethnic, low income areas	1.8

ACORN neighbourhood types			% Social grade
A1	1.1	Wealthy suburbs, large detached houses	2.2 AB
A1	1.2	Villages with wealthy commuters	2.8 AB
A1	1.3	Mature affluent home-owning areas	2.7 ABC1
A1	1.4	Affluent suburbs, older families	3.4 ABC1
A1	1.5	Mature, well-off suburbs	2.9 ABC1
A2	2.6	Agricultural villages, home-based workers	1.5 ABC2D
A2	2.7	Holiday retreats, older people, home based workers	0.7 ABC2D
A3	3.8	Home owning areas, well-off older residents	1.5 ABC1
A3	3.9	Private flats, elderly people	1.3 ABC1
B4	4.10	Affluent working families with mortgages	1.8 ABC1
B4	4.11	Affluent working couples with mortgages, new homes	1.3 ABC1
B4	4.12	Transient workforces, living at their place of work	0.3 –
B5	5.13	Home-owning family areas	2.5 ABC1
B5	5.14	Home-owning family areas, older children	2.6 C1C2
B5	5.15	Families with mortgages, younger children	1.9 C1C2
C6	6.16	Well-off town and city areas	1.1 AB
C6	6.17	Flats and mortgages, singles and young working couples	0.9 ABC1
C6	6.18	Furnished flats and bedsits, younger single people	0.5 ABC1

Table 4.3 Continued

C7	7.19	Apartments, young professional singles and couples	1.4 ABC1
C7	7.20	Gentrified multi-ethnic areas	1.1 ABC1
C8	8.21	Prosperous enclaves, highly qualified executives	0.9 ABC1
C8	8.22	Academic centres, students and young professionals	0.6 ABC1
C8	8.23	Affluent city centre areas, tenements and flats	0.7 ABC1
C8	8.24	Partially gentrified, multi-ethnic areas	0.8 ABC1
C8	8.25	Converted flats and bedsits, single people	1.0 –
D9	9.26	Mature established home-owning areas	3.4 ABC1
D9	9.27	Rural areas, mixed occupation	3.4 –
D9	9.28	Established home-owning areas	3.9 C1
D9	9.29	Home-owning areas, council tenants, retired people	3.0 ABC1
D10	10.30	Established home-owning areas, skilled workers	4.3 C2
D10	10.31	Home owners in older properties, younger workers	3.2 C1C2
D10	10.32	Home-owning areas with skilled workers	3.3 C2DE
E11	11.33	Council areas, some new home owners	3.7 C2DE
E11	11.34	Mature home-owning areas, skilled workers	3.3 C2DE
E11	11.35	Low-rise estates, older workers, new home owners	2.9 C2DE
E12	12.36	Home-owning multi-ethnic areas, young families	1.0 C1
E12	12.37	Multi-occupied town centres, mixed occupations	2.0 –
E12	12.38	Multi-ethnic areas, white-collar workers	1.0 C1
F13	13.39	Home owners, small council flats, single pensioners	2.3 C2DE
F13	13.40	Council areas, older people, health problems	2.1 C2DE
F14	14.41	Better-off council areas, new home owners	2.0 C2DE
F14	14.42	Council areas, young families, some new home owners	2.7 C2DE
F14	14.43	Council areas, young families, many lone parents	1.6 C2DE
F14	14.44	Multi-occupied terraces, multi-ethnic areas	0.7 C2DE
F14	14.45	Low-rise council housing, less well-off families	1.8 C2DE
F14	14.46	Council areas, residents with health problems	2.1 C2DE
F15	15.47	Estates with high unemployment	1.3 DE
F15	15.48	Council flats, elderly people, health problems	1.1 C2DE
F15	15.49	Council flats, very high unemployment, singles	1.2 DE
F16	16.50	Council areas, high unemployment, lone parents	1.5 DE
F16	16.51	Council flats, greatest hardship, many lone parents	0.9 DE
F17	17.52	Multi-ethnic, large families, overcrowding	0.5 DE
F17	17.53	Multi-ethnic, severe unemployment, lone parents	1.0 DE
F17	17.54	Multi-ethnic, high unemployment, overcrowding	0.3 DE

and it divides the country into five categories, 17 groups and 54 types of neighbourhood based on enumeration districts (average population about 460). The full ACORN profile based on 1991 census data is shown in Table 4.3. ACORN is linked with syndicated services such as TGI, BMRB (Tel: 020 8566 5000, Fax: 020 8579 9208, E-mail: web@bmrb.co.uk) and NRS, and with the postcode system. This means that it can be used to identify areas of relevance for most product and service groups, and direct communication to those areas is possible through the postcodes.

ACORN has been used by local authorities to isolate areas of deprivation and by marketing firms seeking to identify areas of greatest demand for their products and services. Major retailers, banks and building societies use the service for site analysis and the mix of products appropriate to each branch. It is also used to target local advertising, posters, leaflet distribution and direct mail. Researchers can also use the system to select representative samples for questionnaire surveys.

Variations on the ACORN system have been introduced to serve the classification needs of specific markets, including Investor ACORN, Scottish ACORN and Financial ACORN. ACORN services have also been extended to Northern Ireland, with the consequent addition of six more neighbourhood types. Workforce ACORN compares the differing profile of an area in a given location during working hours and weekends. Custom ACORN links company data to the ACORN system to create a bespoke targeting classification.

CACI has also produced systems that look at individuals. People UK is a good example of this; it looks at 46 types and eight life stages.

MOSAIC

Experian (Tel: 01159 410 888, Fax: 01159 685 003, E-mail: corporate.communications@uk.experian.com). This system is based around 87 variables, producing 12 groups and 52 types of neighbourhood.

The MOSAIC system includes 52 consumer types that are aggregated into 12 groups:

L1   High Income Families
L2   Suburban Semis
L3   Blue Collar Owners
L4   Low Rise Council
L5   Council Flats
L6   Victorian Low Status
L7   Town Houses and Flats
L8   Stylish Singles
L9   Independent Elders
L10 Mortgaged Families
L11 Country Dwellers
L12 Institutional Areas

Sources of MOSAIC's data include:

- Census Statistics
- Electoral Registers
- The Lord Chancellor's Office
- Companies House
- Retail Data
- Land Registry
- DVLA

MOSAIC has also developed Financial MOSAIC and EUROMOSAIC.

Financial MOSAIC has 36 cluster types aggregated into 10 main groups. It has been developed from data from the Census, along with credit application and County Court Judgements (i.e. debt records), shareholder registers, director registers and unemployment data. The 10 groups are:

A   Adventurous Spenders
B   Burdened Borrowers
C   Capital Accumulators
D   Discerning Investors
E   Equity Holding Elders
F   Farm Owners and Traders
G   Good Paying Realists
H   Hardened Cash Payers
I   Indebted Strugglers
J   Just About Surviving

The above groupings are designed primarily for the use and needs of the financial services industry.

The *EUROMOSAIC* system is based on individual systems that have been developed for 16 developed countries. It consists of 10 cluster groups describing neighbourhood types across Europe.

Experian's website is an excellent source of information on the MOSAIC system and its applications:

www.micromarketing-online.com
www.uk.experian.com

Claritas (Tel: 020 8213 5500 E-mail: info-uk@clatritaseu.com). Claritas' systems include Super Profiles, Lifestyle Universe and Prizm.

Web address: www.claritas.co.uk

Other companies working in this area include Equifax with Microvision, FRuitS and Gems and Eurodirect with CAMEO.

4.6 Summary

Before embarking on original research, an organization is well advised to discover whether the data it requires is already available. There are four sources of 'off-the-peg' research data. Secondary desk research includes the use of published or online data from a range of identified sources covering data about companies, industries and markets. Syndicated research services produce current market data that is available for purchase, and a list of services and suppliers is given. Omnibus research services provide an off-the-peg vehicle for asking questions of specified groups. A list of services and suppliers is given with web addresses. Expertise exists in many research areas and the types of specialist research services available through the Market Research Society are described. This chapter concludes with a look at commonly used bases for consumer classification and provides some examples.

5 'Made-to-measure' research

5.1 Introduction

Chapters 3 and 4 were concerned with the use of data from within the organization, or data and specific services already available 'off-the-peg' from outside bodies. Inevitably, there are many situations for which existing information is too specific, too general, out of date, unavailable, or in some other way inappropriate for providing a solution to a specific problem with which a manager is faced. This is when it is necessary to consider generating original first-hand data, which is collected with the special data requirement that the manager has, as its sole objective. This type of research is referred to as primary research, because it is first-hand. It is also known as field research, because it generally involves going out into the marketplace, or field, to gather data. The term 'made-to-measure' research underlines the fact that the research programme is tailored to meet the precise information needs for which it is required.

5.2 Buying a 'made-to-measure' research survey is just like buying a 'made-to-measure' suit

The suit	*The research survey*
People decide to get a new suit when the old one wears out, or there is a special occasion or a new fashion is introduced. They may decide to get a quote from a tailor. This tailor will ask:	Organizations decide to use research when things go wrong, or they decide to enter a new market, or launch a new product. They may decide to get a quote from a research agency. The agency will ask:
1 What is the suit for? 2 Let us take your measurements. 3 Did you have any particular style in mind?	● What is the problem? ● What data is needed to solve it? ● How will the data be collected?
4 Did you have any particular colour in mind?	● Who will provide the data?
5 Did you have any particular material in mind?	● How will the questions be asked?
6 Did you have any particular cutter in mind?	● Who will ask the questions?
7 Should it be machine-stitched or hand-stitched?	● How will the answers be processed?

8 Will he give the job to the tailor, or decide to get it done at home? Tailor-made or hand-made? Depends on cost, how big a job it is, and how good a job he could get done at home.

9 Will the suit be worn?

10 Will the client like it, and get another one, or decide something was wrong with it that should be changed next time: the colour or material, perhaps. If it's bad enough, maybe the client will change the tailor!

- Will they give the job to a research agency, or get it done within the organization? Agency job or in-house job? Depends on cost, how big the job is, and how much relevant expertise there is in-house.
- What action will result?
- What will be learned from the process? Was it a good piece of research or not? Should the sampling procedure be improved, or the questionnaire? Should the research agency be used again?

In buying a suit, the client decides what he wants the suit for, and the measurements will fit him closely, although the tailor will measure up. He is likely to take the tailor's advice on technical aspects of the suit, although it helps to know something about these things if you're going to get a good job, say on material qualities. Whether it's worn when it arrives depends on whether it's really what was wanted, and both the client and the tailor will learn from the experience. Whether a tailor is really necessary depends on whether professional expertise is worth paying for.

In buying research, the client defines the problem and the data that will be needed to fit the problem, although the research agency may suggest data requirements. The client will probably take the agency's advice on technical aspects of the survey, although it helps to know something about these things if you're going to get a good job, say on data collection methods or questionnaire design. Whether the survey results are used in decision making depends on whether they are really what was needed, and both the client and the agency will learn from the experience. Whether an agency is really necessary depends on whether professional expertise is worth paying for.

5.3 The 'made-to-measure' research process

It is helpful to begin with an overall view of the research process. Six stages in the research process are identified, and 12 related questions that must be given consideration. These form the framework within which the content of this and the following five chapters are set.

A clear definition of the problem, and the data needed to produce a solution to it, are the starting point of the research process. This is also the

Table 5.1 The 'made-to-measure' research process: six stages, twelve questions

Stage	Question	Chapter
1 Defining the research required	1 What is the problem?	5
	2 What data are needed to solve it?	5
2 Planning the research	3 How will the data be collected?	6
	4 Who will provide the data?	7
	5 How will the questions be asked?	8
	6 Who will ask the questions?	9
	7 What will happen to the answers?	10
	8 Will the plan work?	
3 Carrying out the fieldwork	9 Is it going according to schedule?	(9)
4 Analysing, interpreting and reporting	10 What are the results?	(10)
5 Using the research	11 What action will result?	
6 Feedback	12 What can be learned from the process?	

most important part of the process from the point of view of the manager who must play a dominant role in it if the research is to produce the right kind of data for the organization's needs. This chapter is concerned with defining the research requirement, and deals with Questions 1 and 2: What is the problem? and What data are needed to solve it?

The next stage is the planning stage. At this point decisions must be made about technical aspects of the research survey. In practice, the manager who requires research information is unlikely to have more than a controlling involvement in the research process from Stages 2–4. The research itself and the major technical decisions about research method, sampling, questionnaire design, fieldwork, data analysis and report writing are usually undertaken by research professionals, either within the research department of an organization or in research agencies.

Managers who need to commission and use research will be more effective in making use of this business tool if they know more about it. Each of the significant decision areas in the planning and operation of research surveys is explained in the following chapters: research method in Chapter 6, sampling procedures in Chapter 7, questionnaire design in Chapter 8, fieldwork in Chapter 9, and analysis, interpretation and reporting of results in Chapter 10.

The aim of these chapters is to enable the non-research manager to become a more informed research user and buyer, and to equip him or her with appropriate criteria for judging research quality. This will allow the individual to deal more competently and confidently with research agency personnel, and the matter of selecting a good research agency to carry out the research is covered in Chapter 11.

Stage 5, using the research, is the subject of Chapter 16, where a range of research applications in making marketing decisions is dealt with. Stage 6, feedback, is always important, but perhaps particularly so for the new research user. After a made-to-measure research survey has been conducted, it should be critically analysed by the manager personally, in order to learn from it. Approaches, methods or techniques that worked well can be noted for use again in similar circumstances, and those aspects of the research process that did not work so well should be noted and avoided in future. It is always helpful to share this analysis with the research agency, if one was involved, in order to build a constructively developing and improving research expertise relevant to the organization's specific needs, within the agency. Alternatively, it may be that sharing the post-research analysis with an agency may explain to them why they are unlikely to be involved again. The purpose of critical feedback from the research process is for the manager to develop personal skills and experience as a research user, ready for when the process begins again from Stage 1.

5.4 Stage 1: Defining the research required

Before any research programme can be undertaken, its scope and objectives must be defined. Too often, research surveys are undertaken with insufficient clarification of their objectives, with the result that the findings are found to be too vague, too narrow or entirely inappropriate. The responsibility for defining the research objectives lies mainly with the manager who initiates the research and wishes to apply its results in decision making. A non-specialist manager may know very little about research, but is likely to be the only person with a clear idea of why the research is needed and how the findings will be used. If this is not communicated adequately to the researcher, the research programme that follows may be entirely misdirected.

Answering the following questions can help in arriving at a more precise definition of the research required.

5.4.1 Stage 1: Question 1, 'What is the problem?'

This should be stated as specifically as possible. For example, a cinema chain faced with the problem of declining audiences decided that its problem was, 'to identify ways in which more people could be attracted to attend the cinema'. An alternative statement of the problem which was rejected was 'to discover why cinema audiences are declining'. Although the two are obviously very closely related, the outcome of the research as defined was specifically directed to be action-orientated in its findings, in a way that the more general statement was not.

5.4.2 Stage 1: Question 2, 'What data are needed to find a solution?'

Deciding the data requirement

The first step is to review the information that already exists. In the cinema example, there was already some data about cinema attendance. The present state of knowledge should form the starting point for the search for new information, since it can often guide further research into those areas most likely to be fruitful in producing worthwhile data. Cinema audiences were known to be typically young, and so it was clear that the views of this group must be adequately represented in the survey.

The second step involves generating a list of necessary information. In doing this, it is important to distinguish between what is essential to know, and what it would be nice to know, and to delete the latter. This can be accomplished by going back over the first list of necessary information and deleting from it those bits of information that are inessential. The resultant list of essential information now forms the basis for deriving research survey objectives, and makes it possible to redefine the original problem in marketing research terms.

The cinema chain management realized that although they already knew what kind of people attend the cinema, and how often, the further information they needed concerned people's attitudes and motivations for cinema going. This information would enable them to identify what factors attract people to the cinema.

A 'crunch' question in deciding whether a research survey is really required is to ask, 'What would happen without the information?' If the answer to the question indicates that the absence of research information will not materially affect the decision-making process, then the research programme should not be undertaken. It may well be that other routes to problem solution would be more effective, less costly, less time-consuming, and maybe all three. Wasting money on research is as undesirable as wasting it on any other area of business, and just as easy.

If a research survey is to be undertaken, then a definition of who or what is to be surveyed must be drawn up. All decisions about survey content and coverage must be made explicit. For example, in a survey about farms, the group to be surveyed was 'all farms'. Specifically excluded was 'small-holdings'. This made it quite clear to the researcher how the terms were defined. In this example, the definition of 'farms' would be further improved by greater precision: including the minimum acreage or minimum turnover to be considered, and indicating whether all arable, dairy and mixed farms were included, and how other specific classifications were to be treated.

The outcome of this procedure should be a clear and concise written statement of the objectives of the proposed research survey and its scope. To complete the definition of the research required, any constraints must be clearly spelled out at this early stage, since they are likely to affect materially the nature of the research that can be undertaken.

The two most important constraints are time and money. If the decision for which the research input is required has to be made by a particular deadline, then this must be made clear at the outset, for it will affect the choice of research method. Some methods are more time-consuming than others. Similarly, if the budget available for research is limited, then the amount that can be spent must be stated in broad terms. As with any other commodity, in research one gets largely what one pays for. An organization not prepared to spend much cannot expect to acquire very much good research information. Hundreds of pounds saved in research costs must be weighed against possibly hundreds of thousands of pounds lost in the results of wrong decisions.

The high marketing costs of failure, and the damage done to a company's reputation in the marketplace as a result of wrong decisions, are illustrated by the following rather painful example.

A manufacturer of industrial contract materials produced a new flooring material. The success of the product was very important to the organization because markets for most of their product ranges were in decline. Management had high hopes for the new product, which produced a more durable floor with a better finish than existing materials, although it was more expensive. Laying the flooring required a completely different technique to that of traditional floorings, but it was not a complicated process. The manufacturer felt that an industrial market research survey to predict demand for the new material would be too expensive, but some 'market research' was required in view of the importance of the new product launch to the company as a whole. As a result, six good customers for the company's products were given samples of the new material and asked to try it out. Some time later, one of the company executives called on the customers and asked how they rated the material. The customers confirmed the company's own view that it was a good material. On the strength of this 'research', the product was launched nationally. It was a flop. The 'research exercise' was repeated with different customers. They also reported liking the material, and it was relaunched. Another flop. Finally, in desperation, the company undertook a formal survey of the market for flooring materials to discover whether there was a market niche for this material, and if so, how to relaunch the product into it for the third time.

Their research indicated that the conservatism of the building trade was a major stumbling block. The benefits of the new material all came in use. When a floor was being laid the product was seen as expensive and the differences required in laying technique met with resistance from the floor-layers. The company discovered that to make a success of this product their marketing should be aimed at architects so that they would specify the new material for its good appearance and durability. Builders, to whom the product had

> been launched, could see little reason for bothering with it. At the same time, the instructions could be vastly improved so as to make it clear that the material was *different* to lay, but not difficult and no more time-consuming than traditional materials. The message was clear: it was a good product, but needed marketing in ways that the company had not previously been aware of.

If a company cannot afford, or does not wish to pay for, the type of research necessary for a particular decision, then it may be better to have no research at all than an inappropriately small research programme. Beautifully presented research reports have a way of being believed by those who wish to do so, however uncertain the methodology or base data. At least with no research information at all a company knows that its decisions have no affirmative background, and they are therefore more likely to be made with greater caution.

The research required can now be defined in terms of its objectives, scope and practical constraints. This definition forms the framework within which the research will take place. It is therefore essential for the manager to be satisfied that the data requirement is correctly specified. In this situation, more heads are better than one, and it is a useful discipline to discuss the proposed project with others. This has a number of advantages. First, the project benefits from additional input: new and useful suggestions. Second, it benefits from external criticism: any points that are not as clearly defined as they should be will be queried. Third, the very process of articulating and defending the approach to others is most valuable in clarifying and distilling the essence of the research required.

The need for careful consideration at the definitive stage of a research project is emphasized because it is the easiest stage to skimp in practice, and one of the most damaging to the final outcome if not done properly. Research that starts off unsure where it is going is unlikely to arrive in the right place. Defining the research required is a task about which the decision maker personally must be really precise. The main means by which control can be exercised over the execution of the project is through the framework of a clear and correctly expressed statement of research required.

Deciding on the type of data

From the starting point of a well-defined statement of the research required, the next step is to consider what kind of research data would be most useful in improving the decision to be made. Research is often categorized as being either 'qualitative' or 'quantitative', and the distinction is an important one.

Qualitative research

Qualitative research is so called because its emphasis lies in producing data that is rich in insight, understanding, explanation and depth of information, but which cannot be justified statistically. Qualitative research is typically carried out with only a few respondents: often fewer than 50 individuals may be surveyed. While the findings from this number of people may be very important to the researcher in giving clues to the thinking of other members of the target group under investigation, the database is far too small to make such statements as, '10 per cent thought this . . .' and '15 per cent did that . . .'. It is in this sense then, that the data is qualitative rather than quantitative: the emphasis is on meaning rather than number.

The main methods used in qualitative research are depth interviews and group discussions, and these are described in Chapter 6. Their relatively small scale means that qualitative studies can generally be completed more quickly and less expensively than quantitative surveys. They can be used early in the research process to generate hypotheses which a subsequent quantitative survey will investigate further.

Quantitative research

Quantitative research is the kind of research that the layperson brings to mind with a stereotyped picture of the researcher, with questionnaire and clipboard, interviewing people in the street. It involves the research techniques of representative samples, questionnaires, interviewers, data processing, and so on. These are all necessary to make it possible to express the results quantitatively, with such statements as, '25 per cent of the population own . . .' and '37 per cent of machine tool buyers think . . .'. The word 'population' is used here in the research sense, meaning 'the whole group under consideration'. It can, therefore, refer to the human population of a country, but the 'populations' considered by management decision makers are usually more restricted than that. They may include only the buyers of the company's products, all housewives aged 16–45 or all personal digital assistant owners. The population being surveyed may be non-buyers, or potential buyers of a product or service not yet launched, and so on. The definition of the population being considered must be specifically described for the purposes of each particular research survey.

If a population is to be surveyed it would be unacceptably expensive, time-consuming and difficult to organize a census in which questions are asked of every individual in the target population. It is also unnecessary, since sampling theory makes it possible to select a limited number of respondents who are representative of the whole group, i.e. a sample. Carrying out a sample survey is cheaper, quicker and more efficient than a census, but equally effective if an appropriate procedure is used for selecting the sample. Details of sampling techniques are discussed in Chapter 7. It is important to note that as well as being representative, the sample must be sufficiently large for statistical generalizations from it to be valid. In consumer research surveys this usually means several hundred respondents, and for large surveys several thousand. Industrial and other specialized surveys often have smaller, but still adequate, samples. Questionnaires are the device used to ensure that all respondents are asked precisely the same question, so that their responses can be added together meaningfully. Questionnaire design is considered in Chapter 8, and techniques of interviewing and data processing are discussed in Chapters 9 and 10, respectively.

The outcome of the research procedure outlined is that the researcher is able to use the results from this type of sample survey to predict, with a known level of statistical accuracy, what the results would be if the whole group being considered had been asked the questions, whether that be all housewives, all drivers, all retired persons, and so on. The practical limitations of the questionnaire itself – it cannot be too long or respondents will refuse co-operation – mean that data collected this way cannot usually produce the richness of insight that comes from the qualitative approach, but the results have the great advantage of producing quantitative estimates of known reliability. When the decision to be taken is itself a quantitative one, for example, deciding on production levels for the next period, or the levels of social amenities to be provided, then quantitative research is the most appropriate route to providing information input to the decision-making process. In general, the scale of quantitative research means that it is more expensive and more time-consuming than qualitative research. A survey of 500 consumer respondents might take two to three months from commissioning to final report.

In a major study, both qualitative and quantitative approaches may be used. For example, if information is needed about a subject with which a manager is largely unfamiliar, he or she might begin with a qualitative survey. This will generate ideas and insights, and give sufficient familiarity with the area under study to make it possible to formulate a more systematic approach to data collection. It may even be possible to develop research hypotheses from qualitative research which can be tested using an experimental approach. The great advantage of initiating a research programme with qualitative methods is that little prior knowledge of the area is required. On the basis of the knowledge gained in this way, a quantitative follow-up study can be designed to measure the importance of variables identified in the initial study. Qualitative research used in this way is referred to as 'exploratory research'.

Alternatively, in an area with which the manager is already familiar, the research programme may begin with a large-scale quantitative study. In the course of this study some findings may emerge for which there is no apparent explanation. In this case, qualitative research may be used to generate explanations of findings from quantitative studies.

Deciding on the research method

It is apparent from the preceding section that the type of data produced depends not only on the approach chosen, but also on the method of data collection used. Different methods will produce data of differing depth, breadth, quantity and content, as well as differing in levels of accuracy, speed and cost. In this section the types of method in common use are introduced, and in Chapter 6 the methods themselves are described.

There are many ways of categorizing the various methods of collecting data. The descriptions 'primary or secondary' and 'qualitative or quantitative' have already been referred to. The scheme used here classifies methods as using *interviews, observation* or *experiments* as the means of data collection. For the research user, it is important to have some feel for what each method can accomplish, in order to select the appropriate method for the needs of a particular problem.

Interview research

The basic assumption of all interviewing techniques is that to obtain information about people, you simply ask them for it. This could be information about what type of people they are, how they behave (usually in terms of purchase behaviour) or what their likes, dislikes, attitudes and opinions about the subject under study may be. Very often, this basic assumption is a realistic one, which explains why interviewing is the most commonly used technique of social research, i.e. any research concerned with people. The advantage of interviewing techniques is that it is often possible to discover not only *what* people are, do or think, but also *why* this may be so. This makes it a very rich data source in terms of the quantity and quality of data generated.

There are, however, occasions when the basic assumption is unjustified, and people either will not or cannot give, or will falsify, the information required. Some categories of information cannot be gathered by the interview method and other approaches are needed.

There may be occasions when people cannot say what they do, often because the information, which is so important to a decision maker, is of such trivial interest to the individual that it simply is not recalled. A manufacturer may wish to know exactly how many packets of biscuits, and what type, each household buys in a month, and whether this changes over the year. Only the individual whose biscuit-buying behaviour is unusually regular and stable would be able to answer such a question accurately. For those households where biscuits are bought as required, and where several different types may be bought in the course of a year, the best answer to the question could only be an approximation. Manufacturers facing increasingly tight profit margins may find that the difference between decisions based on purchase approximations and reality is the difference between profit and loss.

Observation research

It is for situations such as this that observation techniques are particularly valuable. 'Retail audit' research is now largely based on computer observation of retail sales. Grocery retailing is at the forefront of techniques in this area. Deliveries are now made just in time, using information provided by state-of-the-art stock-control systems. These are allied to the highly sophisticated electronic point of sale (EPOS) systems that transmit data directly from electronic store checkout tills, which read bar codes from goods purchased. Linking this system to in-store loyalty programmes or special offers measures how customers respond to the loyalty programme or how successful special promotions are at generating product purchases.

In areas that are not covered by this service, diary methods and physical observation of how products are bought, stored and used may be made.

Observation techniques are also used a great deal in social planning: in traffic counts, for example, or observation of hospital out-patient departments to investigate ways of minimizing waiting time, and therefore saving the space taken by large waiting areas.

Observational research in online markets may include monitoring browser behaviour through a website or key-stroke recording.

> Increasingly, observation is being undertaken electronically rather than by people, as in store layout investigations using cameras, television-watching measurement or website usability studies. As well as overcoming the limitations of memory, the other important advantage of observation as a method of data collection is that the behaviour of the individual is not influenced by the research process. For behaviour that the individual feels reflects badly on him or her, such as smoking or drinking, observation may give a more accurate picture than personal interviewing. Doctors believe that patients' estimates of drinking and smoking are under-estimated by 100 per cent.

The main limitation of observation methods is that while they may provide good information on *what* people do, they offer no explanation as to *why* that might be so. If observation data is interpreted subjectively with incorrect explanations of the behaviour observed, then the advantages gained by use of the method are lost. For this reason, observation methods are often combined with other sources of data. As an example, the management of a chain of bingo halls initially assumed that regular attenders were primarily gamblers and more could be attracted with higher prizes. When this approach failed, subsequent group discussion indicated that many people play bingo for its social benefits. More money spent on decor and 'ambiance' would attract higher attendance from this group, who were put off by the rather seedy appearance of some bingo halls.

Research experiments

Research experiments involve a more rigorous approach to research design than is necessary in straightforward interview or observation research surveys. The point of research experiments is that they make it possible for the experimenter to investigate cause-and-effect relationships between variables. What factors influence sales, and by how much, for example? Since almost all real-life situations, particularly sales, are the outcome of interaction of many variables, it is necessary for the research programme to be designed in such a way that the variables under test can be controlled by the experimenter and the effects of other identified variables measured independently. To identify the effect of advertising on sales, for example, price, distribution levels and external factors such as weather must also be measured, to isolate their effects. When several interacting variables are under consideration, specific experimental approaches need to be used to make it possible to isolate statistically the effects being measured. Some of the experimental approaches in common use are discussed in Chapter 12.

Although these are the most technically complex studies to mount, they are the most rewarding because they make cause-and-effect relationships statistically explicit. For the manager wishing to exercise control through decision making, such knowledge is invaluable. Knowing how responsive a market is to advertising, price cuts, and so on, makes for greater marketing precision. The difficulty in practice lies in the fact that the more important management problems are typically multivariate. Even if the manager were able to identify all the relevant variables, many of them would be difficult to measure precisely, for example, the 'innovativeness' of buyers in an industrial market. Interaction between variables, such as price and sales support, will also complicate the picture. The more complex and imprecise the measurement of variables becomes, the less easy it is to justify the time and expense demanded by experimental research.

Experiments known as 'testing' are used heavily in the area of direct marketing. Traditionally, direct marketing has invested a large amount in testing creative formats, the timing of campaigns, offers, pricing and audiences. Test programmes may use samples of 20,000 or more to ensure that the limits of accuracy (explained in Section 7.4) associated with any results are very small. This allows subsequent rollout of the full programme to be profitable at perhaps very small margins.

5.5 Summary

'Made-to-measure' research surveys are designed to meet the precise data needs for solving a particular problem. The first stage is to define the research required, and this begins with precise specification of the problem. It is followed by specification of the data required to answer the problem. Decisions must be made about whether qualitative or quantitative data, or both, will be needed. The method to be used in generating the data must also be determined and three approaches are introduced: interview research, observation research and research experiments.

6 How are the data collected?

6.1 Introduction

This chapter reviews the main methods of data collection for primary research. Interview methods are the most widely used, and there are several ways in which interviews can be conducted. These methods involve personal, face-to-face contact between the interviewer and the respondent, and can therefore be both expensive and time-consuming. The non-personal contact research methods attempt to overcome these problems, but in doing so, other problems arise. The major non-personal contact methods are postal research, diary panels, telephone research and observation research. Data is now often gathered using electronic media including laptop or palmtop computers. The Internet is becoming a major data collection method. There is still some uncertainty about the reliability of the Internet as a data collection method.

6.2 Interview methods

Interviews are the most flexible of data collection methods. They are of general application for differing information requirements and differing situations and as a result are very widely used. They can be divided into two categories: those that require direct personal contact between the interviewer and respondents, and those where the contact is through non-personal and indirect means, such as postal questionnaires or the telephone.

6.2.1 Interviewing individuals

The advantage of the personal contact methods is that they normally produce a high response rate, and this means that error, which might be introduced by many people refusing to co-operate in the survey, is minimized. The main disadvantage of the personal contact interview is that it is expensive. Survey costs are influenced by the complexity of information sought, the nature of the sample and the ease with which effective replies can be gathered.

To give some idea of the level of cost likely to be involved, in 2003 the cost per completed interview for a 20-minute structured questionnaire administered to consumers was £30–35. This includes all executive and administrative overheads. A survey of 750 consumer respondents commissioned from a research agency which is required to present a research design proposal, design the questionnaire, carry out the fieldwork, analyse the data and prepare a report, would result in a bill in the order of £26,000.

For industrial research, which requires more technically qualified and skilled interviewers and where respondents are more difficult to obtain, the cost could be very much higher per completed interview, although the generally smaller sample sizes used in such research may compensate for this. In international research the cost will vary. In the USA research costs are two to three times higher than in the UK, whereas in the developing world they are usually much cheaper. In carrying out an international survey co-ordinated from London, for example, the costs will be significantly higher than for a single-country survey.

Personal interviews may be carried out in a number of ways, as follows.

Fully structured interviews

In fully structured interviews, the situation is 'structured' or controlled through the medium of the questionnaire. The interviewer must read out the questions and notes to respondents exactly as they appear on the questionnaire form, and may not add anything else, even by way of explanation to the respondent. This ensures that the responses, from many individuals, are given to precisely the same question, even though many interviewers may be involved in the data gathering process. In a fully structured interview, the respondent may only give one of the responses already listed on the questionnaire. This means that neither the interviewer nor the respondent may introduce material not previously originated by the researcher in designing the questionnaire.

Such questionnaires are used most commonly in 'head-counting' exercises, when the researcher wants to answer the question, 'How many people do this, or think that?' Fully structured questions are easy to ask and easy to answer. This makes it possible to use less technically qualified interviewers, since there is very little that they can do to bias the answers. Interviews can also be completed relatively quickly. Both of these factors will reduce fieldwork costs, which is why fully structured questions are used whenever possible.

Another practical advantage is that data processing and analysis of answers to this type of question are also relatively straightforward. Responses can be 'precoded' on the questionnaire, and all the interviewer has to do is to put a ring around the code number of the answer given. The completed questionnaire can go straight to the data-processing department where those numbers will be entered directly from the questionnaire for computer analysis. This can be done manually or through the use of scanners. The elimination of any intervening coding process between fieldwork and data processing is important in reducing both the time and costs of research. Computer-assisted personal interviews (CAPIs) using laptop or palmtop computers can save significant time in the processing of the questionnaires. Responses can be coded directly onto the computer and fed from anywhere in the world to the controlling office for central processing.

The main limitation of fully structured questionnaires is that they can only collect the data made possible by the content of the questionnaire. The respondent may only choose one of the answers given, not provide his own. If the questionnaire designer has erred, the final data collected will be erroneous. For example, a question may be presented in the form, 'Which of these six items is most important to you when considering the purchase of a camcorder?' and go on to list on a show card six possible factors which seem to the questionnaire designer to be the most important. The answers will make it possible to rank those six factors in order of their importance to respondents. However, if there is some other factor equally important as the six selected, it will not be discovered because respondents are given no opportunity to make this point. Many research designers attempt to resolve this problem by adding an 'Other response' category, but this too has limitations, as will be discussed in Chapter 8. In summary, then, there are practical advantages to using fully structured interviews, but the onus for the quality of data produced is most fully on the questionnaire designer, who is responsible for providing all possible answers as well as the questions.

Semi-structured interviews

In semi-structured interviews, fully structured questions, as described above, are combined with 'open-ended' questions. These questions are easy to design and to ask, but require more of the respondent in answering, and of the interviewer in recording those answers. Structure is still present from the interviewer's point of view, in that the question wording shown on the questionnaire may not be departed from. The respondent is free to answer in whatever way he or she pleases, since no direction or structure is implied by the question. For example, 'What factors would you personally take into account when considering purchase of a camcorder? This is followed by a space in which the interviewer is instructed to write down exactly what the respondent says. The interviewer may be required to encourage the respondent to think about the question by using probing questions like 'What other factors are there?' after one or two have been given. The use of interview 'probes' demands a higher level of technical expertise from the interviewer than in fully structured questioning. The use of open-ended questions and probes in questionnaire surveys goes some way towards making it possible to collect both qualitative and quantitative data in the same survey. The main difficulty lies in analysing and interpreting the responses to open-ended questions. This is discussed more fully in Chapter 8.

Unstructured interviews

In this type of interview, neither the interviewer nor the respondent is bound by the structure of the questionnaire. Interviewers have only a topic guide or checklist of questions that must be asked, or subjects that must be covered. They are normally free to word the questions as they please, and to vary the order in which the questions are asked rather than disrupt the 'flow' of the respondents' answers. Respondents may answer at considerable length, and are encouraged to explore all their thoughts on a particular topic. Unstructured interviews are often used in industrial marketing research, for example, in surveys of managerial, professional or technical groups such as purchasing managers, architects or civil engineers. Unstructured interviews are used to provide qualitative data. They also make it possible to identify the relevant points that must be included in subsequent structured or semi-structured interviews if quantification of the data is needed.

Depth interviews

This approach to the interview situation has been borrowed from the methods of psychoanalysis. It is called 'depth research' because the pattern of questioning encourages respondents to go deeper and deeper into their levels of thought. Respondents move beyond the first thoughts generated by structured and semi-structured interviews, on to second and further thoughts, where the real motives and explanations for behaviour often lie. This is why depth research is used as one of the tools of motivation research.

It is obvious from the description given that the quality of depth research is largely in the hands of the interviewer, and depth research interviewers need to be experts in using the technique. They normally have specialist, and often psychological, training in the methods of depth interviewing. Since the method is so time-consuming and requires such a high calibre of specialist skill, it is usual for fewer than 15 depth interviews to be carried out in any particular survey, particularly if it is a survey of consumers. Costs per completed interview of this type of research are very much higher than for fully or semi-structured interviews, at around £500–700 per interview in 2002. Analysis of depth interviews, which are often recorded on tape with the agreement of the respondent, is also a specialist task, usually carried out by the same person who conducted the interviews. This individual has both the behavioural science expertise to interpret the findings, and the advantage of having been present at the interview, which means that nuances of the interview situation can be included in its interpretation. The costs quoted would include all preparation and design of the fieldwork and subsequent analysis and reporting.

6.2.2 Attitude measurement

Attitude and behaviour

To make good decisions, it is often helpful to understand why the group that will be affected by those decisions behaves in the way it does. The attempt to understand behaviour brings us to a consideration of attitudes. An attitude is 'a predisposition to act in a particular way'. Knowing attitudes can therefore be useful in predicting what people are likely to do, as well as explaining what they have done. Indeed, it was the belief that individuals with favourable attitudes towards products or services were more likely to buy them that led to the importance of attitude measurement as a method of data collection. Unfortunately for decision makers, attitudes do not operate quite this simply or directly in influencing behaviour. Strong personal or social influences may cause an individual not to act in accordance with his or her general attitude. When the behaviour is relatively unimportant to the individual he or she may act first and form an attitude later, based on the outcome of the action. However, for actions that are costly or important to the individual there is evidence that attitudes often precede behaviour. Hence the management decision maker's interest in attitude measurement.

For example, a factory manager may *believe* a fire safety manu-facturer's claims that its products will reduce the risk of fire in the factory. He may *feel* a greater sense of security and less anxiety if safety equipment were installed. This would make him favourably *disposed towards* the idea of installing the equipment. He may not do so, of course. The cost or disruption of installing the equipment may be too high, or his levels of anxiety about fire risk may be too low, and prevent him taking any action at all. Bringing the factory manager to the point of being *favourably disposed* towards the idea of installing fire safety equipment is a first step for the equipment manufacturer, who will want to measure what the factory manager's *beliefs* about the efficiency of the equipment are and how he *feels* about the idea of installing it.

This example illustrates the three components to attitude:

$$\text{Attitude} = \begin{cases} \text{Cognitive component:} & \text{What the individual} \\ & \textit{knows or believes} \text{ about an object or act} \\ \text{Affective component:} & \text{What the individual} \\ & \textit{feels emotionally} \text{ about an object or act} \\ \text{Conative component:} & \text{How the individual is} \\ & \textit{disposed to behave} \text{ towards an object or act} \end{cases}$$

An important assumption of attitude measurement techniques is that 'attitudes' are multidimensional. That is to say, we notice more than one aspect about most objects, and our decisions to buy are often a compromise between the different aspects that make up our attitudes. The researcher is interested in uncovering all the relevant aspects of attitude towards a particular brand or service, and identifying which will be most important in a particular choice situation. For this reason, attitude measurement often involves the use of scales that measure many dimensions of attitude to the same object, be it a product, brand, service or act. Two of the scaling techniques commonly used in attitude measurement are Likert scales and semantic differential scales.

Likert scales

A list of attitude statements about the topic under investigation is generated from depth and semi-structured interviews. This list is then tested on a sample of, say, 100 respondents. Each respondent is asked to score every statement on a five-point scale:

1 agree strongly
2 agree slightly
3 neither agree nor disagree
4 disagree slightly
5 disagree strongly.

Results from the sample are analysed and some statements are eliminated from the scale, so that the statements remaining are those which discriminate best in measuring attitudes to the topic under test. The scale is then administered to a representative sample of respondents, usually as part of a wider questionnaire survey. Responses are scored from 1 to 5. The final result is an average score that represents overall attitude on the subject and measures the degree of respondents' feeling about it. However, since the score total can be arrived at in a number of ways, it is usually useful to look at the pattern of responses as well as the total. (In the example shown in Figure 6.1, it would be interesting to see how different age or social class groups in the sample answered the question, as well as looking at the overall response.)

Statistical analysis (see Chapter 10, Section 10.3.3) of this multi-dimensional data can also identify groups of responses that have something in common. If these grouped responses are held by a sufficient number of the sample, they can indicate separate market segments. Since the attitude clusters of these segments are different, it follows that they are likely to respond to different marketing approaches. This information is extremely useful to the marketing planner.

Semantic differential scales

As their title suggests, these scales measure the difference between words. Prior research with members of the target group is undertaken to generate the 'constructs' or dimensions that people use when thinking about products and services. The semantic differential scale presents these bipolar constructs on a scale, with up to 20 scales on a page, forming an 'attitude battery'. The name of a brand at the top of the page appears, and the respondents are asked to rate that brand on each of the scales. Figure 6.2 shows an example.

EXAMPLE

INTRODUCTION The new houses in the Bridleway development are attractive

Q.1 SHOW CARD B

Look at this card. Which phrase describes your reaction to this statement

	CODE
	(22)
Agree strongly	1
Agree slightly	2
Neither agree nor disagree	3
Disagree slightly	5
Disagree strongly	5

SHOW CARD B

Agree strongly

Agree slightly

Neither agree nor disagree

Disagree slightly

Disagree strongly

Figure 6.1 Likert scales. These are used to qualify the respondents' reaction to a question on a scale ranging from one extreme to the other; for example, from 'very good' through 'good', 'fair', 'poor' to 'very poor'

If a representative sample of respondents is asked to complete the same attitude battery, then the results can be computed and a 'brand profile' drawn. Brand profiles can also be drawn for other brands used in the exercise, and this can help to explain the strengths and weaknesses of brands in the marketplace, particularly when considered in conjunction with their sales figures. It is also useful to add to the attitude battery scaling exercise a set of ratings for 'your ideal brand'. The profile for this can be compared to the profile achieved for the company's brand in order to pinpoint ways in which the company's product differs most from the consumer's ideal. The profiles that might result for two brands of skin-care product are shown alongside the attitude battery in Figure 6.2.

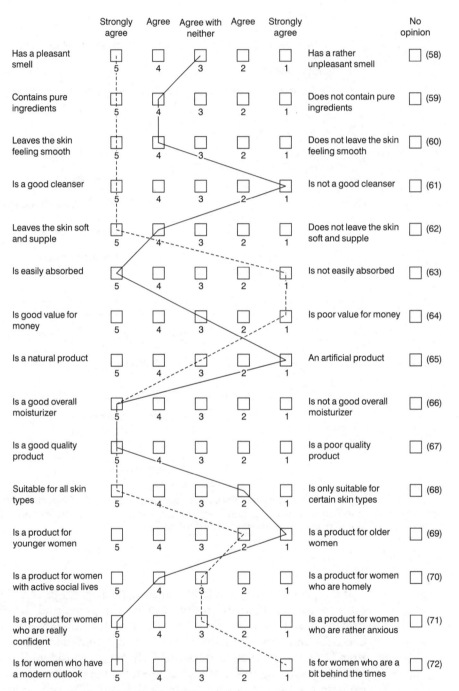

Figure 6.2 Example of a self-completion attitude battery for a skin-care product, and showing brand profiles constructed from it

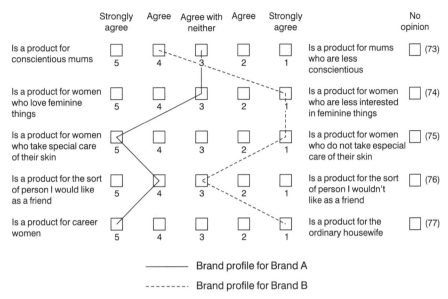

Figure 6.2 (Continued)

The data from semantic differential scaling can also be plotted on two dimensions simultaneously, showing how competing products, brands or services relate to each other in the consumer's mind. This technique can be computer based (see Chapter 10, Section 10.3.3) to make multidimensional maps of the consumer's positioning of products, and is called 'perceptual mapping'. It can indicate close competitors that the manufacturer may not have identified. In a perceptual mapping exercise on food, using data from a survey of housewives, the closest competitor to lamb chops was found to be fish fingers. It also indicates products that the manufacturer may have believed to be competitive, but which the consumer does not perceive as such.

> For example, a holiday survey indicated that short-break holidays in the UK are not seen by consumers as an alternative to two-week package holidays abroad. If bought at all, short UK holidays would be in addition to, rather than instead of, package holidays abroad.

This kind of information is very illuminating both about market behaviour and for marketing strategy. Figure 6.3 shows a hypothetical perceptual map for canned beers.

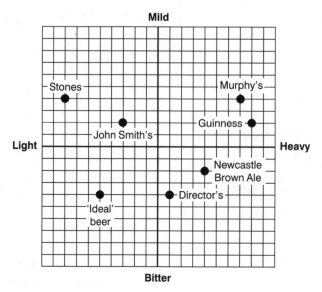

Figure 6.3 A perceptual map

6.2.3 Projective techniques

The interviewing techniques discussed so far rely on the basic assumption that, if you want to know what people do or think and why this is so, you should go out and ask them. In some cases, however, this basic assumption is unjustified. People may not tell you what they do or why they do it, either because they do not wish to do so (they may feel the information is too personal, or reflects on them badly) or because they are unable to do so (the information you require may be difficult to articulate, or if it is to do with motives for action it may be impossible to verbalize the subconscious). To overcome the difficulties in articulating complex or subconscious motivations, researchers have 'borrowed' some approaches and techniques originated by clinical psychologists in their studies of mentally disturbed individuals, who have similar problems in explaining their behaviour to others. These techniques are often called 'projective techniques'. They set up a situation in which the individual is required to bring his or her own point of view to interpret or complete an ambiguous stimulus provided by the researcher. In these situations respondents draw on their own attitudes, opinions and motivations and 'project' them in their reaction to the stimulus. Thus, although they may not be talking about themselves consciously, respondents reveal to researchers what their own views are. Some of the techniques used are briefly described to illustrate the way in which the approach works.

Third person

This is sometimes referred to as 'friendly Martian'. This is particularly useful for products and services in which the individual has very little interest, and if asked for a view might answer, 'I just don't think about it'. The question requires the respondent to explain what someone else, or a 'friendly Martian' might do. For example, 'Suppose someone living round here wanted to buy a car, how would they go about it? What next? How would they decide which manufacturer? Which retailer?' The 'friendly Martian' version of the question would go, 'Suppose a friendly Martian were to land and ask you how to set about buying a car round here, what would you suggest?'

Word association

This is based on the assumption that if a question is answered quickly and spontaneously, subconscious thoughts are revealed, because the conscious mind does not have enough time to think up something else. This approach is sometimes used to test proposed brand names and ensure that they have favourable and appropriate associations for the new product or service.

> For example, 'What is the first thing that comes into your mind when you hear the word "Sharran"?' could have been used to test the UK launch of the Volkswagen MPV. Test names are normally included in a list of other words.

Sentence completion

As in the previous technique, the individual is asked to respond without thinking so that underlying attitudes and motives are more likely to be revealed. 'Men who drink lager are ...?' 'People who have American Express credit cards ...?' 'People who go to art galleries ...?'

Thematic apperception

Thematic apperception tests are usually referred to as 'TATs', or 'picture interpretation'. The individual is shown a picture and asked to say what is going on in the picture, what happened just beforehand and what will happen next, or is asked to tell a story based on the picture.

> The original clinical TAT used 20 standard cards, but when used in market research it is more usual for fewer pictures to be used, and for them to relate to the specific topic under investigation. In a picture interpretation test used by a public library, a picture was shown of an individual going into a library. Both users and non-users of libraries were asked to describe the events that had led up to that individual going to the library, what would happen while in the library and what would happen next. A comparison of responses revealed differences in attitude among library users and non-users, and suggested ways in which non-users might be attracted to use library services.

Story completion

In this technique the respondent is told a story giving an outline of a set of events. The respondent is asked to say what he or she might have done in a similar situation, or to complete the story by relating what will happen next. The respondent might also be asked to give reasons for the behaviour of the people described in the story.

Cartoon completion

This test shows the respondent a cartoon drawing in which one individual is talking to another. The speech for one of the individuals is shown in a 'balloon', and the 'balloon' for the reply of the other individual is left blank. The respondent is asked to fill in that reply. An example might show two housewives talking as one of them unpacks her shopping basket. As she takes out a particular product, her friend asks, 'Why did you buy that brand?', and the respondent in providing a reply will give clues to purchase motivation.

Psychodrama

This is also called the 'fantasy situation'. Respondents are asked to imagine that they are products or services themselves, and to describe their feelings about being used. Examples commonly quoted are motor cars, lawnmowers or boxes of chocolates. This is intended to uncover people's attitudes toward the products: whether using the lawnmower is an inconvenient chore, or an enjoyable fresh-air experience, for example. An alternative approach is to ask the individual to imagine that a particular brand is a person, and then to describe what that person would be like. When repeated for other brands in the market, this provides considerable insight into the mental images that consumers have of the various brands. 'If "CK" perfume were a woman, what would she be like?' 'How would she differ from "Chanel" if she were a woman?' The establishment of a brand personality is a vital part in marketing brands, and creates the platform from which communications strategies, in particular, can be launched.

A major reservation with these projective techniques lies in the fact that answers given by the respondents can rarely be taken at face value: some interpretation is usually necessary. This opens up the possibility of misinterpretation. Trained psychologists are usually employed both to carry out and to interpret the projective techniques used in motivational research, but it should be recognized that these methods are most valuable in the extent to which they provide insights and clues, rather than answers.

6.2.4 Interviewing groups

Situations in which people are interviewed in groups always produce qualitative data, i.e. findings that cannot be treated statistically. This is because they are typically carried out on a small scale, and because the method does not allow for the collection of individual responses that could be summed. Three approaches are described here, of which group discussions are by far the most commonly used.

Group discussions

A group discussion usually consists of about eight respondents and an interviewer, usually called a 'group moderator'. The role of the moderator is to introduce the topics for discussion, and then only to intervene in the conversation to guide the discussion on to other topics or to curtail discussion that moves too far away from the subject. The aim is for the group members to discuss the topic among themselves, unlike the individual interview situation when the dialogue consists of questions from the interviewer and answers from the respondent. Here, the members of the group stimulate, encourage and spark ideas off each other. It is this process of group interaction that makes group discussion so rich in content. In addition to the spontaneity and frankness generated in group comments, it is also interesting to observe the process by which a group consensus is arrived at when there is an initial wide diversity of opinion within the group. To maximize contribution from each of the group members, it is important to ensure that members of the group are sufficiently similar in 'status' to feel free to make their points without inhibition. This usually implies that working-class and middle-class respondents should not be mixed in the same group, and that doctors and hospital consultants should be interviewed in separate groups, and so on. Whenever any members of a group are unduly influenced by the views of other members of the group, the process of free discussion is inhibited and the point of the exercise lost. Another role of the moderator is therefore to ensure that individuals with a powerful personality do not dominate the group to the exclusion of points of view that do not match their own.

Group discussions are commonly held at the outset of the research process since they give such a good 'feel' for the topic being discussed, and can generate possibilities for more structured investigation later in the research process. Often, only four to eight groups may be held, and each group normally lasts for one or two hours. Such small-scale research means that care must be taken not to generalize too much from so few respondents, even though they will have been selected for their representativeness of the wider group being studied. Care is also necessary in the interpretation, organization and reporting of data generated in group discussions. This is normally carried out by the group moderator personally. Group discussions are usually tape-recorded and often videotaped, to enable post-discussion analysis. Specialist research companies will also provide rooms with one-way mirrors which allow the discussion to be monitored and to be steered by an 'independent' moderator, and sometimes the client, via a private voice link to the 'in-room' moderator.

The quality of data from group discussions is largely in the hands of the group moderator, who conducts, interprets and reports on the whole exercise. Group moderation is a skilled task, for which psychological training is useful and experience essential. An advantage of the small-scale nature of group discussion is that it is a fairly speedy form of research. The whole process from briefing the moderator to final report may take only a matter of three to six weeks. It is also a relatively inexpensive form of research, particularly considering the richness of its output. The cost in 2003 was around £2500–3000 per group, including recruiting and paying group members, organizing an appropriate venue (usually a house in the neighbourhood from which respondents are recruited, or a hotel for professional people), providing refreshments to put group members at ease, taping content, analysis and reporting. A typical four-group survey of housewives would therefore cost around £10,000–12,000. Industrial, professional or other specialist groups are likely to be more expensive. The additional costs come from using a hotel venue, more substantial refreshments, higher payments to group attendees and the generally longer duration of group sessions, which may extend to three or even four hours.

Synectics

These are a special form of group discussion, in which the aim is to generate creativity, rather than to collect existing thoughts and attitudes. Synectics are therefore most commonly used to generate new product ideas, or new ideas about provision of services. They were originally used in high-technology markets and carried out using highly qualified technical respondents. They have also been applied in consumer markets using 'ordinary' consumers to generate new product possibilities, with some degree of success. Although it is rare for non-technical respondents to achieve completely innovative idea breakthroughs, they can provide valuable insights into the way in which new product development might go, and suggest a general outline of what a new product might be like. Synectic groups, even with consumers, are more intensive and usually longer than group discussions, lasting for three to four hours. The group structure is different, in that group members are selected deliberately to reflect difference rather than similarity. In the purest form of this method group members are screened for 'high creativity'. They may also meet on more than one occasion, and so increase the generative capacity of the group.

Large group testing

This method is sometimes used for groups that may be difficult to convene because they are widely dispersed. A large group is brought together and some questions are asked of the whole group, to which members are usually required to write down answers or press a code number on a handheld electronic device which will transmit the large group response instantly. This can provide useful demographic and background data about the group members, together with their individual responses to a few questions. The large group is then broken down into a number of smaller groups for group discussions in which the same and other questions can be explored in more depth. It can also be seen whether, on exposure to other points of view, individuals are prepared to change their originally stated positions. Large group testing is not a very commonly used form of research. It has most application in industrial and professional research, where the method is sometimes used at conferences. In this case the results can be transmitted immediately to large screens so that there is instant feedback to the researcher and groups.

6.3 Postal or self-completion research

In postal research the respondent is sent a questionnaire for self-completion through the post. The category also includes other means of distribution such as leaving questionnaires in hotel rooms, or giving them out as people enter museums or department stores. Perhaps 'self-completion' is a better descriptive term since the essence of the method is that the individual completes the questionnaire alone, and then returns it either through the post, or by leaving it in an indicated place. The fact that many of those sent or given self-completion questionnaires fail to return them is the major limitation of postal research. Response rates for completed questionnaires as low as 5 per cent are not uncommon, although the range is very wide. When topics are of particular interest to the sample the response may be much greater. An industrial distributor achieved 85 per cent response in a recent survey of customers, although this is unusually high. A well-run postal survey of interest to respondents, not too demanding of them, with some specific incentive for completion and with follow-up reminders, can expect to achieve a response rate of over 50 per cent.

Self-completion questionnaires work best when they are fully precoded so that all the respondent has to do is tick boxes. The layout should be clear and spacious. If the appearance of the questionnaire suggests that a lot of time will be needed to fill it in, it is less likely to be returned. For these reasons, the type of data that can be collected using postal research is limited in both quantity and quality. When a postal survey is used, evidence suggests that a covering letter explaining the purpose of the survey, and suggesting advantages for the respondent in co-operating, has a very important influence on the response rate. Normally, a second questionnaire is sent to non-responders about three weeks after the first, and then a third. These follow-ups are useful in pushing up the overall response rate. Some argue that separate analysis of the late responders from early responders will reveal differences in response, and that non-responders are likely to be further in the direction of late responders. This allows some subjective estimation to be made of the likely bias present in data from a non-representative sample. Essentially, those who return the questionnaire are self-selected, rather than selected by the researcher, and so may not be representative of the whole group. The lower the response rate, the more of a limitation this becomes. In practice, there is often a bias in such respondents, since individuals who feel more strongly about the topic under investigation are more likely to complete and return questionnaires about it.

Despite this limitation, postal research is quite widely used, for several reasons. It can reach all types of people, in all geographical areas, for the same cost, and does not involve personal interviewers. This makes it much less expensive than other methods. It is also comparatively speedy, since the majority of questionnaires will be returned within the first few weeks if they are going to be returned at all. Sometimes, postal research can be used to reach respondents who would not see an interviewer or accept a telephone call, particularly senior business and professional people. For certain basic factual types of data, postal research may be quite useful, and in these circumstances its advantages over other methods are most evident. The method is often used in industrial research. This is particularly so when an industrial supplier wants to identify ways in which services to customers can be improved. Customers are generally quite ready to respond to this type of research, which is in the interests of both parties. Whether postal research can be used depends on whether an appropriate and up-to-date mailing list exists. Once again, this explains why the method is used in business research, since either customer lists or classified business directories can be used, which make it possible to mail to selected types of company or regions. Whether for industrial or consumer application, postal surveys are most readily completed by enthusiasts and so certain subjects are more likely than others to be successful in using this method; for example, those addressed to specialist groups or concerned with hobbies.

6.4 Internet and e-mail research

Self-completion questionnaires have been taken a step further by the introduction of direct computer interviewing via the Internet or associated e-mail systems. Here the respondent works directly with the computer, following instructions presented on the screen. This technique has also been transferred to telephone research, where responses generated via the telephone keypad initiate the next phase of the interview. The questions are prerecorded. The growth of wireless and cable networks, and applications such as interactive television and mobile telephony on Wireless Application Protocol (WAP) or third-generation mobile devices, means that the potential for development in this area is large. However, the impersonal nature of the process means that some respondents find this interview method intimidating, or simply beyond their level of technological know-how.

Growth to date has been steady, although this is changing. The advantage of direct response by electronic means compared with postal systems is clearly speed. The major problems in using the Internet as a data capture tool are similar to those associated with postal methods. E-mail address lists are even less reliable than some postal mail lists and e-mail users may have multiple e-mail addresses, so there is a lack of suitable responders. On the Internet those who do respond are a self-selecting sample. Currently, home use of the Internet is skewed towards a younger, wealthier and predominantly male audience. In business-to-business research the levels of Internet penetration are much higher and this means that research using the Internet is perhaps more representative. This is still a young and emerging area of marketing research, which clearly has a great deal of potential. However, the same methodological rules about sampling and representativeness apply. With the reach and potential of this medium these rules are often neglected, and this can produce seriously distorted results leading to the wrong management decisions being made.

A different situation applies to panel research and to research based on a known population, for example a company's existing customers. In this case, the use of the Internet or e-mail can generate excellent information, very quickly. This is particularly the case in dot-com companies or companies whose products and services are distributed or supported by the Internet or e-mail. Rather like fax research several years ago, the method also has the advantage of being relatively new to the market and response rates can be higher than using mail. Several companies have developed online panels, and these are outlined in Chapter 4.

In the 2002 Market Research Society (MRS) *Research Buyer's Guide* 60 organizations had the capability of offering computer-assisted web interviewing (CAWI) and 211 could administer online or e-mail surveys. Before conducting research using these media it is advisable to contact these companies for advice.

6.5 Diary panels

In the methods discussed so far it has been assumed that the research is being carried out on an ad hoc basis, i.e. a 'one-off' piece of research carried out when the decision maker has a particular need for a piece of information. However, there are situations in which it is useful to have a continuous series of measurements of the same piece of data, so that any change can be monitored. This is particularly true, for instance, when the decision maker wishes to discover what effects the decisions have on price changes, advertising campaigns, and so on.

One of the most important sources of continuous data is the diary panel. These panels are usually run by independent market research agencies, who sell the results to interested companies. Increasingly, the media are also setting up diary panels, the results of which are available not only to the media owner, but also to advertisers who use the medium. This service has been run for television for some time, and in recent years diary panels have been set up by a number of local newspapers and by local commercial radio stations. The way in which a diary panel operates is that a representative sample of respondents is selected and visited by an interviewer. If they agree to co-operate they are recruited on to the panel and left a diary or other means of recording data. In this they record their behaviour and sometimes that of other members of the family as well, relevant to the subject of the panel.

Most panel systems are computerized, including one of the largest, Superpanel (Taylor Nelson Sofres. Tel: 020 8967 0007, Fax: 020 8967 4060, E-mail enquiries@tnsofres.com), which uses a sample of 15,000 homes providing data on a range of consumer goods. Purchases are scanned using a handheld barcode reader and sent electronically to Taylor Nelson Sofres for central processing and analysis. The obvious advantages of this system are the speed with which information can be generated and the potential for detailed analysis. The service also covers influencing factors in the markets under review.

Nielsen Homescan (Tel: 01865 742 742, Fax: 01865 742 222) is a similar service. Examples of panel data available are those on buying of household consumer goods, personal consumer goods such as toiletries, baby products and motoring products. Examples of the types of data produced from Nielsen's Homescan service are shown in Figure 6.4.

Purpose

To quantify the importance of individual retailers to a market/brand both in terms of expenditure and number of households using particular stores. Comparison against total purchasing quickly establishes strengths and weaknesses.

Key measures

For each retailer group:

- Percentage of households purchasing (penetration)
- Percentage of expenditure
- Average number of visits per buyer
- Average spend per buyer
- Average spend per visit

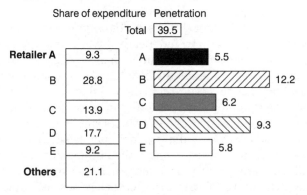

Figure 6.4 Share of trade analysis. *Source*: Nielsen Homescan

Several of these services have been established internationally. ETCD/ PCP is a Taylor Nelson Sofres usage tracking study covering toiletries and cosmetics. It examines the behaviour of 14,000 individuals.

Further information on this type of service can be found in Chapter 4.

Sometimes specific companies may set up short-term panels to monitor the effects of some particularly important decisions, as in test marketing or launching a new product. The information is usually returned to the research company on a weekly basis, either by mail or electronically, and reports are available of monthly or quarterly data.

Diary panels are an excellent method of providing regular data on a range of behaviours that would otherwise be difficult to collect. This is particularly true for buying of items that are easily forgotten, such as chocolate, confectionery and other small purchases. Impulse is a panel system from Taylor Nelson Sofres examining the behaviour of 5250 individuals in the difficult-to-measure impulse market, which includes products such as ice cream, confectionery and snacks, as well as the national lottery. Diary panels are also extremely valuable in that they are 'single-source' data, i.e. the behaviour of the same individual is monitored over time, and this makes it possible to do some very interesting analyses of 'brand-switching' behaviour, that is, the way in which the same consumers choose different brands or a small range of brands over time. Media-use data is also sometimes recorded, which adds further to the value of the data.

When diary panel data are used in conjunction with retail audits (see Section 6.6.2) they are particularly useful in identifying market segments. Retail audits measure what is being bought; diary panels describe who is buying. Diary panels are also useful in showing differences in response among different consumers, say to price, packaging or advertising changes, and this represents a useful diagnostic tool. Most of the syndicated panel research surveys available are listed in Section 4.3.

There are two main problems in diary panel data. The first is a concern over the behaviour of the members: the 'guinea-pig' effect. Does someone recruited to the television-viewing panel exhibit atypically high viewing levels of documentary and news programmes, rather than soap operas and sports programmes? Tests conducted on this aspect of panel behaviour suggest that it may happen with new panel members, but that the effect quickly wears off. Research companies therefore exclude the first four weeks' diaries of new panel members from analysis. The second problem with diary panels lies in maintaining interest in the membership of the panel since, if the drop-out rate becomes too high, the advantages of continuous data from the same individuals are lost. Research companies operate incentive schemes both to encourage prompt return of data and to keep interest in and involvement with the panel going. These may take the form of regular 'lucky draws' and a points system that can be used to buy items from a catalogue.

Companies that decide to operate a panel of customers or trade intermediaries 'in-house' will need to give careful consideration to the cost and mechanics of operating the panel and handling the data generated, since both can escalate beyond expectations.

6.6 Telephone research

The great advantages of telephone research are its speed and relative economy compared to personal interviewing, particularly when only a limited amount of information is required. It has the added advantage for industrial research that individuals difficult to reach by personal interview, e.g. the more senior executives, may respond to telephone surveys, which are less demanding of their time.

An important factor in the growth of telephone research is the wide acceptance of the telephone as a means of communication and the development of sophisticated technical support systems for researchers. With mobile technology the telephone is associated with the person who owns it rather than the building in which they live. This, and the ever improving ability to access the Internet and to transmit pictures, means that mobile telephony could be the next big area for technical change in the research industry, although general consumer penetration of these sophisticated devices remains limited.

A problem, however, is the number of unlisted numbers, which may create difficulty in selecting a representative sample. It is often hard to construct a sample of the wealthier members of society for this reason. Even today, telephone owners tend to be better off than the population as a whole. However, for products and services aimed at this group, telephone research among consumers is possible and growing.

For most marketing purposes widespread telephone ownership makes the method adequate in terms of its representativeness across all social classes. The swiftness of the method is often illustrated during election campaigns, where issues raised on the previous day are reflected in the morning newspapers' opinion polls.

From its small beginnings in 1979, telephone research among consumers has grown rapidly. Ownership of telephones has continued to increase, giving greater representativeness of samples. In the 2002 MRS *Research Buyer's Guide*, 184 of over 800 organizations listed had the capacity to carry out computer-assisted telephone interviewing (CATI) and significantly more were able to gather data by telephone. CATI systems offer the chance to combine the cost and flexibility advantages of telephone contact with increased control, and hence improved data quality, of the computerized interview. The systems operate by showing the questionnaire on a visual display unit from which the interviewer reads the questions. Answers are keyed directly into the computer by the interviewer, and the next question is displayed on the screen. Since the computer can handle complex questionnaire routeing systems (e.g. if answer to Q. 15 is 'Yes' then go to Q. 16, if 'No' go to Q. 27) by only displaying the correct next question, the possibility for interviewer error is reduced.

Telephone interview costs in 2003 ranged between £40 and £70 per interview, depending on whether the sector was consumer or business-to-business.

Many research companies maintain a panel of telephone interviewees who can be accessed at short notice on behalf of their
clients. The panel is maintained to reflect the structure of UK
society as a whole, so representative samples can be selected.
Research International (Tel: 020 7656 5000, Fax: 020 7201 0700,
E-mail: info@research-int.com), one of the major UK-based
research agencies, maintains a panel of 12,000 potential telephone
respondents.

6.7 Observation research

The quality of data collected using interview methods is dependent on
individuals being willing and able to report their behaviour or attitudes
verbally. In certain circumstances people may be unable to do this, not
because they are unwilling to do so, but simply because they do not
mentally record the data required, and are therefore unable to report it. An
example of this would be if you wished to know what items a housewife
had taken from a supermarket shelf and considered purchasing, but had not
actually purchased; or if you wished to know the path an individual had
taken around an art gallery, what exhibits they stopped to look at, and for
how long. In both instances it would be highly unlikely that the individuals
concerned could give an accurate account of their behaviour. Such
information can be readily obtained by observation. Observation techniques
are also widely used by social researchers, in road planning and underpass
siting for pedestrians, for example. They can be used by industrial firms to
check interest in exhibition stands. The method is therefore of wide
application, and where the data required is about what people do rather
than why they do it, it can provide accurate data, free of the possible biases
of interviewer effect and faulty memory. These advantages make observation especially useful in collecting data about routine consumer behaviour
on a continuous basis.

6.7.1 Observation panels

There are several panels in operation in which observation is the primary
method of data collection. These cover household consumer goods,
shopping behaviour and television viewing. For the first of these a panel of
informants is recruited who agree to allow an auditor to come into the home
each week and check what products are in the house in the product fields
being investigated. Informants are given a plastic bin in which to place
discarded wrappers and packets of products used during the week. From
this data both purchase and usage rates can be calculated. These are
sometimes referred to as 'pantry checks' and 'dustbin checks'. The research
company collates the data and presents monthly reports to clients
purchasing the service. Shopping behaviour is observed by recruiting a

panel of housewives who agree to do all their shopping in a travelling shop. This is a mobile shop laid out inside to look like a supermarket. The housewife simply shops in the usual way. From time to time new brands are introduced on to the shelves to test how the housewife reacts to them in a purchase choice situation, and more importantly, whether she buys the product next time or goes back to her original brand.

One of the advantages of observation techniques is that in an age of sophisticated electronic technology it is not always necessary for an individual to collect the data, since this can be done using the appropriate hardware. Television viewing is a case in point.

> PeopleMeter is a recording device that is attached to the television. It records data on when the set is on, and which channel it is tuned to. This gives a measure of 'sets tuned'. To convert this to 'viewers', members of co-operating households push buttons on the meter as they enter and leave the room. The system also allows guests' age and gender to be entered and additionally video playback is monitored.

Observation by hardware is also useful for all kinds of 'flow counts'; for example, to investigate traffic and pedestrian flows past poster sites, or around supermarkets or exhibitions. Usually the recording periods are randomized to give flow patterns on different days of the week and at different times of day.

6.7.2 Retail audits

An important application of the 'audit' method of observation research is in the field of trade research. An example of this is that organized by ACNielsen UK, Nielsen's Retail Measurement Services.

A representative sample of grocery shops is recruited to the panel. At each visit auditors record the amount of stock in the shop, and check computer records, invoices and delivery notes for deliveries made since the last visit. Sales in the intervening period can then be calculated. Where Nielsen is denied access to data, the interviewers will question customers outside those outlets about purchases made. In-home checks are also carried out to cover less frequently purchased products. ACNielsen measures and tracks sales volume, selling price, observed promotion and merchandising execution, encompassing an organization's own brands as well as competitive brands. A wide range of analyses can be derived from this data. Retail Measurement Services help to gauge product penetration, overall product performance, distribution, promotion effectiveness and price sensitivity

A similar method is employed by Nielsen, covering chemists, confectioners/tobacconists/newsagents (CTN), DIY, home appliances, sportswear, liquor and cash-and-carry trades. This is an important service for manufacturers of products covered, since it is one of the ways in which they can measure consumer sales reaction to advertising, price changes and other marketing tactics. Ex-factory sales do not provide this kind of feedback because of the length of the marketing channel, which may include stock buffers at both wholesale and retail outlets. This can mean that after leaving the factory it could be six weeks before a product reaches the retail outlet shelf. The introduction of direct electronic links from checkout points is improving the quality and speed of retail audit data. Increasingly, data is received electronically from the point-of-sale equipment installed in most major supermarket chains. Other research agencies also produce retail audit data and are listed in Section 4.3, since they are usually made available on a syndicated basis, as is Nielsen data. An example of results is shown in Figure 6.5.

Purpose

To measure the strengths and weaknesses of brands/sectors/variants within individual retailers, including own label.

Key measures

For each reported item:

- Shares and expenditure by individual retail group
- Average RSP

Retailers

	X	Y	Z
Brand A variant 1	5.4	6.3	6.6
2	7.9	7.6	8.4
3	16.4	20.1	25.2
Brand B variant 1	23.0	30.8	10.6
			9.0
2	10.6	10.2	
			40.2
Own label	36.7	25.0	

Figure 6.5 Source of purchase analysis. *Source*: Nielsen

6.8 Summary

Interviews involving personal contact between interviewer and respondents are the most versatile and widely used method of primary data collection. They may be carried out in a variety of ways, and descriptions are given of types of individual interview, attitude measurement and projective techniques. Group interviewing methods, of which group discussions are the most important, are also mentioned. The non-personal research methods covered are postal research or self-completion, Internet and e-mail research, diary panels, telephone research and the observation methods of panels and retail audits.

7 Who provides the information?

7.1 Introduction

This chapter is concerned with sampling: the process of actually selecting those individuals whose views will be collected in the survey in order to be representative of the whole group whose views are being sought. Good sampling practice is the key to the ability of large-scale quantitative surveys to represent the views of the population being studied to a known and calculable degree of accuracy. Sampling theory has at its heart probability theory and it is on probability theory that the validity of large-scale surveys rests. If you like, it is probability theory that allows large-scale market research surveys to 'work'. A complete understanding of sampling theory therefore demands an understanding of basic statistical probability theory. However, it is possible for an individual without a statistical background to appreciate what sampling theory is able to do and how samples are selected without necessarily getting involved in the intricacies of the statistical basis for this. Those wishing to read a statistical treatment of sampling are recommended the appropriate chapters in the books by Chisnall, and Worcester and Downham, listed in Chapter 17. This chapter will answer four questions:

- What is a sample?
- Why use a sample?
- How is the sample selected?
- How big does the sample need to be?

In Section 7.4, describing how samples are selected, the three main methods of sampling will be discussed: random sampling, quota sampling and judgement sampling.

7.2 What is a sample?

A sample is a limited number taken from a large group for testing and analysis, on the assumption that the sample can be taken as representative of the whole group. Most people are familiar with the concept of sampling and its application in many everyday areas of life. For example, we take a sip of a drink or a bite of food to determine whether or not we are going to enjoy it. We are also familiar with the idea that scientists wishing to check the quality of a production batch will take a small sample from a large batch of product, and subject the sample to analysis to determine the constituents and their proportions in the whole batch. It is exactly this procedure which the marketing researcher is seeking to apply when sampling is used in survey research. From the example given it is easy to see that the major constituents of the production batch will only be represented in the correct proportions if the sample selected by the scientist for test was from a well-mixed batch, i.e. is representative of the whole content of the batch. The techniques of sample selection seek to ensure that the members of a survey sample are truly representative of all the members of the population from which they are derived. This therefore underlines the importance of correct sampling procedures in research. Without them the sample selected will not be representative and the answers gathered from them will not be a good guide to what the population of interest would say if all of them were asked.

7.3 Why use a sample?

In survey research, samples are used to make an estimate of what the whole population of interest is like or what it thinks or does. In theory, it would be possible to measure or to question all members of the population of interest; this is known as a census, but in practice this would prove difficult. It is the practical advantages that account for the fact that samples are the normal method of collecting data, rather than censuses in which everyone must be included. The smaller the number of people from whom data is to be collected, the cheaper and quicker the process will be. Analysis of the data will be more manageable and control of the whole procedure more effectively achieved. Added to these highly practical advantages is the fact that good sampling procedures allow a high degree of precision in estimating the results that would have been achieved from a census, and so the argument for sampling becomes overwhelming and explains its almost universal usage.

7.4 How is the sample selected?

Samples are selected from populations, and the term 'sample' has already been explained. In marketing research, use of the term 'population' refers to the whole group whose views are to be represented. For example, some surveys are interested in the views of the general population of the country. More commonly, marketing researchers are interested in the views of populations with characteristics of special relevance: the population of motorists, the population of housewives, the population of retail outlets for a particular type of goods, the population of suppliers of a particular type of industrial machinery, the population of professional groups such as architects, or users of social services, and so on.

Data collected from the sample are referred to as 'statistics' and these sample statistics are used to estimate the 'population parameter'. That is, results obtained from a sample are used to calculate the results that would have been obtained from the underlying population had a census been used. The degree to which it is possible to use sample statistics to estimate population parameters with an acceptable degree of accuracy depends on the sampling procedures used and on the size of the sample. The three main methods used in selecting samples are called *random sampling*, *quota sampling* and *judgement sampling*. The method whose statistical validity forms the foundation for the whole practice of survey research is random sampling, and for this reason it is the best known and most commonly described method of sampling. However, in practice, quota sampling has been found to give perfectly acceptable results for commercial purposes and at a cheaper cost than random sampling. Quota sampling is therefore the most commonly applied sample selection method in market research, despite its lack of statistical purity. Judgement sampling is also commonly applied in practice simply because, as its title suggests, it is often the most sensible way of approaching the sample selection problem, although it has theoretical limitations. Because of the lack of statistical purity in their manner of sample selection, quota and judgement sampling methods are sometimes referred to as 'non-probability' sampling procedures and, referring to the element of personal discretion used, they are also called 'purposive' sampling procedures.

7.4.1 Random sampling

Random sampling, based on statistical probability theory, has two characteristics that make it extremely useful in practice to the decision maker. These are that it is possible to calculate the level of confidence and limits of accuracy of the results.

The 'level of confidence' refers to the fact that from a randomly drawn sample it is possible to work out the statistical probability that the sample is a good one. Very much like that famous toothpaste 'ring of confidence', it is heartening for a decision maker to hear from the researchers, 'these results are correct to the 95 per cent level of confidence'. What they are in effect saying is, 'there is only a one in twenty chance that this sample is a bad one'. The 95 per cent level is the most commonly used level of confidence in research and most decision makers in organizational settings are satisfied with data in which they can be assured of having this level of confidence, simply because so much other uncertainty surrounds the decision-making environment.

The second practical outcome of sound sampling practice referred to is the 'limits of accuracy'. Common sense dictates that when 1000 respondents are used to calculate the views of the 3,000,000 members of the population whom they represent, then the calculation is likely to be only an approximate one. This is, sample statistics can be used to calculate population parameters only within certain limits of accuracy, rather than with spot-on precision. It also makes sense that the more respondents included in the sample, the more accurate the calculation of the population parameters is likely to be, i.e. the larger the size of the sample the narrower the range of limits of accuracy. The relationship, however, is not in direct proportion. From a sample of 1000, results may be within limits of accuracy of + or –10 per cent. To reduce that by half, i.e. to results of + or –5 per cent, it would be necessary to include four times as many individuals in the sample, i.e. 4000 respondents. This point about the relationship between sample size and accuracy is considered further in Section 7.5.

The third, and important, practical advantage of sampling theory is that the level of confidence and limits of accuracy required in the results can be decided in advance of the survey. Use of the appropriate statistical calculations makes it possible to determine what size of sample will be required to produce findings to those specifications. While it is not essential to be able to perform personally the statistical calculations referred to, it is important to note that the quality and validity of the findings from large-scale quantitative research surveys are determined by the appropriateness with which these calculations are carried out and statistical concepts applied.

This book aims only to introduce marketing research and does not expect the reader to be equipped with a statistical background. Nor is it felt feasible or desirable to attempt to teach that statistical background in an intro-ductory book. In the authors' experience it is those horrifying pages of statistical calculations that cause managers who started off with an interest in learning more about marketing research to decide that perhaps the subject is not for them. However, the authors are also aware of the desire of managers in very many types of organization to undertake their own research. Advice to the would-be 'do-it-yourself' researcher is that he or she needs to know far more about sampling theory and practice than the introduction given in this chapter will provide. The same advice holds for students of market research. The purpose of the following explanation of sample selection procedures is to provide a basis for understanding why particular selection techniques are used in sample surveys and to judge their appropriateness. It will also give an appreciation of the advantages and limitations of each method.

To summarize, the great advantage of random sampling techniques is that they allow statistical calculation of the appropriate sample size for predetermined levels of confidence (usually set at the 95 per cent level) and limits of accuracy (set to meet requirements of the decision to be made). It must be stressed that these calculations are only possible when random sampling techniques are used because random sampling is the only one of the three methods discussed in this chapter that is based on probability theory, from which the appropriate calculations derive. So, random sampling may be called 'probability sampling'.

The sampling frame

A randomly drawn sample is one in which every member of the population has a calculable chance of being included in the sample. If every member of the population is to have a chance of being included in the sample then it follows that every member of the population must be known in order to have that chance. So, the first step in drawing a random sample is to make a list of all the members of the population; this is referred to as the 'sampling frame'. The term 'frame' is used rather than 'list' because for certain types of sample the frame may be a map rather than a list. It is at this point that many attempts to apply random sampling techniques will flounder, simply because a sampling frame cannot be constructed. Commonly used frames are: the electoral register, for sampling households or adults over 18 years of age; trade directories, for sampling manufacturing, retailing and other organizations; and customer lists, for sampling customers of a particular firm. Difficulties arise, however, when the population to be sampled cannot be listed; for example, owners of digital personal assistants, buyers of office supplies or people who have taken more than one holiday in the past 12 months. Even when a sampling frame can be constructed it may turn out to be unusable in practice because of out-of-date addresses, incompleteness, duplication of entries, lack of geographical clustering or poor list organization. The greater any of these problems, the less reliable the frame as a basis for sampling. If the frame is not representative of the population of interest then any sample drawn from it will not be.

Simple random sampling

The point of any random sampling procedure is that there should be no personal influence in the selection of individuals to be interviewed. The simplest way to achieve this in theory is to cut up the population list into separate individuals, put all the strips of paper into a large container or tombola drum, give them a good mix round and then draw out the number required. Although straightforward in theory, this procedure is less so in practice, particularly on a windy day! Nowadays the most common method of drawing a simple random sample is to assign a number to every item on the list and to select the required number at random by using random number tables. (These are available in books and electronically. The numbers in them are produced by electronic means and checked for randomness.) There is also a number of computer packages that will generate random numbers.

Systematic (quasi-) random sampling

The most commonly used method of systematic random sampling is to select every nth number from the frame by dividing the number of items on the list by the number required in the eventual sample. In the earlier example, if the sampling frame contained 3,000,000 names and if we required 1000 respondents, then dividing 3,000,000 by 1000 would indicate that every 3000th name on the list must be selected. This is achieved by selecting the first name at random out of the first 3000 names and thereafter selecting every 3000th name. So, using a simple random method the first number selected might be 111; thereafter, the second number would be 3111, the third number 6111, and so on, and by the time the end of the list was reached 1000 names would have been drawn from it.

Random sample interviewing

Since the whole point of random sampling is that respondents are selected without any personal bias creeping into the process, it is important that the individuals selected are actually included in the samples by being interviewed. In practice, this means that interviewers must call back on the address they are given until they make contact with the individual named, and it is normal procedure to insist that three callbacks are made by the interviewer before giving up on an individual. The need for callbacks in the field is one of the reasons why random sampling is the most expensive form of sampling to use, but if the named individuals are not contacted then the whole point of using a random sampling selection procedure is lost.

Practical limitations of simple random sampling

While simple random sampling methods may be the most elegant in theory, they often turn out to be the most expensive to apply in practice, for several reasons. First, there is the time and expense involved in drawing up the sampling frame in the first place, particularly if it is a large one which has to be compiled from a number of different sources. Second, for a national sample it would be reasonable to expect that the respondents selected would be randomly distributed on a national basis. This will make the cost of fieldwork very high, since separate trips will need to be made to each location and, as has already been mentioned, up to three callbacks may have to be made in each location. To overcome these limitations two refinements in methods of random sampling have been developed. They are widely used in commercial research practice and have been found to yield results of acceptable accuracy, bearing in mind that most research is done to represent the views of typical members of the population under consideration, rather than its unusual members.

Random route sampling

In this form of sampling the district within which an interviewer will work is determined by random methods. However, within that district the interviewers must follow a prescribed 'route'. That is, they are given a set of instructions such as, 'Take the first turning on the right, the third on the left', and so on. The instructions contain details about where to start trying to obtain interviews and how many houses to leave before trying again after a successful interview has been achieved. The practical advantage of this system is that interviewers do not make a callback if they get no reply and this therefore reduces the time and cost involved in the survey. The possibility of bias arising from some individuals being more likely to be found at home than others can be overcome by setting controls on the numbers of, say, working women who must be included in each interviewer's required number of interviews.

Random location sampling

In simple and systematic random sampling procedures the final sampling unit selected is the individual to be interviewed. In random location sampling the sample is selected in such a way that the final unit of selection is a geographical unit rather than an individual. The interviewer must complete a given number of interviews within the geographical area, which is usually an enumerator district of about 150–200 homes. Which actual respondents should be selected within that location is determined by giving the interviewer a target number of individuals meeting specified age, gender, class and other relevant characteristic requirements. These targets are called 'quotas' and are further explained in Section 7.4.2. Random location sampling is a hybrid between random sampling and quota sampling which attempts to combine the best aspects of both sampling methods, i.e. the objectivity of random sampling combined with the cost-efficiency of quota sampling.

Stratification

The point of sampling is to represent the characteristics of the population of interest in the correct proportions but, because a sample is being used, only an estimate of the characteristics of interest can be derived from it rather than a precise value. However, it is often the case that certain characteristics of the population of interest are already known. In the case of the general population these characteristics are known from census data. In industrial and trade research certain characteristics of the population may be known from existing secondary sources or from previous original research data. When the proportions of certain important and relevant characteristics in the population being surveyed are known with certainty, then it makes sense to use this information as a way of improving the quality of the sample. The technique used to do this is 'stratification'. For stratified samples, the sampling frame is rearranged so that particular attributes of the population are grouped together in their known proportions. The sample is then selected by a random method from each group or 'stratum' in the same proportion in which the stratum exists in the population. One of the most common stratification systems used is to stratify by geographical regions, taking account of the population density. The proportion of survey respondents within each region is then calculated in proportion to the percentage of the population living in that region. By ensuring that each known segment of the population of interest is correctly reflected in the make-up of a sample, one possible source of inaccuracy in the sample is avoided.

The method of stratification is commonly applied in sampling wherever possible since it improves the accuracy of the sample. Age, gender, region and social class are four commonly used stratification variables in commercial market research. In industrial research, manufacturers may be stratified by standard industrial classification (SIC) grouping, number of employees or size of turnover. In trade research, retail outlets may be stratified by size of turnover, square footage of floor space, and so on. Whenever the proportions of relevant characteristics about the population are known with certainty it makes sense to apply them. This method of determining the allocation of a sample of respondents is also referred to as 'proportionate sampling'. This is because it has the effect of ensuring that important characteristics of the population are proportionately represented in the sample.

Multi-stage sampling

The method of stratification referred to above is often used as a basis for multi-stage sampling. This is a refinement of the random sampling technique which attempts to reduce the cost of random sampling at both the selection and fieldwork stages, without losing the element of randomness. In the case of sampling UK households, for example, at the first stage of the process a simple random sample may be taken of all parliamentary constituencies in the UK. For each constituency selected at the first stage a list of wards is compiled and a simple random sample selected of wards within each constituency. At the third stage each ward is divided into groups of streets known as polling districts and a simple random sample taken of these streets. This technique forms the basis for random location sampling, since the group of streets selected at the third stage forms the area used for interviewers to carry out their quota of interviews. The process could go one stage further and the selection of individual respondents be made from lists of names and addresses for the polling districts identified at the previous stage.

An advantage of multi-stage sampling is that compilation of the sampling frame is very much reduced. Even when the individual sampling unit is of names and addresses this does not arise from the need for a complete listing of all addresses in the UK in the first place. At the first stage the frame is restricted simply to a list of constituencies, electoral registers of names and addresses only being required for a limited number of areas at the final stage. A second advantage of the technique is that the final interviews end up being geographically clustered. This considerably reduces the administrative and travelling costs of carrying out the fieldwork in these areas.

Weighting

It may be that the research user is not equally interested in the views of members of all subgroups of the population, or that the user is particularly interested in analysing the views of just one small subgroup.

In a general survey about financial services, some information was required about those individuals using pension services. It was estimated that only 5 per cent of individuals in the target sector used pension services, so in the sample of 1000 respondents only 50 could be expected to be within this subgroup, which would not have been sufficient for detailed analysis of their views in isolation. In order to have a minimum of 100 respondents in this minority group for detailed analysis, it would be necessary to start off with an original sample twice as big, that is to say of 2000. This would have obviously undesirable effects on the timing and costs of the survey. An alternative way of overcoming the problem was simply to increase the number of respondents in the minority group to 100 without changing the rest of the sample. So the total sample size was actually 1050 respondents, of whom 100 were users of pension services.

For the purpose of analysing the results of the whole sample, the subgroup of users of pension services would have twice the representation of any other group. To correct this imbalance when analysing the content of the survey as a whole, results from this group were weighted downwards by a factor of two. However, with 100 respondents there was a sufficient number for a limited amount of analysis within the responses of that group. They could therefore be used for separate consideration as a group.

The procedure described is known as 'weighting'. It may be used, as in the example, to explore the particular views of minority groups without overinflating the total size of the sample. It can also be used to reduce the number of respondents selected from particularly large subgroups of the population, so as to reduce the overall cost of the survey. Results from this group are then weighted up by the factor with which they have been underrepresented in the original sample.

A trade survey of grocers' attitudes was carried out using Nielsen data. This indicated that co-operative and multiple shops accounted for 6 and 14 per cent, respectively, of all grocers, the remaining 80 per cent being independent grocers. The sample included 100 respondents from each type of outlet. In analysing the results for grocers generally, weighting factors were applied to reduce the input from co-operative and multiple shop respondents and to increase that of independent grocers. Each subgroup could also be analysed separately to identify differences between them. Had the sample wished to take account of differences in turnover rather than number of shops, the weighting factors would be based on Nielsen data showing that for share of turnover co-operatives represent 11 per cent, multiples 73 per cent and independents 16 per cent.

7.4.2 Quota sampling

To ensure that respondents to a random sample are genuinely representative of the population from which they are drawn, it is common practice to calculate the proportions of respondents by age, gender, class, region and so on, and check that these are in line with the known figures of census data. Since this has become routine procedure for checking the accuracy of random samples it is a very short mental step from here to suggest that if applying the proportions of known characteristics of the population to the results of random samples is valid as a check for their accuracy, then why not simply select the sample so as to represent those characteristics in the known proportions in the first place? This reasoning forms the basis for quota sampling. The reasoning is that if the known characteristics of the population are represented in the correct proportions then all other data collected will be represented in the correct proportions. Stating its underlying assumption in this way also illustrates the main reason for criticism of quota samples. It could happen that even though known and measurable characteristics are distributed in the correct proportions, unknown characteristics relevant to the subject of the survey may not be.

A quota sample based on interviewing people at home is likely to underrepresent those who go out a lot. A quota sample based on interviewing people in the street may underrepresent those who do not go out a lot. If behaviour relevant to going out or not going out is important to the context of a quota sample survey – perhaps it is about leisure activities in general, or frequency of visits to pubs, or the amount of TV viewing – then important aspects of the data may be misrepresented, resulting in the collection of biased data which will mislead the decision maker. When the significance of the limitations of the sampling procedure is as obvious as in the example suggested, then common sense can go a considerable way to overcoming this disadvantage. The theoretical danger of quota sampling is that some hidden bias may exist which will not be discovered.

Quota sampling is considerably influenced by the researcher, in ways that random sampling is not. In the first place, the researcher determines which characteristics should be used as a basis for setting quotas. Next, the actual selection of respondents is left to the interviewer rather than determined by the sample selection procedure as in random sampling. In quota sampling the interviewer is presented with a set of target interviews to complete, and the interviews are described in terms of the characteristics of the respondents required. For example, the interviewer may be told that he or she has to complete 30 interviews in three to four days' work, the 30 interviews to be completed as shown in Figure 7.1.

Once the interviewer has these quotas it is up to him or her to locate the appropriate number and type of people within the working area in the required time. Most interviewers knowing their area well will know exactly where to go to collect the type and age of person specified. Everyone knows for their own home town where the middle class and working class areas are. One can think of the place one would go to if one were particularly

Your assignment is to interview 30 respondents to the sex, age and class quotas detailed below.

Sex

	Required	*Achieved*	*Total*
Male	15		
Female	15		
			30

Age

	Required	*Achieved*	*Total*
16–34	13		
35–54	12		
55+	5		
			30

Class

	Required	*Achieved*	*Total*
ABC1	12		
C2	11		
DE	7		
			30

Figure 7.1 Quota sheet

interested in collecting the views of younger people or of older people. Applying exactly that kind of local knowledge, the interviewers quickly and efficiently complete the quota set for them. The problem is that by selecting respondents from such stereotyped areas they are not entirely representative of the whole population, which is more mixed than the method described might reflect. What of the middle-class individual living in a generally working class area, or vice versa? What of the young person not to be found with the majority of young people, and so on?

Recognizing that a possible weakness in the validity of quota sampling lies in the degree to which the interviewer is able to influence the selection of final respondents, hybrid systems of sample selection have been developed. In random location sampling the interviewer is given a quota of interviews to complete, but may only do this within an area of named streets. Other quota controls may be established, perhaps to limit the proportion of respondents with easy-to-interview occupations such as men working on outside jobs or public transport. Quota controls are also used to include the correct proportion of working housewives, and of other characteristics relevant to the purpose of the survey.

The great advantages of quota sampling are its quickness and cheapness, both in generating the sample in the first place and in completing and controlling the fieldwork. In order to select the sample, no sampling frame needs to be devised. This is not only a saving in cost and time, but in certain circumstances it makes sampling possible when a sampling frame cannot be established and yet some important characteristics of the population to be sampled are known. In industrial and trade research, quota sampling is particularly useful since sampling frames are often difficult to construct yet the major characteristics of an industry or trade may be known. Another advantage of quota sampling is that it overcomes one of the problems of random sampling, in that although sampling frames may be quickly outdated, the population characteristics used as the basis of allocating quota samples are far more stable.

In carrying out the fieldwork the most important advantage of quota sampling is that interviewers do not have to find named individuals. This accounts for the greatest cost and time savings of the method. The interviewer simply screens likely individuals with a small number of classification questions and, if they meet the requirements of the quota, goes on to complete the full interview. If they do not meet the quota requirement, the interview is terminated and the interviewer continues knocking on doors or stopping other individuals in the street until he or she finds someone who does. This reduces the costs of quota sampling to about one-third to one-half that of random sampling.

As far as the quality of data is concerned, studies that have tested the results of quota samples against those of random samples have suggested that for the majority of commercial purposes these are perfectly acceptable. In these applications the cost benefits of the method outweigh the theoretical disadvantages, provided adequate control is exercised. This will include adequate training of interviewers for their important role in this type of sample selection procedure. The cost saving made in the application of quota rather than random sampling can be used to improve the quality of the data generated in other ways, say by increasing the sample size. Quota sampling is mainly used as an acceptable but cheaper alternative to random sampling for the purposes of most ad hoc market research surveys. The fact that this is the major method now in use appears to underline its widespread acceptability. Presumably its army of regular users has found that the system works well in practice. For social surveys, however, when it is often the views of minorities rather than majorities which it is required to represent, it is possible that quota sampling may not be sufficiently sensitive.

7.4.3 Judgement sampling

Judgement sampling is a move further away from the unbiased attempt to provide a representative sample of the population to be surveyed. In theory, it is only the random sampling methods that do this. Quota sampling is an attempt to replicate what random sampling achieves at a lower cost, and it has some success in doing this. An element of judgement comes into the method in deciding which quota controls should be used in selection of the sample. Nevertheless, the basic aim of the method is to attain the representativeness of random samples.

Judgement sampling, like quota sampling, is a form of purposive sampling but differs from both quota sampling and random sampling in that the attempt to achieve statistical representativeness of the population as a whole is largely abandoned. The aim is still to produce data representative of the population to be sampled, but judgement is used in the sample selection procedure to make the data more useful to the decision maker.

Judgement sampling is commonly applied in industrial and trade research when a few large manufacturers or retailers may dominate the market. In this case the sample might include all the major manufacturers or retailers in a trade and then a sample of other organizations. This will ensure the inclusion of those major organizations whose activities are of such significance in the marketplace that any survey not including all of them could not hope to give a valid picture of what is happening in that market.

> A manufacturer of china included all the major department store buyers in a sample together with a random sample of specialist china outlets. The purpose here, as is usually the case in trade and industrial research, was to give additional weight to the views of more important members of the trade in terms of their size or share of turnover.

A similar approach may be taken by an industrial supplier surveying its own customers. Once again, the supplier may wish to seek the views of all the important customers and sample the rest.

Judgement sampling may be the only practical approach for sampling populations if no sampling frame can be constructed for random sampling and insufficient data is available about the population for quota sampling.

This is often the case in the preliminary stages of a survey and judgement sampling is the main technique used in small-scale exploratory research surveys. A programme of 'key interviews' might be carried out to generate some ideas about what the views of members of the population might be with respect to the topic under discussion. This is the sampling basis for the interviews described in Section 6.2.1.

The manufacturer of a new type of hard-wearing floor covering conducted a depth interview survey among architects working for local authorities. After interviews with only 10 architects about the new material, it seemed that the concept of the material was generally acceptable. The case quoted is an actual example in which the company went ahead and launched the product on the basis that most of the architects interviewed had expressed an interest in it. Unfortunately, that interest was not directly translatable into product sales in the marketplace. The company is now in the process of improving its sampling procedures for a second attempt to survey the market, since its own belief in the product remains unshaken. This time it will not be using a qualitative approach to make quantitative decisions. This highlights the danger of judgement sampling as a form of research. Such research is so small scale and unrepresentative that false readings can be obtained.

Judgement sampling is used as the basis for surveys using the method of group discussions. As discussed in Chapter 6, group discussions are a very widely used form of research. They give the decision maker some insight into and understanding of the attitudes, opinions and feelings of members of the market about the organization's own, or competing, products. In a survey of housewives about consumer goods it is not unusual for a qualitative survey using group discussion to include only six to eight groups. Eight groups containing eight people is only 64 individuals, and so inevitably the findings cannot be 'representative' in the same sense implied by the use of random or quota sampling methods. However, the attempt is made to generate as wide a range of views as possible by using judgement to decide the type of individuals who will be used for each group.

In order to give a breadth of opinion a cake manufacturer commissioning a survey including eight groups spread them as follows. Four were held in northern towns and four in southern towns. Each group of four interviews was split into two of middle-class respondents and two of working-class respondents. Each pair of groups included one with respondents aged under 30 and one with respondents over 30. The attempt here was to collect the widest possible range of views from a national, class and age spread of respondents.

Typically, judgement sampling is used in the conduct of smaller surveys. When these are particularly small and qualitative in nature, it is most important not to confuse the attempt to represent a wide range of views with the concept of 'representativeness' implied by random and quota sampling methods. If judgement sampling is used in small-scale surveys the results should never be used in a quantitative way. If half the members of a set of group discussions agree on a particular point, it should not be assumed that 50 per cent of the target population will also agree with that point.

Judgement is used in sampling as a way of overcoming practical difficulties or limitations in using other sampling methods. It is also used for 'toe in the water' exercises and, just like using a toe to measure the temperature of water, it is equally unreliable if used in place of a thermometer. It produces a 'feel' rather than a measurement. A toe can give some idea of general hotness or coldness but if placed in the edge of the sea or a cold eddy of a river will not give a reliable measure for the whole body of water. In the same way, the results of small-scale judgement sample surveys cannot be used as representative of the population as a whole, although they do give some guidance about what the population might be thinking, feeling or doing.

7.5 How big does the sample need to be?

A very commonly held fallacy is that there needs to be some relationship between the size of the sample selected and the size of the population of interest. This is only the case when sampling very small populations. The point has already been made that random sampling has a sound statistical basis which allows the researcher to have confidence in the fact that results from randomly selected samples are truly representative of the population being studied. The researcher can calculate the degree of confidence which he or she can have in the fact that this is so, and can calculate a range of accuracy within which the results obtained from the sample would be likely to hold in the population from which the sample was drawn. These factors are linked in a statistical formula which indicates that sample size is dependent on the following three factors.

7.5.1 Variability in the population

The first factor affecting the size of the sample is the proportionate distribution of the characteristics of interest, for example, the proportion of people who are boat owners or holiday takers. When the proportion is either small, as in the first instance, or very large, as in the second instance, the size of sample required to measure this accurately is smaller than when the population is more or less equally split between having and not having the attributes under consideration. Thus, predicting the outcome of a general election accurately, with support for the two major parties more or less equally split, requires a larger sample than when support is heavily in favour of one party rather than the other.

7.5.2 Required level of confidence

In discussing the virtues of random sampling earlier in this chapter, it was pointed out that one of these lies in being able to calculate the level of confidence one can have that the results achieved by the sample are likely to give a true indication of results in the underlying population. Common sense, and the statistical formula, indicate that the higher the level of confidence required in the results then the larger the size of sample necessary. What common sense does not make clear but the formula does, is that to increase the level of confidence from the 68% level (i.e. a 1 in 3 risk of the sample not being a good one) to the 95% level more commonly used (i.e. only a 1 in 20 risk that the sample is not a good one) it is necessary to multiply the sample size by a factor of 4. If a survey of 100 respondents indicated that 28% of all households had a separate freezer at the 68% level of confidence, to increase the level of confidence in the results to the 95% level, a survey of 400 respondents would be required.

7.5.3 Required limits of accuracy

It also makes sense at an intuitive level to accept that the larger the size of the sample the more accurate the results are likely to be as a predictor of population values. Once again, the statistical formula of sampling theory makes it possible to quantify this relationship. The relationship is inverse and square. That piece of statistical jargon simply says that to double the accuracy in the results (i.e. to halve the allowable range in the limits of accuracy) it would be necessary to multiply the size of the sample by 4. In the example above, if the sample of 400 respondents indicated that at the 95% level of confidence 28% of all households had a separate freezer within limits of accuracy of 10%, this would indicate between 25.2 and 30.8% of all homes have separate freezers. For greater precision the limits of accuracy must be reduced. To halve this to +5 or −5% (i.e. between 26.6 and 29.4%) a sample size of 1600 would be required.

To summarize, then, sampling theory indicates that in random samples three factors should be taken into account in deciding the size of the sample: variability in the population, the level of confidence wanted in the results, and the limits of accuracy acceptable to the decision maker. All of these can be decided before the survey takes place, and the sample size calculated to meet the requirements for confidence and accuracy in the results.

However, three further factors need to be considered before the size of sample can be determined, as follows.

7.5.4 Allowance for non-response

Inevitably, some non-response will be experienced in applying any field research method. If this is estimated at, say, 10 per cent, then if the final number of successfully completed interviews required is 1000 it will be necessary to arrange for 1111 interviews to be attempted.

7.5.5 Subgroup analysis requirements

The calculations referred to above are concerned with calculating the sample size required for precision in the analysis of the answers to one particular question. The calculation has to be repeated for every question in the questionnaire. In practice, this turns out to be a largely unmanageable amount of calculation and is rarely undertaken. The size of a sample needed to meet the requirements of every question on the questionnaire is determined by the smallest proportion of respondents likely to answer any particular question on it.

For example, information may be required from both users and non-users of a product. The questionnaire will be devised to ask all respondents the 'filter' question, 'Do you drive a company car?' In 2001 it was known that approximately 6 per cent of households had access to a company car. In a random sample, therefore, 6 per cent of the sample were expected to answer 'yes' and go on to give further information about how they made the decision to take advantage of the company car scheme, whether they owned a private vehicle in addition and so on. In a sample of 500 respondents only 30 were expected to give the data we require about company cars. To expand this number to a more statistically viable level the survey started with a sample of 1800 respondents, anticipating a subsample of 108 households with a company car. If it wanted to identify company car owners who drove five-door hatchbacks, which accounted for 50 per cent of the market, it would have been necessary to start with an overall sample size of 3600 respondents in order to end up with 108 respondents in this category.

It is considerations such as these that determine the overall size of a sample, by working upwards from the analysis requirements of particular subgroups within a sample. As discussed in Section 7.4.1, weighting can also be used in determining sample size when subgroup analysis is required.

7.5.6 Practical factors

As with much else in organizational life it is often the practical considerations that, in the end, dominate many decisions. Cost, time and the availability of suitable personnel cannot be ignored. Cost is often the dominant factor in determining how many interviews are undertaken.

For all the reasons given above, cost is not a relevant determination of sample size, but this ignores practical reality. Some trade-off must be achieved between increased reliability and accuracy in the data arising from a larger size sample and increased cost, so that an optimum level is achieved. If cost is allowed to be the determinant of sample size then the implications for reliability and accuracy must be recognized and not ignored as is so often the case. It cannot be expected that the same quality of results will be achieved from a small sample as from a large sample. However, it is unnecessary to generate a high level of precision in research results when other areas surrounding the problem under consideration are subject to an even higher degree of error. Time is another important element in that the shorter the time in which results are required, then the less time available for fieldwork and the smaller the size of sample that can be achieved in the time limits set. Finally, suitably trained interviewers may simply not be available to meet the needs of a very large and widely spread sampling requirement.

A number of factors have been shown to be relevant in determining sample size. This demonstrates that the appropriate sample size must be worked out with respect to the needs of each particular survey. However, most beginners in a subject area like some rough clues as to the order of size that may be 'usual'. As 'rule of thumb' guidelines only, the following points may be helpful. In general, for acceptable statistical validity of results generated from quantitative surveys, any subgroup containing fewer than 100 respondents should be treated with extreme caution in statistical analysis. Numbers below 50 respondents should not be subjected to statistical analysis at all. The normal range of sample sizes used in national samples for many consumer goods is 1500–2000 respondents. Minimum sample sizes for quantitative consumer surveys are in the order of 300–500 respondents. The upper limits of size of sample have been pushed very high by the Government's National Housing Survey including 100,000 households, but this is most unusual.

The points made above with respect to sample size have been derived from sampling theory, which forms the basis for random sampling. In the case of quota sampling, or of variations to the random procedure such as multi-stage and random location, it is usual to increase the size of the sample to compensate for any inaccuracies introduced by the sampling procedure. Alternatively, a 'design factor' may be used to reduce the confidence level and accuracy in the results, and compensate for the limitations of the non-random sampling techniques in this way.

As a final note on sampling, it should be mentioned that the only time when the size of the underlying population needs be taken into account in considering the size of the sample to be drawn from it, is when the size of the sample required is likely to account for 10 per cent or more of the population.

7.6 Summary

Sampling is the process of selecting the individuals who will provide the data required in a survey. The term 'sample' is defined and reasons for its use in research are given. The main techniques of sample selection are discussed: random sampling and its variants, quota sampling and judgement sampling. The size of the sample needed is shown to be dependent on factors of population variance, required confidence levels and limits of accuracy, allowance for non-response and subgroup analysis requirements.

8 How do you ask the questions?

8.1 Introduction

Chapter 6 introduced interviews as the most versatile and widely used method of primary data collection. The device used by interviewers for delivering questions to respondents and recording their answers is a questionnaire. This chapter considers the use, design and content of questionnaires. Questionnaires are also used in telephone research and, without interviewers, in postal or self-completion research. They are also used in online research. These questionnaires may or may not be supported by interviewers, depending on the approach. Some guidelines for questionnaire construction are given, but in large-scale quantitative survey research questionnaires are usually written by research specialists and a framework for vetting questionnaires is suggested at the end of this chapter.

8.2 Why use a questionnaire?

Questionnaires have four main purposes in the data collection process: to collect relevant data, to make data comparable, to minimize bias and to motivate the respondent.

8.2.1 To collect relevant data

Since data collection is structured by the questionnaire it is a most important element in the research process. The quality of the data gathered is highly dependent on the design of the questionnaire and the questions it contains. A poorly designed questionnaire will collect inappropriate or inaccurate data and so negate the whole purpose of the research, even though the major costs will have been incurred. No amount of good analysis can retrieve bad data. The first stage in designing a questionnaire is to clarify its objectives. The 'Definition of research required', discussed in Section 5.4, would form the basis for this. The role of the research user is to ensure that research specialists responsible for questionnaire design are fully and adequately briefed. Once the questionnaire objectives have been agreed, they form the framework within which all subsequent decisions about the questionnaire structure and question content are made. This mechanism ensures that the data collected is directly relevant to the problem.

The relevance of information produced is also determined by the analysis and interpretation to which it can be subjected. For this reason question design must be clearly linked to schemes for processing and analysing the data. There is no point in including questions that cannot be analysed to produce usable information. A readership study for a local newspaper wanted to measure the appeal of various items to different class, age, region and special interest groups. The questions about liking of editorial, sport, women's and motoring sections were made relevant to the purposes of the survey by analysis against the descriptive variables. All had to be included in the questionnaire.

8.2.2 To make data comparable

A questionnaire makes it possible to use tens of interviewers and hundreds of respondents, with the main variable being the variation in response. It is then possible to add up similar responses and say, '10 per cent say this'. This requires the questionnaire to be constructed in such a way that the words used have the same meaning for all respondents and all interviewers. To ensure that all interviewers do ask precisely the same question of all respondents it is usual to instruct them to read out the question from the questionnaire exactly as written. If a respondent has difficulty in answering, the interviewer is instructed simply to read out the question again and to add no words of clarification or explanation. Clearly, this procedure will only work if questions are well written and use everyday language. If it becomes necessary for the interviewer to assist the respondent in answering, then the questionnaire has failed and the comparability of data is lost. Variations due to different interviewer interpretations will have been introduced, but these will not be known by the data analyst and may result in misleading conclusions being drawn. Questionnaire piloting is an essential procedure in ensuring that the questions work.

8.2.3 To minimize bias

In a research interview, bias is defined as the difference between the answers given by respondents and the 'truth'. It is minimized by paying particular attention to the sequence and wording of questions, and to the words themselves. The questionnaire should make it easy for respondents to give true answers and care must be taken to avoid questions or words that may lead respondents into giving answers that do not reflect their true opinions.

8.2.4 To motivate the respondent

Answering a questionnaire requires a respondent to give time, attention and thought to a subject which, though of great interest to the researcher, may not be of much interest to the respondent. It is important to remember this when designing a questionnaire. The length should be kept to a minimum, although some topics will of themselves maintain the respondent's interest for longer than others. Questions should be as easy for the respondent to understand and answer as possible: an uncertain respondent is more likely to terminate the interview. Explanations should be included to bridge what might appear unconnected changes of question topic: a respondent who feels the overall content makes no sense is again more likely to cease co-operation. As much as possible, the format and type of question used should be made varied and interesting for the respondent.

8.3 Getting the questionnaire content right

For ease of explanation the questionnaire design process is discussed as a staged progression. In practice, like much research procedure, it is an iterative process. Decisions made at one point may affect what has gone before as well as what comes after, so that continual revision and refinement of the questionnaire is going on throughout the process.

In Chapter 5, the first step in the whole research procedure was to define the problem and the data required to solve it. From this statement of general research objectives it is now necessary to specify exactly what information is to be collected using a questionnaire survey. The manager involved should personally give adequate time and attention to ensure that the objectives set for the questionnaire will result in production of the information required. Faults in questionnaire design commonly occur because this important stage has been completed too hurriedly. What may happen then is that the objectives are never properly clarified. The researchers do what they assume is required, and this can result in expensively produced information, which at best leaves some questions unanswered, and at worst answers none of them. The decision maker has a prime responsibility for ensuring that if the survey objectives, as defined, are carried out, then this will meet the information need precisely.

Once the survey objectives have been agreed, they form the framework within which the rest of the process is set. All subsequent stages are measured against the objectives to see whether they help to fulfil them. The next step is to transform the survey objectives into a list of data requirements and then into a list of questions. Each question on the list must be checked against the research objectives: does the information it will generate contribute directly towards meeting those objectives? If the data that will be generated is interesting, but not essential, then the question should be deleted. Asking non-essential questions will only lengthen the questionnaire and potentially reduce the quality of the rest of the data gathered, by increasing interviewer and respondent fatigue. Decision makers commissioning research will often think 'Well, while we're out there, let's ask . . .', and so the questionnaire grows. However, it should be noted that the greatest costs in survey research are the fieldwork costs, so if the basic data required will only take a few minutes of interviewing time, then it may be reasonable to add further questions. For short factual data requirements, the use of an omnibus survey could be a more efficient way of generating the required information (see Section 4.4).

After ensuring that every question is essential to the purposes of the survey, and checking that all the purposes of the survey will be met by the questions to be included, the process of questionnaire construction can begin.

8.4 What types of data can be collected using a questionnaire?

Three types of information can be gathered using questionnaires: fact, opinion and motive.

8.4.1 Fact

This includes what is often termed 'classification data', i.e. facts about respondents that are used to describe them: demographic information such as age, gender, social class, geographic location, and so on. It also includes information relevant to the survey, such as ownership of a washing machine, garden, library ticket, credit card, etc. Facts may also refer to behaviour, 'Have you ever bought a book online?', 'Have you ever visited an art gallery?', and so on.

Factual information is relatively easy to ask and to answer, providing the respondent knows and can remember. To be most useful the questions need to be quite specific. For example, a publisher may be more interested in current online book buyers than knowing whether the individual has ever bought a book through any distribution channel. In this case the question would be, 'Have you bought any book online in the last month?' Or it may be that the real interest lies in people who buy books online for their own use rather than for someone else; 'Have you bought any book online in the last month for yourself?' then becomes the question, and so on until the question specifically asks for the information that is required.

Factual information can be described as 'hard' data, because it is data that can be relied upon: people are or are not in a particular category; possess or do not possess a particular item; have performed or have not performed a particular action. This gives reasonable quantitative estimates for the subject under study, and gives some bases for cross-tabulation of results. In the example, it was possible to look at the ages of online book buyers against non-book buyers, and be fairly confident that the findings were relevant, given that the sample was a good one.

8.4.2 Opinion

Included in this category are beliefs, attitudes, feelings and knowledge. Opinion data can be very useful to decision makers, in giving under-standing of the background to behaviour. However, the findings should be treated with rather more caution than factual data. In asking people what their opinions or feelings are about a subject the question itself assumes that they have opinions. This 'cue' will be picked up and answers to the questions given. If respondents actually had no opinion before the questions were asked, the researcher has collected data that appears to measure something, but does not in fact do so. Also, in answering questions of the form, 'What do you feel about . . .?', people tend to give answers making only one or two points about their feelings. Feelings and attitudes are generally rather complex, having a number of dimensions, and so this kind of answer is only a limited and sometimes inaccurate reply. It is for this reason that the multidimensional scaling techniques, discussed in Section 6.2.2, are commonly used to collect attitudinal data.

The results of opinion questions are described as 'soft' data, because they are far less reliable as a base for decision making than factual information. Disasters have befallen decision makers who believed that the sum of the 'yes' answers to the question, 'Would you buy this product?' is the same thing as a demand forecast. Hypothetical responses rarely provide a good indicator of subsequent behaviour. Nevertheless, opinion data is extremely good at suggesting new ideas and approaches which are a valuable input to decision making.

8.4.3 Motive

Knowing people's reasons for a particular belief or action can be important to those wishing to influence them.

> It is quite easy to ask, 'Why do you do that? . . . buy slimming aids? . . . read a newspaper?' or 'Why do you think this? . . . like/dislike your local public house?' The difficulty lies in answering this kind of question. It is often hard to explain fully why one does or thinks a particular thing. If asked, 'Why are you reading this particular book?' it is probable that you can give a reason quite readily. It is usual to explain behaviour, when asked, using only one reason. You may be reading this book because you have a particular problem at work, which you hope this book will help to solve, but there will be other, less immediate, reasons. Maybe you are preparing for a job change, or trying to impress your boss. Probably you have reasons relevant only to your own situation.

This illustrates another problem with questions about motive: the answers are likely to be so diverse that they are difficult to compare and analyse. The analysis is inevitably subjective and the results are impressionistic rather than certain.

To produce quantitative data about motives, possible reasons for behaviour can be explored using small-scale qualitative techniques such as group discussions or depth interviews (discussed in Sections 6.2.1 and 6.2.4). From these, the categories of reason most relevant to the objectives of the survey can be determined. Specific questions, designed to measure how many people share these motives, can then be included in a representative sample survey which will produce quantifiable results.

8.5 What does a questionnaire contain?

There are three parts to a questionnaire:

1 Identification data
2 Classification data
3 Subject data.

8.5.1 Identification data

This section is usually completed by the interviewer, and identifies one particular interview. It usually contains the name and address of the respondent, perhaps the date, time, length and place of interview, and the name of the interviewer. An example is shown in Figure 8.1. This data is required in case any checkback is needed, either to ensure that the interview took place, or if questions are missed out or completed incorrectly. Usually, these questions are asked right at the end of a personal interview, when sufficient rapport exists between interviewer and respondent for assurance that replies will be treated in confidence, even though a name is being requested.

8.5.2 Classification data

This is the data required to classify the respondent, and is often used as the basis for analysis of the subject data sought in the body of the questionnaire. It includes data such as age, gender, occupation of the head of household, income group, marital status and other data thought to be relevant, which helps to define the individual for the purposes of analysing responses. In a personal interview this information can be left until the end if the respondent has been selected on a random sampling basis, but if the interviewer must select the respondent for a quota sample, then it is necessary to ask some of the classification questions at the outset. Classification data is also used in checking the representativeness of the sample. A typical identification and classification page from a questionnaire is shown in Figure 8.1.

8.5.3 Subject data

This refers to the information being gathered to meet the survey objectives, and forms the major part of the questionnaire. It is often helpful to begin by constructing a flowchart diagram. This is useful in planning the sequence of the questionnaire when different questions need to be asked of different respondents, e.g. 'Have you made any journeys by bus this week?'

If 'YES' go to Q. 2
If 'NO' go to Q. 8

The question used in this example is described as a 'filter' question, or 'skip', because it filters respondents into or out of subsequent question sections. Great care must be taken if several filter questions are to be used, to ensure that it is quite clear what route the respondent must follow through the

MORI/9312   Q'aire   CORE   Serial No . . . .
             Number   1996 OMNIBUS - WAVE 12   (OUO)   (5-8)

☐☐☐☐ ☐☐☐☐☐☐☐☐☐☐☐☐ ☐☐☐☐☐☐☐☐☐☐☐☐☐☐☐☐
(9)   (12)   (14)   First name   (24) (26)   Surname   (40)

Title (eg Mr/Mrs)

Tel no: ☐☐☐☐☐☐ ☐☐☐☐☐☐☐☐
        (42)   STD Code   (48) (50) (10)   Number   (57)

Telephone: In household 1
             None 2
(SINGLE   Refused to say 3
CODE)   Yes, but ex. dir 4
             Yes, but refused to give number 5

                                              | CARD 1 | 9 |

Address . . . .

. . . .   Post Code ☐☐☐ ☐☐ ☐☐   11-17

Sex (18)		**Total no. In household (incl. respondent)**	
Male 1		1 2 3 4 5 6 7 8 9+	26
Female 2	18	**Children** (under 15) 0 1 2 3 4 5 6 7 8 9+	
Respondent is: (19)		(Remember to circle '0' if no children in HH)	27
Chief Income Earner 1		**Ages of children (in household)** (28)	
Not Chief Income Earner 2	19	Aged 0-4 1	

Occupation of Chief Income Earner

Position/rank/grade:

. . . .

		Aged 5-6 2	
Industry/type of co.		Aged 7-8 3	
		Aged 9-10 4	
		Aged 11-13 5	
Quals/degrees/apprents.		Aged 14 6	28

How many cars or light vans are there
in your household   (29)

No of staff responsible for		1 car or light van 1	
(PROBE FULLY FOR PENSION)		2 cars/light vans 2	
Class of CIE (CODE FROM ABOVE) (20)		3+ cars/light vans 3	
A. 1		None 4	29
B. 2		**Home is:** (30)	
C1 3		Being bought on mortgage 1	
C2 4		Owned outright by household 2	
D. 5		Rented from Local Authority 3	
E. 6	20	Rented from Housing Association/Trust. . . 4	
		Rented from private landlord 5	
Respondent is: . . . . (21)		Other 6	30
Housewife 1		**Date of interview:** ☐☐ ☐☐ 96	31/34
Not housewife 2	21	Date Month	

Day of interview
 1   2   3   4   5   6   7
(Mon)   (Thu)   (Sun)   35

Age

| EXACT AGE   WRITE IN | 22/23 |
| **Marital Status**   (24) |

Sample Point No ☐☐☐☐☐☐☐   36/42

| Married . . . . 1 |
| Living together . . . . 2 |
| Single . . . . 3 |
| Widowed . . . . 4 |
| Divorced . . . . 5 |
| Separated . . . . 6 | 24 |

District Name . . . .

Interviewer declaration
I confirm that i have conducted this interview
face-to-face with the the above named person at
the above address and that I asked all the relevent
questions and recorded the answers in conformance
with the survey specifications and the MRS Code
of Conduct

Respondent is: (25)
Working full time (30 hrs/wk+) 1
Working part time (8-29 hrs/wk) 2
Not working (ie under 8 hrs/week)
- housewife 3
- retired 4
- unemployed (registered) 5
- unemployed (not registered but
  looking for work) 6
- student 7
- other (incl disabled) 8   25

Interviewer Signature . . . .

Interview End Time . . . .

Length of interview ☐☐ monutes   43/44

Interviewer no ☐☐☐☐☐/☐   45/49

Interviewer name (CAPS)

THIS FORM IS THE PROPERTY OF MARKET & OPINION RESEARCH INTERNATIONAL (MORI)
95 SOUTHWARK STREET, LONDON SE1 0HX

Figure 8.1

questionnaire. Arrows appearing on the questionnaire are sometimes used to aid the interviewer and ensure that sections are not missed completely. Devices to ensure that sections are not missed are particularly important in self-completion questionnaires, and sometimes differently coloured pages are used to help respondents to identify which sections to complete. Online questionnaires can build skips automatically into questionnaires by inserting links to subsequent questions based on response to a question. Instructions to the interviewer are normally shown in capital letters. Figure 8.2 illustrates the use of skips.

In thinking about the order of questions, it is important to remember that the respondent's reaction to the first few questions will determine whether he or she decides to continue co-operation throughout the interview. These early questions should therefore be of interest to the respondent and be easy to answer. This latter point is an important one, since many respondents initially regard a research interview as being a test of their knowledge, and on being approached may say, 'I can't help you. I don't know a lot about it'. When they realize from the first couple of questions that the questions are really quite easy, and well within their experience, then they will relax and the interviewer's task is made easier as the respondent's confidence grows. For opposite reasons, questions that are either uninteresting or rather personal in nature should appear as late as possible in the questionnaire. The assumption is that a good interviewer will have built up sufficient rapport by this time to carry on through less interesting material which might earlier have caused the respondent to terminate the interview.

Another point to bear in mind is the influence of each question on succeeding questions. It is pointless to present a respondent with a show card listing brands and ask about brand attributes, then later in the questionnaire ask what brands the respondent can recall. The recall question must come first.

Every attempt should be made to ensure a logical sequence to the questions so that the respondent is aided in thinking about the subject and is more likely to produce reliable answers.

8.6 What types of question can be used?

There are four main question types: dichotomous (or yes/no), multiple-choice, open-ended and rating scales.

8.6.1 Dichotomous questions

These are questions with only two possible answers, e.g. yes/no questions. For use of these questions to be valid the answer must fall unambiguously into one of the two categories offered, e.g. 'Do you buy ready-made biscuits rather than bake your own?' is ambiguous because many people do both and so could not answer 'yes' or 'no'. Similarly, if qualified answers to the question are possible, then the answers may be invalidated. 'Do you intend

	CODE	ROUTE
Q.30 Have you ever received any training, either while you were working or in order to get a job? No –	(48) X	Q.37
YES: ASK: How many periods of training have you done altogether? 1 2 3 4 5 OR MORE (DON'T KNOW/NOT STATED)	1 2 3 4 5 A	Q.31
IF THE ANSWER IS 'YES' ASK ALL THE FOLLOWING QUESTIONS. IF THE ANSWER IS 'NO' TO Q.30, SKIP TO QUESTION 37.		
Q.31 How useful do you feel this training could be to you now? ASK ABOUT 'LAST TRAINING' IF MORE THAN ONE VERY USEFUL FAIRLY USEFUL NOT VERY USEFUL NOT AT ALL USEFUL (DON'T KNOW/NOT STATED)	(49) 1 2 3 4 A	Q.32
Q.32 What job or skill was that training for ? WRITE IN _____ _____ _____	(50) (51)	Q.33
Q.33 How long did the training last? LESS THAN 2 WEEKS 2 WEEKS BUT LESS THAN 1 MONTH 1 MONTH BUT LESS THAN 3 MONTHS 3 MONTHS BUT LESS THAN 6 MONTHS 6 MONTHS BUT LESS THAN 1 YEAR 1 YEAR BUT LESS THAN 2 YEARS 2 YEARS OR MORE (DON'T KNOW/NOT STATED)	(52) 1 2 3 4 5 6 5 A	Q.34
Q.34 Was it full-time, or part-time (30 hrs or less, per week)? FULL-TIME PART-TIME (DON'T KNOW/NOT STATED)	(53) 1 2 A	Q.35
Q.35 Was it 'on-the-job' training or 'off-the-job' training (........................... away from the normal job situation)? CODE ALL THAT APPLY ON THE JOB OFF THE JOB (DON'T KNOW/NOT STATED)	(54) 1 2 A	Q.36
Q.36 How long ago did you finish it? 1 YEAR BUT LESS THAN 2 YEARS AGO 2 YEARS BUT LESS THAN 5 YEARS AGO 5 YEARS BUT LESS THAN 10 YEARS AGO 10 OR MORE YEARS AGO (DON'T KNOW/NOT STATED)	(55) 1 2 3 4 A	Q.37
Q.37 ASK ALL Now I'd like to ask you a few questions about your health. Thinking of the present, do you have any handicap or illness which affects your activities in any way? YES – HAVE HANDICAP OR ILLNESS NO (DON'T KNOW/NOT STATED)	(56) 1 2 A	

Figure 8.2 Filter questions or 'skips'

to invest in new IT equipment?' is an example of a question that for many companies would be answered, 'It depends'. However, when a straight yes or no is appropriate, dichotomous questions are easy to ask, easy to answer and easy to analyse statistically. For completeness in recording responses, a 'don't know' category is included on the questionnaire. The three possible responses, 'yes/no/don't know', can be assigned code numbers which are printed on the questionnaire so that the interviewer just rings the response given. This *precoding* saves time, effort and therefore cost in processing responses. Code numbers can be entered directly from the completed questionnaires for computer analysis. Precoding is explained further in Section 8.9, and questions 34, 35 and 37 in Figure 8.2 are examples of precoded dichotomous questions.

8.6.2 Multiple-choice questions

These questions are deceptively easy to ask. In fact, they are one of the most difficult types of question to design, because the question designer has to know not only what to ask, but also all the possible answers. The range of answers provided must be comprehensive (no respondent should want to give an answer that is not offered) and mutually exclusive (no respondent should feel that the answer could be in more than one category).

In practice, these requirements are very difficult to meet. One has only to think of occasions when a multiple-choice question has been presented for which none of the offered responses exactly matched one's own point of view, to know that this type of question is commonly asked rather badly. The danger is that the researcher collects nice, neat data, where people are tidily classified into boxes, and may not appreciate that respondents have squeezed themselves into boxes that do not really fit them. Attempts to avoid this problem by offering a category saying, 'Other (please specify)' will introduce further complications. How many of those who have used one of the classifications offered would have used these additional classifications suggested by some respondents?

Nevertheless, where it is possible to design a valid multiple-choice question, such questions are easy to analyse and are less open to interviewer bias since respondents select their own response category. Processing responses is also easy since precoding can be used on the questionnaire. In Figure 8.2, questions 31, 33 and 36 are examples of precoded multiple-choice questions. It is usual to present the alternatives to respondents written on a 'show card', to avoid the problem of respondents forgetting some of the possible responses. When a number of responses is presented, the order in which they appear can affect their likelihood of being selected. Items that appear at the beginning and end of lists are more likely to be selected. Show cards with the responses listed in different orders are therefore produced so that these 'order effects' are randomized and cancel each other out. Figure 8.3 illustrates interviewer instructions on using show cards, and gives an example of a multiple-choice question with its accompanying show card.

SHOW CARD C

Q.2   Which of these building materials do you
        mainly prefer to see used in the
        construction of a building?

RING ONE ONLY

	CODE
	(13)
STEEL	1
GLASS	2
CONCRETE/CEMENT	3
BRICK	4
TIMBER	5
STONE	6
INDIFFERENT	7

SHOW CARD C

STEEL

GLASS

CONCRETE/CEMENT

BRICK

TIMBER

STONE

INDIFFERENT

Show cards. These are used as visual aids during interviews. They help the respondent to choose a statement in answer to a question – if the statements are simply read out he or she may not be able to remember all the alternatives long enough to make a decision. They *must always be used* where indicated on the questionnaires.

They should be shown to the respondent and read aloud. (The order of statements on the card may be different from the order on the questionnaire so care must be taken to ring the correct code.) Never make the respondent aware of the 'Don't know' code or he/she may constantly say, 'Don't know'.

A respondent may appear to be looking at a show card, but in fact is not reading it at all. People who cannot read are reluctant to admit it, and it is very important that the card be read aloud to respondents in case they have difficulty in reading, or poor eyesight.

Figure 8.3 Interviewer instructions on the use of show cards

8.6.3 Open-ended questions

These are questions in which possible answers are not suggested, as they are by the two previous types of question. The respondent is free to respond in any way at all, and so response variation may be extreme. The interviewer must record all that the respondent says, which can introduce bias if he or she decides to record only what seems relevant. When the completed questionnaires are returned, the responses require manual analysis, which is time and labour consuming, and therefore expensive. Since there is likely to be a high degree of variation in response, the results will be qualitative rather than quantitative. These practical limitations usually mean that not more than one or two questions on a questionnaire are open-ended. Wherever possible, qualitative work is carried out before the stage of questionnaire design, so that multiple-choice questions or attitude scales can be used to quantify qualitative findings and avoid the need for open-ended questions on large-scale surveys. In smaller scale surveys when statistical validity is not a prime objective, open-ended questions are of great value in exploring complex and variable topics.

An example might be, 'What are the things you take into account when buying aircraft components?'

8.6.4 Rating scales

In Sections 6.2.2 and 6.2.3, attitude measurement and motivational research were discussed. Commonly, these techniques involve the use of rating scales or projective questions. Where special question techniques are used in a questionnaire, it is important that the interviewers are trained in the application of the technique and are quite clear about what is required both from them and from the respondent. The great value of rating scales is that they make it possible to quantify complex and multidimensional concepts. The dimensions themselves are uncovered in preliminary research using qualitative open-ended question techniques. Analysis of answers to rating scales requires the application of special statistical techniques, and these are discussed in Section 10.3.3. Two kinds of rating scale are commonly used. One is the semantic differential scale discussed in Section 6.2.2 and illustrated in Figure 6.2. This requires respondents to assess each brand separately on a number of dimensions. An alternative approach is shown in Figure 8.4, where all the brands are assessed on one dimension at a time.

8.7 How should questions be worded?

8.7.1 Meaning

The key to question wording is to remember that words are not precise descriptive instruments, and so it is necessary to ensure that the words selected have the same meaning for the respondent as they have for the

Q.14 I am now going to show you some ranges of packs for different brands of shampoos and read out some comments other people have made about them. As I do so, I want you to tell me, just going by the appearance of the packs of each range, to which of the ranges of packs each comment applies. You may feel a comment applies to all the ranges or to just some or to none at all.

ALLOW RESPONDENT TIME TO VIEW ALL BRANDS

Q.15 First of all which of these packs do you personally think look ...... (READ OUT)

	A	B	C	D	E	F	All of them
Modern and up-to-date							
Rather ordinary							
Easy to tell for which hair types							
Gimmicky							
Feminine							
Not for me							
Particularly attractive							
Poor value for money							
Distinctive							
Expensive looking							
Easy to handle							

Q.16 Which of the packs looks as if they would contain a shampoo which would ...... (READ OUT BELOW)

	A	B	C	D	E	F	All of them	None of them
Be different from other shampoos								
Be really good for your hair								
Have a fresh and natural perfume								
Be a thin, weak shampoo								
Be a high quality shampoo								
Be made with good ingredients								
Will leave hair looking really nice								

Figure 8.4 Example of a rating scale

Q.17 Now I am going to read out some descriptions of several different people or personalities all of whom use shampoo. For each description I would like you to tell me, just by looking at each of the ranges, which ones you think would most likely be used by .... You may give as many as you like for each range. (READ OUT BELOW)

	A	B	C	D	E	F	All of them
A teenage girl							
An older woman							
A lively, youthful person							
A young woman							
A working woman							
Men as well as women							
A natural self-confident woman							
Anyone in the family							
A price-conscious person							

Figure 8.4 (*Continued*)

researcher. For example, 'dinner' may be a meal one has in the middle of the day, or in the evening; it may be different for children and adults, and different on Sunday from the rest of the week. 'Supper' and 'tea' are equally imprecise terms. The point of these examples is to illustrate that even the most common of words can be a source of misinterpretation in the context of a questionnaire. In the examples used, the terms most usually applied are, 'midday meal', 'main evening meal', and so on.

When a respondent is being asked about a particular piece of behaviour, the issue must be clearly defined. It is often useful to apply the 'who, what, where, when and how' checks to what is being asked by the question, and if these questions cannot be answered, then the question needs to be reworded so as to be more specific about exactly what is required.

> For example, 'How many times have you personally attended an exhibition of industrial equipment, of any kind, in the UK in the last 12 months?' This question makes it quite clear to whom the question refers, 'you personally'; what information is sought, 'attended an exhibition of industrial equipment of any kind'; where the relevant behaviour occurred, 'in the UK'; when it took place, 'in the last 12 months', and 'How many times'. In this example, 'Why' the individual attended such exhibitions could be a subsequent question.

All questions should be kept as short as possible, and should use everyday language. Every part of the questionnaire must communicate effectively with the least educated member of the sample.

8.7.2 Ambiguity

Ambiguous terms should be avoided, or a definition included. 'Do you read a daily newspaper regularly?' What does 'regularly' mean? For some it might mean 'every day', but a person who regularly buys the paper on Friday could answer 'Yes', and other patterns might be included also. Normally the qualification, 'By "regularly", I mean three or more days each week', is added. But what does 'read' mean in this context? 'Look at?', 'Scan?', 'Read from cover to cover?', 'Buy, but don't actually get round to looking at?', and so on. So the qualification, 'by "read" I mean read or look at' is added. Now the question reads, 'Have you read, or looked at, a daily newspaper on three or more days in the past seven days?'

8.7.3 Leading

Leading questions and loaded words should be avoided. These are questions or words with meanings that invite particular responses.

'Do you think that the United Kingdom should stay in the European Community (the Common Market)?' was the question posed in the 1975 referendum. To ask, 'Do you think the United Kingdom should enter the European Community?' would probably have generated differences in response. The use of the word 'stay' in the actual question invited support for the status quo, and received it.

Many words are 'loaded' in the sense that they have associative meaning beyond their strict dictionary definition, and individuals tend to respond to the associations the word has for them. The choice of word must therefore be considered from this point of view. 'Bosses', 'managers' and 'administrators' could all be descriptions of the same group of 'workers' (another loaded word). The selection of a term used to describe them is likely to affect responses to questions about the group. The problem is that almost all words are loaded in one direction or another. The aim must be to select words least likely to bias response, and also be aware of the possibility and potential direction of bias and treat the results with corresponding caution.

8.7.4 Generalization

A common problem in question wording is the use of generalizations such as 'On average, how often do you buy sweets in a week?' Unless the relevant behaviour is extremely regular, this question is likely to produce bad data, since the respondent is asked to generalize about behaviour. What they are really being asked to do is to calculate their frequency of sweet buying over the last year and compute the arithmetic average per week: a patently unreasonable and probably impossible request. They will either respond using last week's behaviour, or pluck some hypothetical figure out of the air. It would be better to ask, 'On how many occasions have you bought sweets during the past week?' An average frequency of purchase can then be calculated from the spread of data generated by the sample.

8.7.5 Unidimensionality

Sometimes it is necessary to ask more than one question. As well as asking, 'What names of airline companies can you recall?', it would be useful to ask first, 'Do you ever travel by air nowadays?' Analysis of recall among travellers and non-travellers could then be carried out. A check should also be made to ensure that the question is only asking about one dimension, e.g. 'Do you think cream cleansers get surfaces clean without scratching them?' In this case a 'No' answer could mean that cream cleansers do not get surfaces clean, or that they do scratch. Most questions of the form, 'Why did you choose a particular product or service?' have two possible lines of reply. One relates to the perceived attributes of the product or service, and the other describes the circumstances leading up to its choice and how the respondent came to hear about the product or service. It might therefore be better to use the two questions, 'How did you first come to use this product or service?' and 'What do you like about using the product or service?' Unidimensionality refers to the need for each question to be asking about only a single point.

8.7.6 Cushion statements

When a questionnaire covers a number of different topics, it is helpful to 'cushion' changes in subject with an introductory phrase, such as, 'Now I'm going to ask a few questions about leisure facilities in this city . . .', and when the next section comes up, 'Now I'm going to ask a few questions about transport facilities in this city . . .'. This helps respondents to follow what is going on, and to switch their thinking from one, otherwise unrelated topic to the next, without becoming too confused. In general, respondents are more likely to co-operate if they feel they understand what is going on in the questionnaire and can appreciate the reason for it. Brief explanations can aid this process, with benefits to respondent, interviewer and researcher.

8.8 Will the respondent answer the questions?

The questionnaire designer must consider whether it is reasonable to ask those questions of respondents. Do they expect too much of the respondent's memory? A travel questionnaire asked, 'How many journeys have you taken by train in the last year?', obviously an unreasonable time span for most respondents.

Is the respondent likely to have the necessary information? This is particularly a problem when a housewife is asked about the purchasing habits of other members of her family. In general, it is unwise to ask about any behaviour, attitude or opinion other than that of the individual being interviewed.

It is also unwise to ask questions which assume that respondents have experience they may not have, e.g. 'Is this make of industrial machine better than competing machines on the market?' This assumes that the respondent has tried all the brands of machine on the market with sufficient depth to be able to draw valid comparisons with the machine under test.

Will the respondent give the information required? Respondents may be unwilling to answer because they regard the question as too personal. This is often the case for financial questions in both consumer and industrial research. Respondents may be unwilling to admit their behaviour, for example, drinking and smoking are typically underreported. Respondents may not answer when it is difficult to explain, say, reasons for doing a particular thing, e.g. 'What do you feel about mowing the lawn?' In these circumstances the projective techniques mentioned in Section 6.2.3 can be useful.

8.9 Allowing for method of analysis

When preparing a questionnaire, a great deal of time and money at the analysis stage can be saved. One of the major ways of doing this is to use precoded questions, as mentioned in Section 8.6.1 and illustrated in Figure 8.2. Not only the question, but also a list of responses appears on the questionnaire. Code numbers for each response appear in the far right-hand column of the questionnaire, and the interviewer simply rings the relevant response. These ringed codes can be entered into the computer directly from the questionnaire. This saves the intervening stage of coding original responses when the questionnaires are returned. By precoding responses, and deciding beforehand how many codes will be allotted to open-ended questions, the whole questionnaire can be laid out in such a way that as much direct input as possible is facilitated. Computer-assisted interviewing either by telephone (CATI), on the World Wide Web (CAWI) or in person (CAPI) clearly facilitates this process further. Questions can be entered directly into analysis programs and results can be processed very quickly.

The requirements for tabular analysis should also be considered at this stage: which answers will be analysed by which classification categories? This is a very useful discipline at the stage of questionnaire design, because it illustrates whether the data produced will be in the form required for analysis to produce the information needed by the decision maker. When the actual stage of analysis comes, it is too late to discover that all the data required has not been collected, or that it is in the wrong form for analysis to produce appropriate information to meet the survey objectives.

8.10 Why does presentation matter?

The physical appearance of the questionnaire affects its likelihood of securing a response, and this is particularly so for self-completion questionnaires. Ease of use and analysis are dependent on good questionnaire layout. The questionnaire should be laid out using adequate space and reasonable quality paper. If it looks too 'amateurish' the respondent is less likely to co-operate. If the questionnaire looks as though its perpetrators attach little importance to it, then why should respondents give up their time?

Also important at this moment of attracting the potential respondent's attention is the verbal introduction used by the interviewer. This must be worked out by the researcher, and should be written on the questionnaire. The form of introduction used is a major influence in securing acceptance, and should not be left to the interviewer's own initiative. Where explanations for the purpose of the survey can be given without possibly biasing response, then this should be done. If a specific explanation is undesirable, then a general statement should be made that gives the respondent some good reason for co-operating. 'To help us produce better products, or services' is often an acceptable rationale. Giving the respondent a good reason for co-operating is especially important in interviewing business and professional people, who generally attach more importance to the value of their time.

In considering the form of the questionnaire, the conditions under which the interviewer is expected to use it should be remembered. If a quota sample is being used, when the interviewer will probably be working outside, possibly in wind or rain, then the questionnaire must not disintegrate or fly off in all directions. This explains the wide use made of clipboards, and sometimes of a book format.

As far as layout is concerned, interviewer instructions must be clearly distinguished from questions, usually by using a different typeface or capital letters. When filter questions are being used, either the arrows referred to earlier can assist interviewers in following the correct path through the interview, or more easily, the number of the next question for each response can be written on the questionnaire. Examples of these points are shown in Figure 8.2.

Using the questionnaire can be made easier for both interviewer and respondent by providing show cards whenever a choice of responses is available. These ensure that the respondent is not reliant on memory when selecting a response, and as the answer is read out, the interviewer can ring the appropriate codes on the questionnaire. Figure 8.3 gives one example of this, and more complicated examples allowing multiple coding are shown in Figures 8.5 and 9.1.

8.11 Will the questionnaire work?

It is both easy and dangerous at the point of having designed a questionnaire to use it in the field quickly, 'before any more time is wasted'. The danger is that faults in the questionnaire will not be discovered, resulting in unreliable

Some precoded questions require that more than one answer be coded, if appropriate. This is called MULTICODING.

	ROUTE
EXAMPLE	
SHOW CARD C	

Q.11a   Please tell me which of these types of people you think would use pastes and spreads?

PROBE: Which others? RECORD BELOW

Q.11b   And are there any types of people on this list you think would definitiely not use pastes and spreads?

PROBE: Which others? RECORD BELOW

MULTICODE	Q11a WOULD USE (55)	Q11b WOULD NOT USE (56)	
PEOPLE WHO ENTERTAIN A LOT	1	1	
WORKING MAN	2	2	
YOUNG CHILDREN	3	3	
PEOPLE WITH A LARGE FAMILY	4	4	
TEENAGERS	5	5	
MOTHERS AT HOME ALL DAY	6	6	
PEOPLE ON A TIGHT BUDGET	7	7	Q.12
OLDER PEOPLE	8	8	
WORKING MOTHERS	9	9	
BUSY PEOPLE	0	0	
PEOPLE LIKE YOURSELF	X	X	
NONE	A	A	

```
            SHOW CARD C

     PEOPLE WHO ENTERTAIN A LOT
            WORKING MAN
           YOUNG CHILDREN
     PEOPLE WITH A LARGE FAMILY
             TEENAGERS
       MOTHERS AT HOME ALL DAY
      PEOPLE ON A TIGHT BUDGET
            OLDER PEOPLE
          WORKING MOTHERS
             BUSY PEOPLE
         PEOPLE LIKE YOURSELF
```

Figure 8.5

data. It is always worth piloting a questionnaire, even if only a handful of interviews is done. For important pieces of research it is advisable to ask for a pilot survey, even though this will add to the cost.

The process of piloting requires interviewers to conduct the interview in the normal way, and to note any difficulties that they encounter in introducing the questionnaire, asking or recording answers to the questions, following the instructions or coping with the layout. They are also asked to note any difficulties that the respondent has in interpreting or answering the questions. When the interview is complete the interviewer may explain that the questionnaire is actually being tested, and ask the respondent, 'What did you think that question meant?', 'What was in your mind when you answered this question?' or 'How did you arrive at your answer?' This last question is particularly important to test questions involving memory.

The feedback from this process readily indicates any ways in which the questionnaire does not work well, and interviewers can be asked what words they found it necessary to use to explain what was required of respondents. It is usually instructive for the manager to try a few interviews personally, if he or she really wants to learn about the research process. Hearing how a questionnaire works in the field can lend insight to the way in which the final results are used in decision making. The interviewers used for piloting should be average rather than good interviewers, so that difficulties they may have can be monitored. When the questionnaire is sent into the field the whole range of interviewer abilities will be working on the survey, and all must be able to use the questionnaire easily.

It is also useful to use the results from a pilot survey for a 'dummy run' of the analysis to check that it, too, will work out. Piloting will lead to revising, modifying and improving the questionnaire until the designer is satisfied that it is a good instrument for collecting the data required in as undistorted a manner as possible.

8.12 Special types of questionnaire

Most of the comments about questionnaire design and content made in this chapter apply generally, however the questionnaire is to be applied. When questionnaires are presented to respondents for self-completion, often through the post, or are used as the basis for telephone interviewing, there are implications for the number and type of questions that can be asked, the way in which they are phrased and the order in which they are presented.

8.12.1 Postal or self-completion questionnaires

As covered in Section 6.3, when an appropriate mailing list or easy mechanism for collecting self-completed questionnaires exists, postal or self-completion questionnaires can be a useful tool for primary data collection.

This is particularly true for executives working on a small budget, or in markets where response rates are likely to be good. Industrial researchers often achieve good response rates from buyers or suppliers. Mail-order companies also use this technique to good effect. Self-completion questionnaires are widely used by hotels and other service-supplying institutions. One of the features of response to postal or self-completion questionnaires is that they are more likely to come from individuals with an interest in the subject, so if this is the group whose views are required the method is particularly appropriate.

The rate of response to postal or self-completion questionnaires is influenced by the covering letter introducing and explaining the purposes of the questionnaire, and also by sending reminder letters to non-respondents to postal questionnaires. At least as much attention should be given to the design of these letters as is given to the questionnaire itself. The letter should be personalized as far as possible, and indicate to the potential respondent the relevance of the enquiry to his or her personal interests and the importance of his or her personal response. Small incentives can also be used to encourage response. These comments apply equally to the introductory part of an e-mail containing a self-completion questionnaire.

As far as length is concerned, if the subject is one of great interest to respondents they may well be prepared to complete a lengthy questionnaire. However, since there is no interviewer present to encourage completion, it is wise to assume that less ground can be covered in a postal or self-completion questionnaire than in a personal interview. The layout should be such that it is easy to answer the questions and easy to follow the sequence, particularly when different questions need to be answered depending on the response to a filter question.

In thinking about question sequence, it must be remembered that some of the facilities available in a personally administered questionnaire are not available in a postal or self-completion questionnaire. For example, it is not possible to ask general questions about a product group and then funnel down to specific questions about a particular brand. Since respondents are able to read through the whole questionnaire before answering any questions, their awareness of the specific brand being researched may influence responses to earlier questions. However, an advantage is that being able to look through the whole questionnaire, and complete it in their own time, can produce more thoughtful responses than a personal interview.

In general, a postal or self-completion questionnaire should give the appearance of being relatively quick, easy and interesting to complete. Precoded dichotomous or multiple-choice questions should be used as much as possible so that the respondent only has to mark responses. The respondent should think, 'I might as well do that now' rather than, 'That looks as if it needs thinking about – I'll have a go at it tomorrow'. The latter is the questionnaire that probably will not be completed at all.

8.12.2 Telephone questionnaires

Telephone research is a relatively low-cost way of achieving high response rates, notably in business-to-business research. In consumer research the cost advantage over the personal interview method is not as great, but the speed advantage can be overriding.

The types of question most appropriate to telephone surveys are brief, and require brief factual answers that the respondent can give accurately without much thought: 'Do you . . .?' or 'Don't you . . .?', 'Have you . . .?' or 'Haven't you . . .?' This is because the telephone call is going to interrupt the respondent in the middle of some other activity. The difficulty of establishing rapport over the telephone also makes it unusual for a long conversation to be practicable. Some companies have managed to avoid this problem by maintaining a panel of respondents from which a sample may be drawn.

Open-ended questions do not work very well over the telephone, because respondents tend to abbreviate responses so depth of response is lost. Similarly, long and complicated questions offering several categories of response should not be used because the respondent is unlikely to be able to remember the whole question by the time the interviewer reaches the end of it. Questions that would involve the use of a show card in a personal interview, or where the respondent may be required to look at a pack or an advertisement before answering are clearly not possible over the telephone. This can be overcome by sending material through the post to respondents and then telephoning to ask questions about it, but this may not work well if the respondent loses the material or reads directly from it when questioned.

Computer-assisted telephone interviewing (CATI) is a service offered by a number of research agencies. It gives advantages in questionnaire presentation since the interviewer reads a question from the screen, types in the code appropriate to the respondent's answer, and the next question appears on the screen. In this way, quite complicated questionnaires using filter questions can be devised without worrying that the interviewer will become lost in the questionnaire. The possibility of questions being missed out is also eliminated since only one question appears on the screen and an answer must be keyed in before the next question will appear.

8.12.3 Online questionnaires

Questionnaires developed and administered online through e-mail on the Internet are becoming increasingly popular in certain markets. The dot-com sector is a major user of this type of questionnaire. However, as the Internet becomes ubiquitous other business sectors are adopting the methodology, exploiting the advantages that this mode of delivery offers. They are cheap and fast to prepare and to administer, and results may be gained very quickly. In addition, the use of hypertext mark-up language (HTML) can create links to help areas for respondents completing self-administered questionnaires, or to video or other audio visual content to support the questionnaire. This means that if respondents have questions they can click on a link that takes them to a site which contains supporting information, or send an e-mail to the researcher asking for help.

Questionnaires can be delivered to potential respondents in a number of ways. They can be sent through a link from a website, as an attachment to an e-mail or as an e-mail, or as a pop-up or an interstitial; this may be triggered by browser behaviour, e.g. a visit to a site post-purchase may drive a pop-up questionnaire to monitor satisfaction with the process. This is generated automatically as a result of a browser's actions and is known as an interstitial or a pop-up as it appears or pops up between the words or images on a site.

A major concern is that a user's browser may not support content-rich questionnaires and this will reduce or distort response.

There are major issues around certain providers of online research services. The online market is beset by the sending of unsolicited e-mail material, also known as spam. Those organizations that abide by the industry codes of conduct and are members of the Market Research Society are reputable, and should provide a methodigically sound solution to the design, delivery and analysis of online questionnaires.

8.13 Vetting questionnaires

Whether the questionnaire has been designed by staff within the company or from a research agency, the individual for whom the research is being conducted should insist on vetting the questionnaire. This is an important control in ensuring that the fieldwork will produce relevant data for the problem needs. Above all, the overall purposes of the research must be borne firmly in mind when vetting a questionnaire, but the subject content and type of respondent will also influence judgements as to whether a questionnaire is a good one. A checklist for vetting a questionnaire is suggested using the points on questionnaire design raised in this chapter.

Questionnaire checklist

- Are the objectives right? ☐
- Will the data specified meet the objectives? ☐
- Will the questions listed collect all the data required? ☐
- Is every question essential? ☐

- Will the right type of data be collected for:
  - fact? ☐
  - opinion? ☐
  - motive? ☐
- Will all the identification data required be collected? ☐
- Will all the classification data required be collected? ☐
- Is the question sequence logical? ☐
- Are the types of question being used appropriate?
  - dichotomous ☐
  - multiple-choice ☐
  - open-ended ☐
  - rating scales ☐
- Is the question wording:
  - simple to understand? ☐
  - unambiguous? ☐
  - clear? ☐
- Have cushion statements been used when necessary? ☐
- Is it reasonable to expect the respondent to answer every question? ☐
- Will the answers be easy to record? ☐
- Will the answers be easy to process? ☐
- Does the questionnaire look good? ☐
- Will it, and any show material, be easy for the interviewers to use? ☐
- Has the questionnaire been piloted? ☐
- Is the right type of questionnaire being used?
  - personal ☐
  - postal ☐
  - telephone ☐
  - online ☐

8.14 Summary

Questionnaires are used to present questions and record answers in quantitative field research surveys, and the quality depends on the design of the questionnaire. Design, content, structure and presentation of questionnaires are discussed. Special aspects of questionnaire design relevant when postal, self-completion telephone or e-mail questionnaires are to be used are mentioned. A checklist for vetting a questionnaire is suggested.

9   Who asks the questions?

9.1 Introduction

An interview is understood as 'a conversation for the purpose of gathering information' and this definition emphasizes the functional nature of the interview situation. Thus, although an interview may have the superficial structure of a conversation, it is actually a situation in which one party to the interchange, the interviewer, is required to obtain the answers to a predetermined set of questions or topics from the other party to the interchange, the respondent. It is this task-related view of the interview situation that is best understood by the researcher using interviews as a method of data collection. However, a sociological definition of a conversation is 'an interpersonal behaviour event: an interaction in which the action of one is both a response and a stimulus to the other'. This draws attention to the fact that when people engage in conversation, however purposeful, there is an undercurrent of social and non-verbal interplay that may affect the nature of their co-operation in the conversation process. It is understanding both the task and social elements of the interview situation that makes interviewing a skilled task.

Good interviewing procedures are of fundamental importance in the data collection process. No matter how good the planning procedures that go before the fieldwork or the analysis that follows it, it is in the process of raw data collection in the field that the quality of research undertaken is determined. The computer acronym 'GIGO' (garbage in, garbage out) holds equally true in data collection. If bad data is collected in the field, bad research information will be produced. For this reason it is necessary to consider who the interviewer should be, the skills and problems surrounding the interviewing process and the characteristics of interviewers themselves.

Since interviewing is a skilled task and since the maintenance of these skills is a lengthy procedure, it is usual in large-scale research exercises for the interviewing to be carried out by interviewers from research agencies, or by specialist fieldwork agencies. It is most unusual for businesses to maintain their own field force. The processes that agencies use to supervise and control interviewers are therefore reviewed, along with advice on selecting and using an agency for fieldwork. The chapter concludes with a brief section on 'do-it-yourself' interviewing.

9.2 Interviewers: 'horses for courses'

Interviewers have two important roles to play in any interview situation. First, they are responsible for delivering the question to respondents, and the degree to which they may be required to intervene in the questioning process to help the respondent answer correctly can vary. Second, they are responsible for recording the answer, and the degree to which they may be required to intervene in interpreting the respondent's answers can also vary. Therefore, before a decision to use a particular type of interviewer can be made, it is necessary to consider what is required from him or her in both delivering the questions and interpreting and recording the answers. The more that is required in either of these areas then the more skilled, and therefore more expensive, will be the type of interviewer needed. Because interviews vary according to the role demanded of the interviewer, so the amount of error and variability the interviewer can introduce into the data varies also. This is why it is important to consider 'horses for courses' in selecting the type of interviewer to be used according to the type of interview to be conducted.

9.2.1 Fully structured interviews

In this type of interview the interviewer must adhere strictly to the questionnaire, and the questions are commonly precoded so that the respondent too is bound by the confines of the questionnaire structure. This would be the case in a questionnaire using mainly dichotomous and multiple-choice questions. There is very little need for the interviewer to intervene either in asking the questions, apart from reading out what is on the questionnaire, or in interpreting the questions, apart from ringing the appropriate codes. In this situation the least skilled type of interviewer may be used as there is very little the interviewer can do to interfere with the quality of data collected.

9.2.2 Using rating scales

The kind of complex scaling exercises often used in attitude measurement are also fully structured in the sense that both the interviewer and respondent are bound by the questionnaire. However, when scaling and attitude battery exercises are used there is a greater need for intervention by the interviewer to ensure that respondents fully understand what they are required to do in order to answer the questions correctly. Once this explanation has been given then recording of respondents' answers is quite straightforward. When using this type of question it is, therefore, sensible to use interviewers who have experience in applying the particular type required.

9.2.3 Semi-structured interviews

This type of interview is normally a mixture of precoded and open-ended questions combined in the questionnaire. The interviewer is bound by the structure of the questionnaire but the respondent is free to answer the open-ended questions in any way. Open-ended questions are relatively easy for the interviewer to ask, but more skill is needed in interpreting the responses. Not least, there is the problem of recording all that a respondent says should he or she speak rapidly. The danger exists that the interviewer will edit the responses to those that seem to be most appropriate, or most required. In both of these situations the interviewer can distort the quality of data obtained. It is, therefore, necessary for the interviewer to be aware of the importance of his or her role in accurately and completely recording the respondent's answers. A higher degree of skill and experience is looked for, and more attention must be paid to interviewer briefing before fieldwork commences.

9.2.4 Unstructured interviews

Depth interviews

These are usually prolonged interviews in which the interviewer has the freedom to phrase the questions as seems most appropriate and to order them and probe them according to the respondent's responses. In this type of interview the interviewer often has only a checklist of points or topics, and will be using mainly open-ended questions. Depth interviews often use indirect and projective techniques, and call on specialized interviewing skills.

Group discussions or focus groups

These are interviews in which one interviewer or moderator asks questions of a group of respondents, usually comprising six to eight persons. The essence of a group discussion is that group dynamics are used to draw out individual beliefs that might not be so freely expressed in a one-to-one interview situation. Once again, an advanced degree of interviewer skill is called upon.

Qualitative techniques of depth interview and group discussion or focus groups are most demanding from the interviewer's point of view. Often the interviewer will have a degree of psychological training, since it requires considerable skill to manage both depth interviews and group discussion or focus groups in such a way as to elicit the detail and freedom of response required. In order to do this the interviewer is free to insert questions as seems most appropriate. Since depth interviews are commonly used in industrial, trade or professional research studies, depth interviewers may be required to have some subject qualifications in addition to their research expertise. In group discussion or focus groups the role of the moderator is often simply to act as a catalyst to the generation of appropriate conversation between members of the group. A good moderator may intervene very little in the discussion process except to keep it on the right lines and to ensure that all required topics are covered.

Interpretation of depth interview and group discussion or focus group sessions is also a highly skilled task and is normally carried out by the interviewer or moderator. For this reason, in this type of research, the quality of data obtained is almost entirely in the hands of the interviewer or moderator selected. These are highly specialist individuals, often working independently and far better paid than the normal interviewer.

9.3 What do interviewers do?

Interviewers can carry out a number of functions in the fieldwork process. Each function requires the application of skill, and interviewers who lack appropriate skills may introduce error into the data collection procedure.

9.3.1 Selecting respondents

When random samples are used, unless the interviewer does not do the callback as instructed, he or she can do very little to affect the selection of respondents, since a list of specific names and addresses to interview is given. However, in quota samples the selection of actual respondents is in the hands of the interviewers. Quota sampling is often used because it is cheaper than random sampling, since it uses interviewer time more efficiently. In practice, the main difference between respondents obtained through the use of the quota sampling and random sampling methods is that when quota samples are used then extreme and unusual types of respondent are less likely to be included.

For example, in the AB class category respondents are more likely to be Bs than As and in the DE class category respondents are more likely to be Ds than Es in quota sampling. The reason for this is that these are the kinds of respondents that it is easier for the interviewer to identify.

If the interviewer has to contact a certain number of respondents of a particular occupation type then most experienced interviewers will know where in their area that type of respondent is more likely to be found. This results in middle-class respondents who live in middle-class areas having a greater chance of being included in the sample than middle-class respondents who live in mixed class areas, and so on. Similarly, certain types of manual occupation are more likely to be represented.

For example, bus drivers are commonly included because interviewers know that they will be able to find them and interview them easily at their place of work. A gatekeeper in a Newcastle factory admitted having been interviewed 60 times in the preceding month since whenever interviewers in his area required an individual for a quota sample which matched his profile they knew just where to find him, a warm fire, a friendly welcome and a cup of tea!

Random route and random location sampling procedures attempt to overcome some of these problems by restricting interviewers' choice of respondent.

9.3.2 Obtaining interviews

There is evidence to indicate that experienced interviewers are better able to obtain interviews than inexperienced interviewers. This is important, since the higher the percentage of non-respondents in a survey, the greater the probability that some bias will be introduced by the fact that non-respondents are different in some relevant way to those who do respond.

> For example, in a survey about drinking habits those most likely to be interviewed are most likely to be found at home, and yet the very fact of their being at home means that they differ in important ways from those who are out drinking!

Although obtaining co-operation from respondents is thought to be becoming harder, it is still true to say that on most consumer-type surveys skilled interviewers can obtain response rates of 80 per cent or better. Response rates such as these obviously minimize the potential errors that might be introduced by non-response bias.

In general, industrial, trade and executive interviews are harder to obtain because the respondent is being interviewed in his or her role as a business person and there is a need to secure their co-operation using working time. In obtaining industrial and executive interviews, it is usual for an appointment to be made by telephone and this may be preceded by an explanatory letter or e-mail. When the interviewer keeps the appointment he or she should be provided with an 'authority letter' which gives the respondent a telephone number to check on the interviewer's credentials. In practice this opportunity is rarely taken up, but it is too minor a detail over which to lose a valuable interview if such letters have not been provided.

In certain kinds of highly specialist or technical interviewing it may be necessary for the interviewer to have appropriate educational qualifications, or the ability to absorb knowledge relevant to the interview, in order to comprehend the answers and be able to frame appropriate supplementary questions.

There is the danger, however, that if the interviewer is too much of a specialist then his or her expertise on the subject will become evident to the respondent and may inhibit replies. If the interviewer is not sufficiently knowledgeable about the subject the opposite danger exists: that it is a waste of time talking with an interviewer who obviously does not understand the subject, and therefore asks inappropriate questions to which incomprehensible replies are given. In general, the industrial trade or executive respondent should perceive the interviewer as being an informed and intelligent person fully competent to explore the subject of the interview and to comprehend the replies, but leaving the respondent feeling the dominant partner to the interchange.

9.3.3 Asking questions

In structured interviewing it is important that interviewers understand the need for them to use exactly the words written on the questionnaire. By changing the words, or even the emphasis that they use in reading the questions, it is possible for the interviewer to change the question and therefore invalidate the use of the answers in quantitative analysis. In semi-structured and qualitative interview techniques, the way in which questions are asked, and indeed whether they are asked at all, is left to the interviewer and hence his or her role in determining what data are collected is a fundamental one. In ensuring that interviewers ask questions correctly, the interviewer briefing process is of great importance.

9.3.4 Probing and prompting

When open-ended questions are used the interviewer is often required to follow these up to obtain more information. There are two ways in which an interviewer can follow up the question with supplementary questions. The first of these is called probing. *Probing* is a non-directional prompt to the respondent. That is, the words used in the probe require the respondent to give additional information without indicating what kind of information that might be. 'What else?' may be used as a probe, or just a waiting silence.

Prompting is a directional supplementary question that indicates the kind of answer which the respondent might give.

For example, a common prompt following the question 'What brands of toothpaste have you ever heard of?' would be to show a prompt card listing the brands of toothpaste and ask the question 'Which of these brands have you ever heard of?' Where either a probe or prompt is used it should be written down on the questionnaire so that the researcher knows whether the information was volunteered with or without aid from the interviewer. Interviewers vary considerably in their skill and conscientiousness at using probes and prompts, and this varies the amount of data that is achieved from each respondent.

Where the use of probes and prompts is of importance in gathering the depth of information required, then these should be written directly on to the questionnaire to ensure that they are used appropriately by interviewers. Figure 8.5 shows an example of the use of probing, and Figure 9.1 illustrates the use of prompting.

Prompt Cards   These are also visual aids and must be shown to the respondent when specified in the questionnaire. Prompt cards must <u>NEVER</u> be shown until the instruction is given as they provide additional information to jog the respondent's memory.

<u>EXAMPLE</u>
Good morning/afternoon. I work for a market research company and we are doing a survey about savoury biscuits. What makes of savoury biscuits can you think of? Any others.

<u>SHOW CARD A</u>
Just to remind you, here is a list of savoury biscuits. Which on this list have you heard of including any you have already mentioned?

<u>SHOW CARD A</u>
And which of these have you ever bought?

	Q1	Q2	Q3
	(13)	(14)	(15)
JACOB'S CREAM CRACKERS	1	1	1
RYVITA	2	2	2
RITZ CRACKERS	3	3	3
CARR'S WATER BISCUITS	4	4	4
KRACKAWHEAT	5	5	5
TUC	6	6	6
BATH OLIVER	7	7	7
JACOB'S ASSORTMENT	8	8	8
OTHER (WRITE IN) _____	9	9	9
_____	0	0	0
NONE/NEVER	X	X	X
U.K./C.R.	A	A	A

SHOW CARD A

JACOB'S CREAM CRACKERS

RYVITA

RITZ CRACKERS

CARR'S WATER BISCUITS

KRACKAWHEAT

TUC

BATH OLIVER

JACOB'S ASSORTMENT

Figure 9.1 Interviewer instructions on the use of prompt cards

9.3.5 Motivating respondents

The interviewer has a role in motivating the respondent to give answers comprehensively, relevantly and accurately. This is achieved through the establishment of *rapport* between the interviewer and respondent. Rapport is an essential ingredient in conducting and completing an interview, but it may also be biasing. Interviewers need to be made aware that if rapport is too firmly established then the danger exists that the respondent will give answers which, it is believed, will reflect more favourably upon the interviewer. Like any other departure from the respondent's own true feelings, excessively favourable responses are as undesirable as excessively negative responses.

9.3.6 Interpreting and recording responses

In fully structured interviews the role of the interviewer in interpreting and recording responses is limited to doing so accurately. However, in open-ended and qualitative interviews the interviewer has an important role to play in correct interpretation and accurate comprehensive recording of responses. In depth interviews and group discussion or focus groups it is usual for a tape recorder to be employed to record responses, but when open-ended questions are used in questionnaires it is more usual for the interviewer to be required to write down exactly what the respondent says. If the respondent speaks fully and quickly this can prove a practical difficulty for the interviewer which may be overcome by editing responses. This may lose some of the quality and detail of information that the researcher would like to acquire. This is one of the reasons why open-ended questions often do not work well when used in fully structured quantitative research surveys. To help overcome this, interviewers are usually instructed to go over the questionnaire as soon as possible after the interview to record anything remembered but not recorded during the interview.

9.3.7 Interviewer bias

Interviewer bias has been defined as 'a unidirectional attitude, opinion or expectation held consistently by an interviewer'. The traditional view is that bias arises through communication to the respondent of the interviewer's own ideology and expectations or through the interviewer's motivation to influence results to confirm with his or her own ideology. In practice it seems that interviewer bias is most likely to be a problem when respondents do not have firmly held opinions or attitudes of their own. It is seen as a problem most seriously in fields of social research, but should also be borne in mind when research is being carried out on subjects that may be controversial, such as drinking and smoking. It is usual when interviewers are recruited for them to be screened for political activity if they are likely to be employed in asking political questions.

9.4 Who are the interviewers?

In the UK the market research industry depends mainly on freelance interviewers. Thus, the interviewers like to retain the freedom of when they will work and when they will not. For this reason most agencies need to have a much higher number of interviewers on their books than they will expect to use at any one time, since some of the interviewers will want to work at a particular time and others will not. Inevitably, there is some degree of lack of control in this type of situation where the interviewers do not see themselves as the employees of the company for which they work and indeed they will usually work for more than one research company. The typical characteristics used for selection of interviewers are as follows.

9.4.1 Gender

Most research interviewers are women, particularly for consumer research. Increasingly, women are also being used for industrial research. There are several reasons why women are more likely to be interviewers than men. First, the work is of a part-time and intermittent nature and is generally rather poorly paid. This may make it an impractical job proposition for many men but may be a highly suitable occupation for those women with family commitments. The part-time and intermittent nature of the work enables interviewers to build sufficient flexibility around their work programme to fit in with domestic commitments. Second, the socialization process results in the fact that women generally find it easier to play the neutral listener role than do men, and women are usually more readily and freely spoken to than men. Increasingly in industrial interviewing where men were used previously, mainly because of the technical knowledge required, it has been found to be easier for women to obtain interviews and they may obtain fuller information.

Conversely, with increasing levels of violence, particularly in the inner-city areas and after dark, men are being used for interviewing in these kinds of situations. High levels of unemployment have also led to more men being recruited as interviewers.

9.4.2 Age

The ideal age requirements for entry to consumer interviewing are between 25 and 45 years. The reasons for these limits are that interviewers below 25 may well have a biasing effect on the information they obtain and interviewers over 45 may be less easy to train for a new occupation. A higher level of training and mental agility is required for the more specialist type of industrial interviewing and this may mean recruiting at the lower end of the age range indicated.

9.4.3 Social background

The ideal requirement for interviewers is that they should not appear to be obviously of any particular social background, i.e. a degree of social neutrality is required. It helps if the interviewer has the ability to be 'chameleon-like' so as to be able to fit in with the respondent. In practice, most interviewers are middle class because of the other requirements for selection.

9.4.4 Education

For consumer interviewing, applicants are required to have at least GCSE qualifications. For specialist interviewing in either industrial or qualitative research, further education qualifications are normally required. In industrial research it helps if the interviewer has some knowledge of the specialist area in which the research will be carried out or is sufficiently well educated to be able to conduct interviews at executive level. For qualitative interviewing the interviewer is often required to have some psychological training.

9.4.5 Job background

The best interviewers seem to be those whose previous occupations have been people orientated, for example, teachers and nurses. Those who have previously held selling occupations tend not to be very good at interviewing, but are particularly successful at recruiting respondents for group discussions. In general, research has indicated that it is rather difficult for salespeople in particular, but often other company personnel as well, to conduct interviews in their own product areas.

9.4.6 Personality

Above all, interviewers need the ability to listen and to record accurately. One agency which uses personality tests to select its interviewers requires that on a neuroticism/stability scale they should be just on the stability side of the scale. Too far along the emotional stability scale and they would be such 'suet puddings' that it would be difficult for them to be able to obtain the interview in the first place. On the extraversion/introversion scale interviewers should be just on the extraverted side of the scale. Too extraverted an individual would not have the sensitivity to listen truly to their respondent, but too introverted an individual would not be able to obtain an interview in the first place. The same agency also uses a lie scale in selecting appropriate people as interviewers.

9.4.7 Training

The Interviewer Quality Control Scheme (IQCS), shown in Figure 9.2, sets out minimum standards. Once selected, interviewers should be trained. For most of the leading research agencies interviewer training involves a two or three day programme.

Under the Interviewer Quality Control Scheme (IQCS) a minimum of 12 hours' training is required by all new field interviewers or by those who have not received training by an IQCS member company. In addition, new interviewers must be accompanied on their first assignment. If this is not possible then the company should make an attempt to validate all the interviewer's work before it is used. On business-to-business assignments interviews should be taped and assessed before analysis. For other areas of research a minimum of six hours' training is required.

The standards of the IQCS are now also incorporated within the Market Research Quality Standards (MRQSA), a broader quality assurance scheme for the industry which covers data processing and the work carried out by research executives, as well as fieldwork and data collection. MRQSA also ensures compliance to standards within the industry in the UK.

Training for field research covers:

- Sampling methods
- Recruitment methods
- Quotas control
- Interviewing courtesy/manner
- Interviewing technique
- Types of questions including prompting and probing
- Questionnaire completion and administration
- Use of visual aids/concepts/products
- Demographics/classification/social grading
- Some practical experience of interviewing/recruiting/auditing

For group research:

- The company's rules for group recruitment
- What happens at a group discussion or focus group
- The importance of maintaining recruitment standards
- How to 'sell' participation
- Group dynamics
- Role of the moderator/researcher
- Viewing facilities, audio and video taping of groups
- Confirming group attendance
- Practical arrangement for home groups
- Hosting

Figure 9.2 The Interviewer Quality Control Scheme

The first part of the training is theoretical. In this part of the programme interviewers are lectured on their importance in the research process and in the special skills they need to acquire. They are fully briefed on the dangers of bias that can be introduced by them. The second part of the training programme is practical. This involves role playing in the classroom situation followed by practice interviews in the field. Finally, for consumer interviewing, trainees accompany the supervisor who carries out field interviews, and then carry out field interviews with the supervisor present. For industrial interviewing the practical training will take the form of listening to and checking off taped interviews before carrying them out personally. The third aspect of interviewer training is that of refresher training. This takes place in three ways: first, when pilot briefings and debriefings are given; second, when personal briefings on important surveys are given; and third, through the provision of a handbook for reference and guidance. Once interviewers have been trained and are working in the field, maintenance of good interviewing practice is ensured through the system of supervision, appraisal and checking of work.

9.5 How are interviewers controlled?

The quality of fieldwork can be controlled in several ways, as follows.

9.5.1 The Interviewer Quality Control Scheme

As good-quality fieldwork is the pivot around which good-quality data collection revolves, it is important that adequate controls be imposed to maintain high-quality fieldwork.

As part of its concern about instituting and maintaining good-quality fieldwork, the Market Research Society (MRS) operates an IQCS and in 2002, 84 companies were members of the scheme.

The scheme covers the following types of fieldwork: consumer, social and qualitative research, consumer and retail panels and audits, hall tests and telephone research. In each case the scheme lays down minimum standards for recruitment, office procedures, supervision, training, quality control (IQCS standards are in line with BS 5750) and survey administration. Each member company is visited annually by an independent inspector and required to produce documentation and other evidence that it conforms to or exceeds the minimum standards. Inspection can be made with a minimum of 24 hours' notice. If accepted as a member of the scheme, the company is shown in the MRS listing of organizations, and if providing market research services, in the *Research Buyer's Guide*. Members of the IQCS are also listed in its own annual handbook, *IQCS Minimum Service Standards for Market Research Data Collection*. That booklet and full details of the IQCS standards will be sent on request, by IQCS, 6 Walkfield Drive, Epsom Downs, Surrey KT18 5UF (Tel: 01737 379 261, Fax: 01737 351 171, E-mail: gwareing@lineone.net).

9.5.2 Field supervision

Most agencies with any size of field force will have a supervisory structure, from a field manager in head office down to a number of area managers or supervisors, each responsible for a number of interviewers. It is usual that the field manager is a full-time employee of the agency and that supervisors work exclusively for one agency. Good practice would require that the area manager who is responsible for the quality of work of a team of interviewers supervises their work in the field by spending a day with them from time to time, by attending area briefings and watching mock interviews, and generally ensuring that the company's standards are maintained.

9.5.3 Postal checking

Under the IQCS a minimum of 7.5 per cent of each interviewer's work is followed up with checkbacks by phone or face-to-face. A minimum of 10 per cent of the sample must be validated overall; up to 25 per cent of these checks may be carried out by post. The follow-up check might contain two questions from the interview, two demographic questions and the questions, 'Did you know the interviewer?' 'Did you see a prompt card?' and 'How long did the interview last?' If any doubts arise as a result of these postal checkbacks then the check is followed by a 100 per cent check on all of that interviewer's work. An example of a postal check form is shown in Figure 9.3.

9.5.4 Telephone checks

Most checking on the interviewer's work will be done by telephone. This will vary depending on the nature of respondents and the probability of their having telephones.

9.5.5 Personal recall checks

As an alternative to telephoning, the interviewer's work may be followed up by personal recall checks, usually carried out by the area supervisor. Once again, a few questions from the interview will be asked, demographics will be checked on and one or two additional questions will be put to the respondent. It is desirable, although unusual, that field checks should be completed before the data analysis so that any errors or mistakes can be corrected or withdrawn from the data analysis process. A personal recall check form is shown in Figure 9.4.

9.5.6 Editing checks

When completed questionnaires are returned to the office, editing checks will indicate something about the quality of an interviewer's work. They will show, for example, how the amount and calibre of original information vary between interviewers as a result of their probing and prompting skills. They will also indicate the accuracy with which the interviewer works, e.g. sections are properly completed, filter questions are not skipped and the questionnaire is generally completed in an appropriate manner.

We understand that you helped one of our interviewers recently by answering some questions on _____

We like to be sure that our interviewers have left a good impression and that their work is accurate. We would be very grateful if you would help us again by answering the questions below. Your replies will be compared with those recorded by the interviewer, as a check.

1 Was the interviewer polite and courteous? _____

2 How long did the interview take? _____

3 May we know your age group (Please tick one box)

☐ 15–24 yrs   ☐ 25–34 yrs   ☐ 35–54 yrs   ☐ 55 yrs and over

Control question (if applicable) _____

_____

Do you live in the constituency of _____

_____

Are there any comments you would like to make concerning the interview?

_____

_____

This card needs no stamp. Just drop it in the post as soon as possible.

Thank you once again for your cooperation.

Interviewer Number	Respondent Number	Job Number	Backchecker Int. No.	Date Posted

Figure 9.3 Postal check form. (Courtesy of MORI)

9.5.7 Computer checks

Once the data from the questionnaires has been entered into the computer another range of checks becomes possible. Once again, checks can be made for completeness and accuracy. Where control questions have been used the computer can check one answer against another. The computer will also check whether the correct sections have been completed following filter questions. Finally, to test the reliability of the interviewers, inter-interviewer

MORI/FIELD & TAB
BACKCHECK REPORT FORM

Interviewer Name: _____   Interviewer Number: □□□□/□

Job Name: _____   Job Number: □□□□/□

Name of Backchecker: _____   Int Number: □□□□/□ Date: _____

Number of questionnaires in quota for checking: _____

Number checked by phone: _____

Number checked face-to-face: _____

Number of postal checks: _____   Posted on (date): _____

NUMBER OF ERRORS	PHONE/FACE-TO-FACE	POSTAL (OUO)
CIE occupation details:	_____	_____
Age:	_____	_____
Social Grading:	_____	_____
Working Status:	_____	_____
Other (write in):	_____	_____

GENERAL COMMENTS (Backchecker)

AREA MANAGER COMMENTS

FEEDBACK TO INTERVIEWER		ACTION REQUIRED	
By phone	□	None	□
By letter	□	Arrange Accompaniment	□
In person	□	Request further B/C	□
By letter from HO	□	Request Edit Check	□
None required	□	Other	□

OFFICE USE ONLY: NUMBER OF POSTAL CHECKS RETURNED: _____   % CHECK _____

ACTION TAKEN BY FIELD MANAGER: Letter Sent □ Other □	QC:

Figure 9.4 Backcheck report form. (Courtesy of MORI)

comparisons are drawn by analysing the results from one interviewer against the results of the whole survey.

9.5.8 Monitoring fieldwork

The good research agencies will normally carry out all of these checks. A manager using an agency for fieldwork should ask to see the fieldwork checks on his or her own survey, and agencies who carry out these checks will be only too pleased to show this evidence of the quality of their work. It is also very instructive to spend a day in the field with one of the interviewers working on the survey. It gives the manager far greater insight into interpreting and understanding results if he or she has seen the survey in the process of raw data collection. Again, the better agencies will be happy to entertain a request to spend a day in the field with one of their interviewers.

9.6 Choosing a good fieldwork agency

It is apparent from the preceding sections of this chapter that whether the research being conducted is a quantitative survey involving several hundred respondents or a qualitative survey requiring specialist qualitative interviewing skills of group moderation, industrial or depth interviewing, better quality fieldwork is likely to be achieved using professional and experienced interviewers. This therefore involves the selection of an appropriate agency to carry out the fieldwork. As with buying most services, it makes sense to ask for quotations from two or three companies to give a basis for comparing both procedures and prices. The first step is to determine which two or three companies should be invited to quote. In making the selection a number of other factors must be considered and the procedure suggested should give a pretty clear idea of an agency's ability to handle the work required and of the quality of work they are likely to produce.

9.6.1 Finding the agency

Finding an agency to carry out fieldwork can be quite difficult for a company that has never conducted research before.

One starting point is to obtain the MRS publication entitled *The Research Buyer's Guide.* This directory is updated each year and is annotated in such a way as to give as much help as possible to the intending purchaser of research services, e.g. membership of the IQCS is shown, and an indication is given of the size of turnover of companies, since a small job is likely to be done better by a small agency. The *Guide* also gives an indication of what services research companies specialize in by showing in bold type those services from which they gain more than 25 per cent or over £100,000 of their income. An initial shortlist can be drawn up by going through the book and noting companies of the right size with the right kind of experience and who have worked in the industry in which the fieldwork is to be carried out.

Areas in which information is presented are:

- Name
- Contact details
- Establishment date
- Turnover
- Parent or principal company
- Associate companies
- Associate memberships
- Accredited standards
- Total employees
- Personnel
- Senior contacts
- Research markets
- Research services
- Research locations
- Promotional statement

The MRS website offers a searchable database of research businesses.

Web address: MRS.org.uk

The ESOMAR website offers a similar service for international research agencies.

Web address: www.esomar.nl

Another approach to generating an appropriate shortlist for invitation to quote is to use business contacts. Most managers will know their opposite numbers in competitive organizations or be familiar through the normal network of business contacts with other managers working in their industry. It is always worthwhile asking these people to recommend agencies that they have used. It is not necessarily the case that an agency that has done a good job for one company will do a good job for another company, particularly if the nature of the research required is different. However, such recommendations offer a starting point to the inexperienced fieldwork buyer. It is also often the case that if agencies believe they could not do a good job for a potential client they are likely to hand the enquiry on to an agency better suited to those needs.

9.6.2 Asking pertinent questions

Once quotations have been obtained from two or three companies, the next stage in evaluating their ability to do work to the standards required is to visit their premises and ask pertinent questions. These are the kinds of question that will be seen as pertinent and discriminating, and therefore approved of, by the good-quality research agency, and will be seen as discriminating, and therefore impertinent and disapproved of, by the poor-quality research agency. At least that is their objective.

The kinds of questions to ask in order to assess the quality of an agency's fieldwork procedures relate to the structure and organization of its field force. For example:

- 'Is there a fieldwork manager?'
- 'How many interviewers have you?'
- 'How many supervisors are there?'
- 'Do the supervisors work exclusively for this agency?'
- 'What is the agency's supervisory structure, i.e. how many supervisors and how many interviewers per supervisor?'
- 'How are interviewers selected?'
- 'How are interviewers trained?'
- 'On average, how long do interviewers stay with your organization?'
- 'How many interviewers work exclusively for your agency?'
- 'What quality-control procedures are used?'

9.6.3 Looking at the evidence

From the questions that have already been asked, providing the right kinds of answer have been obtained, a further check would be to look for the evidence that must exist. For example, if the company claims a certain size field force then it should be possible to see the records containing details of the field force: their abilities, their geographical spread and so forth. Similarly, it should be possible to see the documentary evidence of quality-control procedures, for example, evidence of postal checkbacks. A well-managed field force will be supported by a set of administrative records that can be evaluated for quality.

9.6.4 Membership of the Interviewer Quality Control Scheme

It may be helpful to ask whether the agency is a member of the IQCS. If so, then it should be possible to see the report produced by the scheme's annual inspectors. Non-membership of the IQCS does not necessarily imply a poor-quality fieldwork agency. This is particularly true of small agencies, many of which are not members of the scheme. However, for the inexperienced fieldwork buyer, an agency's membership of the IQCS offers an independent assessment and control over that company's working procedure.

9.6.5 Relevant experience

An important criterion for selecting one fieldwork agency over another is to look for experience related to the needs of the survey. This experience may be of two kinds. First, it may consist of experience in the industry in which the research will be carried out. Most industries have their special language and problems, and an agency familiar with these is more likely to be able to do a good job than one unfamiliar with them. Second, the particular research method required may be better carried out by one type of quantitative attitude battery scaling exercise, or qualitative research of a particular kind. In both cases, interviewers experienced in the technique are more likely to produce a better job than those who are not. Available evidence suggests that interviewers familiar with the industry and technique with which they are working are more likely to produce better quality data than those who are inexperienced. An attempt should therefore be made to identify agencies whose experience is relevant to the particular research problem.

9.6.6 Cost

As in other buying areas, costs may be a useful indicator in making the buying decision. In the case of fieldwork several factors affect the costs:

- the type of sample
- the penetration of the product
- the length of interview
- the type of respondent
- the type of interviewer to be used.

Also relevant will be the method of payment used for interviewers. Interviewers may be paid per interview, per day or per job. With fully structured questionnaires it may make sense for interviewers to be paid per completed interview, as this will encourage them to complete the work as quickly as possible. However, when open-ended questions are included in the questionnaire, the quality of data is likely to be better if interviewers are paid by the day and have no financial incentive to rush the probing of open-ended questions. The agency will decide the most appropriate method of paying its interviewers, but in comparing costs from different fieldwork agencies any relevant assumptions should be checked to ensure that like is being compared with like.

9.7 Using an agency for fieldwork

In using agency fieldwork, the agency and interviewer briefing procedures are the only means by which the intentions of the research initiator are communicated to those responsible for collecting answers to the questions posed. Good briefing is essential to ensure that both agency and interviewers appreciate their role in the research process.

9.7.1 Briefing the agency

The agency should be adequately briefed on the market and marketing background, and on the factors that gave rise to the research. They should be told all pertinent facts, such as the percentage of product users, and also forewarned of potential difficulties that they may meet. This enables them to develop appropriate strategies for dealing with problems that may arise in the field.

9.7.2 Agreeing the procedures

The form of interview to be used must be determined: structured, semi-structured or depth interview, group discussion or focus group, industrial or executive interviewing, and so on. When this has been agreed a check must be made that the agency will be using interviewers capable of doing the job and experienced in the type of interview decided on. Matters of selection and training will have already been discussed. The administrative procedures for handling the project in the field must be agreed, for example:

- Will the first day's work be checked?
- How will fieldworkers be supervised?
- When will quality checks be undertaken?
- What type and percentage of checks will be used?
- What assumptions have been made about the number of interviews to be completed in a day?

All matters relevant to conducting the survey must be agreed and committed to writing in advance of the fieldwork.

9.7.3 Briefing the interviewers

In most routine consumer surveys the interviewers are unlikely to be given a personal briefing. A good explanatory written brief must therefore be developed to be sent to the interviewers with the questionnaires. This may be followed up by a telephone briefing from the area supervisor. In complex or unusual consumer surveys it may be necessary to hold interviewer briefing meetings, and these will have to be paid for to cover the interviewers' time.

In industrial and executive research, briefing the interviewers is of paramount importance and personal briefing is usually essential. The objectives of the research must be made clear to the interviewer. Probes and prompts should be discussed and an indication given of where the areas of greatest potential interest are expected to be. The method of recording the answers must be agreed and this will often involve the use of tape recorders. Possible difficulties and ways in which the interviewer might handle them should be covered. Finally, the importance of establishing rapport in this type of interviewing should be stressed, since without the respondent's wholehearted co-operation much of the point of depth interviewing in business situations is lost.

9.8 Asking the questions yourself

In smaller companies, industrial companies and companies that have not used research previously, there is a strong temptation on the part of the newly appointed and usually inexperienced research executive to carry out his or her own research programme. For large-scale research surveys or for group discussion or focus groups this is unlikely to be viable: in the first case because of the time and expense involved in using one's own time on a routine and repetitive task, and in the second case because the executive is unlikely to have the appropriate skills for the method to work to its best advantage. However, for industrial and trade interviewing when only 20 or 30 depth interviews may be required for an exploratory survey it could well be feasible for the manager to carry these out personally. Indeed, there may be good commercial and technical reasons for doing so for a small project, with no necessity for confidentiality. A desk research exercise followed by 15–20 personal interviews or by a postal questionnaire could readily be carried out by a manager with enough time and motivation, if the following points are borne in mind.

First, serious thought should be given to the real costs of do-it-yourself interviewing. It is too easy to count one's own time as 'free'. Second, the implications for the quality of data to be obtained if the sponsor is identified as personally carrying out the survey must be considered. Third, a manager must objectively decide whether he or she has, or can acquire, the appropriate skills. A manager used to decision making, authority and generally playing an assertive role at work may find the role play required to succeed as an interviewer particularly difficult. Essentially, it is necessary to present to the respondent a neutral, empathetic and passively accepting personality. The questions must be asked in a straightforward manner that gives no clues, either verbal or non-verbal, as to the kind of answers that would be most acceptable. The interviewer must be aware of his or her own effect upon the respondent, and above all, must resist the temptation to 'correct' the respondent who makes remarks that the researcher knows to be factually inaccurate.

Whether a manager is able to fulfil successfully the role of industrial or trade researcher is a matter of individual trial and error. It is, nevertheless, a highly salutary experience to attempt to carry out one's own fieldwork, and certainly increases the manager's insight into and understanding of the market in which he or she operates. It is also a useful learning device which enables managers to appreciate exactly what they are expecting interviewers to accomplish for them. However, if an organization intends to carry out research in any regular way, do-it-yourself interviewing will very quickly become too demanding in terms of time for the manager to carry out all the research personally. Experience suggests that organizations experimenting with the use of research will quickly realize the need to use professional interviewing services.

A situation in which it may be desirable to ask the questions oneself is if one is involved in questionnaire design. Piloting the questionnaire during the drafting procedure is a very worthwhile experience in producing better questions and better questionnaires. It will give a better feeling for the contribution that questionnaire interviews are able to make to the research problem and for what their limitations might be.

9.9 Summary

Good interviewing procedures are of fundamental importance in producing high-quality research information. Different types of interviewer are required for different types of interview. Interviewer skills, characteristics and control procedures are discussed. Selecting and using a research agency for fieldwork is followed by a brief consideration of 'do-it-yourself' interviewing.

10 What happens to the answers?

10.1 Introduction

Chapter 6 indicated two broad approaches to data collection for made-to-measure research. One is the qualitative approach, where a large amount of data is collected from a relatively small number of people in a fairly unstructured way, usually using group discussions or depth interviews. The quantitative approach is where a smaller amount of data is collected from a large number of people in a structured way, usually using questionnaire surveys often involving 500–1000 or more respondents. What happens to the answers will depend on which approach has been used for data collection. In this chapter the analysis and interpretation of both quantitative and qualitative data are explained. The emphasis in the section on analysis of quantitative data is deliberately confined to a straightforward description of what various statistical techniques will do. It aims to introduce the non-statistical reader to the usefulness of these techniques, but does not attempt to teach how they can be applied.

10.2 Analysis and interpretation of qualitative data

Group discussions or depth interviews represent the most common ways in which qualitative data is collected. In both cases it is normal for the moderator, in the case of group discussions, or the depth interviewer, to tape-record each data collection session, which normally will last from one and a half to two hours. Group discussions may also be held on premises where they can be watched through a one-way mirror or recorded by video camera, so that behaviour, as well as verbal responses, can be observed. A typical survey involving group discussions might cover six to eight groups and a typical survey involving depth interviews might cover 10–20 depth interviews. In each case it is usual for the individual who was responsible for the collection of the information, i.e. the moderator or depth interviewer, to carry out the analysis of the tapes. The person who conducted the interviews can bring much greater insight and understanding to bear on their interpretation, since they will have been conscious of the whole range of non-verbal communication going on during the data collection process.

The tapes of an interview with a doctor on the subject of his use of and attitude towards a number of treatments for bronchial disorders apparently revealed an extremely aggressive respondent. The field manager was impressed that the interviewer had managed to complete the whole course of the two hour interview and had doggedly gone on asking questions even after most vehemently expressed negative answers accompanied on the tape by the sounds of violent altercation. In fact, the respondent concerned had leaned forward and thumped the desk close to the microphone in order to emphasize the points he was making. On the tape it sounded quite alarming but the interviewer present was aware from the friendly facial expressions of the respondent that this was just his manner of speech and presentation and not an aggressive response to the interview. If someone else had analysed that tape, quite a different interpretation would have been put on the respondent's approach and attitude to the topic. This illustrates how helpful video recordings can be in improving the analysis of group discussions and depth interviews.

How then does the moderator or depth interviewer go about analysing recorded information? In the first place he or she will listen several times to each interview, making notes on points made and categorizing and classifying the answers into the separate topics covered by the respondent.

An alternative method of analysis is to have the tapes transcribed and perform a 'content' analysis of the transcriptions, perhaps by cutting them up into statements and grouping related statements together for analysis and comment.

Since the research is on such a small scale it is important that all responses are considered. One of the aims of this type of research is to collect the range of possible responses, but not to count them. However, when there is a very clear and strong measure of agreement between respondents, the researcher will indicate this, as well as when there is no clear agreement between respondents.

The results of qualitative research should never be expressed in terms of percentages. This is extremely dangerous because it implies that results are somehow representative quantitatively of what a wider sample of respondents might say. Since no statistical procedure has been used in selecting the sample for qualitative research this is not the case. While the researcher and the immediate user of the research may both appreciate this point, the fact of using percentages in interpreting the data will lead to less informed readers of the report talking about market percentages as if they had representative validity.

The outcome of analysis of qualitative data is a report that indicates the range of views expressed on the topics covered and some indication of whether the views were strongly held and widely supported. When proper interpretation takes place by skilled analysts (usually psychologists) the report goes deeper than this, and underlying attitudes and motivations are 'interpreted' even though not explicitly verbalized. Hence, this is not a game for amateurs. A characteristic of qualitative research reports is that they contain direct quotations to indicate the way in which respondents express their opinions and the language used. It is this aspect of qualitative research that is often of most use, particularly when considering promotional ways of approaching the market: what to say in advertisements, what environment to use as the background for an advertisement, and so on.

Characteristically, then, analysis of qualitative data is subjective and impressionistic. It conveys to the decision maker insights into people's feelings about the market, the product, the advertising and their attitudes towards the use of competitive products. How good the analysis and interpretation of qualitative data is depends on the individual who undertakes both the conduct of the research and analysis of the tapes produced. This introduces a high risk of bias in both the conduct and interpretation of qualitative research. For this reason, once organizations find a qualitative researcher who produces good and useful guidance they will often continue to use the same individual. The advantage of this is that the researcher identifies closely with the organization's interests and is better able to probe areas likely to be of most interest. This also explains why many qualitative research agencies are small one- or two-person consultancies.

Various software packages are available to help the researcher with the analysis of qualitative data. The best known of these are the NUD*IST N6 package and NVivo, both from QSR software. These are valuable in helping the researcher to handle the large amount of data that often derives from extended qualitative research. QSR's software products help the researcher to interpret and manage data and emerging ideas from qualitative data. The software looks for patterns and meanings and places these in a manageable context.

QSR's website has full details of the two products, and the software is downloadable along with tutorials and examples of how the programs are used.

Web address: www.qsr.com.au/home/home.asp

10.3 Analysis of quantitative data

From the discussion in Chapter 5 it will be clear that quantitative data is typically produced using a questionnaire that is either interviewer administered or designed for self-completion by the respondent. In either case, the end result will be a large number (often 500 or more) of completed questionnaires containing both precoded and open-ended answers. To combine all the answers and thus make a meaningful summary of responses, there are several stages in the analysis process: data preparation, data processing, computer and statistical analysis and testing. These are discussed in the following subsections.

10.3.1 Data preparation

This involves ensuring that questionnaires appear to be completed correctly, and that the data they contain are represented in the form of numbers that are suitable for further processing and analysis. The techniques that accomplish this are editing and coding.

Editing

The purpose of editing is to check the returned questionnaires for any errors or omissions. Where possible, minor errors are corrected. If this is not possible the error may be sufficiently serious to result in the whole questionnaire being rejected from further analysis. A high proportion of errors detected at the editing stage may indicate a badly designed questionnaire or poor interviewing techniques. Some feedback system should therefore be introduced to ensure that such avoidable problems are not carried forward into future research undertakings. If an interviewer has skipped a question or a series of questions, he or she can be asked to call again on the respondent and complete the questionnaire, or to telephone the respondent if a telephone number is recorded and collect the missing data. Where inconsistencies or other errors are apparent from the editing process these may also be rectified by recontacting the respondent. Sometimes it is possible to amend data in one question as a result of the answer recorded for another question, but there are obvious dangers in attempting this kind of 'putting answers into respondents' mouths'. Editing is primarily a matter of common sense and experience. At the end of the editing process the editor must decide whether the questionnaire is to be rejected or accepted for further analysis.

Editing may be carried out either manually, by simply reading through each original questionnaire, or more often, by computer. In the latter case the data from the original questionnaire is transferred to a file and a check is carried out on the records for missing data, inconsistencies and so on. The computer will identify those questionnaires in which errors or inconsistencies exist. For example, in a question on health a respondent might say that he does not smoke and will later list a favourite brand of tobacco. It is primarily the responsibility of the questionnaire designer and the interviewer to ensure that these types of mistake do not occur, but the computer programs now available will reject data such as this. The identified respondent may be called back, or the questionnaire may be rejected.

Coding

It was pointed out in Section 8.9 on questionnaire design that, for quantitative data, precoding should be used wherever possible. In this case the code numbers are printed on to the questionnaire and the interviewer carries out the coding process during the interview by simply ringing the appropriate code. This bypasses the coding stage of analysis and explains why the use of precoding reduces the cost of research, because coding is a manual procedure, and therefore expensive. Computer-assisted telephone, personal and web interviews (CATI, CAPI and CAWI) allow automatic coding to take place and the process of editing and rationalizing data is far quicker than with manual coding.

To code open-ended questions, the answers must be analysed for the separate points that they make, and each point assigned a code number that must be written on the questionnaire. The code numbers are allocated from a coding frame. The coding frame is constructed by a research executive selecting 100, or sometimes 10 per cent of the original questionnaires, writing down all of the separate points made in answer to a particular question on those questionnaires and assigning a code number to each point. Responses that occur infrequently may be grouped together under an 'Other' code number. When the coding frame has been

JOB NO 0307

i.e. Card 2
Column 14

JOB TITLE READERSHIP SURVEY

OPEN QUESTION CODING MASTER: CODE ALL THAT APPLY

2/14/1	TIMES	Q
2	GUARDIAN	U
3	TELEGRAPH	E
4	MAIL DAILY PAPERS	S
5	EXPRESS	T
6	MIRROR	I
7	SUN	O
8	STAR	N
9	OTHER DAILY PAPER	Q5.
0	SUNDAY TIMES	Newspapers read nowadays (national)
X	OBSERVER	
A	SUNDAY TELEGRAPH	
	SUNDAY PAPERS	
2/15/1	MAIL (ON SUNDAY)	Q
2	SUNDAY EXPRESS	U
3	OTHER SUNDAY PAPER	E
4	OTHER PAPER, not elsewhere classified	S
5		T
6		I
7		O
8		N
9		Q5. (cont'd)
0		
X	NONE	
A	DON'T KNOW/NOT STATED	

Figure 10.1

derived using this process, a copy of it is given to the coders, who then write the appropriate code numbers for answers to that question given on all the other questionnaires. When the coders come across any answers not included on the coding frame these are passed to the research executive who must decide whether they occur with sufficient frequency to open a separate code number for them. Figure 10.1 is an example of a coding frame, or 'coding master' drawn up in answer to an open-ended question, 'Which daily or Sunday newspapers do you personally read nowadays?'

Whether answers to questions have been entered directly into computers, or are precoded or manually coded, this brings the data on the questionnaire to the point where every answer is represented by a number in the right-hand column of the questionnaire. The questionnaires are then ready for the next stage of analysis.

10.3.2 Data processing

Once the data has been fed into the computer it is possible to carry out many checks on the data and to analyse and cross-analyse it in all sorts of ways. Data can be handled manually, but this is unusual. Computers take the leg work out of survey analysis and allow for a greater sophistication of analysis. However, for simple surveys it may be quicker to process data manually. Statistical tests of the data can be carried out easily, and weighting to remove bias due to over- or underrepresentation in the sample is quite straightforward. The problem that arises from easy access to a vast range of statistical techniques is that of overanalysis. It is possible to generate vast numbers of tables very easily. It must be remembered that the information generated must relate to the research objectives and that the information should be used. That said, most managers with access to standard business software can produce data of great sophistication quickly and cheaply.

Data entry

Direct-entry computer systems enable information from the questionnaire to be entered directly into the computer through a keyboard. A large range of software packages has been developed for the market research industry. Software providers are listed in the Market Research Society (MRS) yearbook.

Optical character recognition (OCR) or optical mark recognition (OMR) systems are also used. In this case, the questionnaire is usually precoded, and the appropriate codes are marked by the respondent (for self-completion questionnaires) or interviewer (for administered questionnaires). The completed questionnaire pages are fed directly into an electronic scanner which reads the codes directly from the questionnaire and stores them in the computer.

In 1998 the Government passed a new Data Protection Act which strengthened rules concerning the storing of data about individuals. While the market research industry is only interested in individuals as representatives of a wider subgroup of the population, the MRS has published a code of conduct relating to the Data Protection Act. This is available on request from the Market Research Society (Tel: 020 7490 4911, Fax: 020 7490 0608, E-mail: info@mrs.org).

The original questionnaires are usually kept for two years in case they are needed. In subsequent analysis of the data, for example, it might be thought useful to identify the actual data coded under an 'Other' code. Respondents may have been asked which brands they used, and it would be normal to assign codes to the most frequently mentioned brands and put all infrequently mentioned brands into an 'Other' code. At some later date it may be useful to know which other brands were mentioned. The computer will be used to identify the questionnaires containing an answer under the 'Other' code for that particular question. These questionnaires can then be analysed separately.

Telling the computer what to do with the data

Once the computer has the data, it needs to know what to do with it, i.e. what calculations to perform, what tabulations to produce and what statistical manipulations to carry out. This is determined by the research executive, often in conjunction with the individual who commissioned the research survey, particularly if the survey is complex or unusual. This is called 'specification writing' because it specifies what the computer must do. The *specifications* are a set of written instructions to the computer in whatever computer language is appropriate for the machine being used. A typical set of specifications might instruct the computer to do straight counts and percentages on the answers to all questions and to produce tables of the answer to each question analysed by the demographic characteristics of age, gender, class and region, or cross-tabulations of these. In addition to this, specifications may instruct the computer to carry out significance tests on any figures that are considered important. 'Spec. writing' is an important part of the researcher's art and one with which the research user should become involved. Either at the briefing stage, or after the fieldwork has been done, the research user should make it plain exactly what analyses are to be carried out on the data.

Computer programs

The computer now has a set of data and a set of instructions about what to do with the data. The program enables the computer to accept and interpret the specifications, to accept the data and to process them as specified. Computer programs consist of instructions that tell the computer what to do with the data it accepts. They are called software, as opposed to hardware, which refers to the machinery itself. Since most surveys have many analysis requirements in common, standard programs exist that will carry out analysis of research data. These are called software packages, and may involve a number of programs being linked together to do the various things required for all the common types of data analysis. Software packages are written by computer programmers, and some research organizations may contract data processing out to a specialist organization. If this is the case then the research user should be informed, in order to ensure that the briefing requirements for analysis are adequately communicated.

Most analysis packages avoid the need to write analysis programs and even simple statistical packages like Microsoft's Excel allow for sophisticated analysis to be made very simply. Occasionally, for highly complex surveys or where a new technique is to be applied, programmers may be employed. Generally, the use of a skilled analyst and a bespoke statistical package will suffice.

A range of software packages is available to the researcher to help in the design and analysis of questionnaires. Some of these are bespoke market research packages such as Snap; others are statistical analysis packages such as SSPS and SAP. Snap manages the whole process from design to analysis and presentation of results. ConfirmIT does the same for online surveys. A full listing of suppliers is given in the MRS *Research Buyer's Guide,* but some of the best known are covered here.

Web addresses:

www.ssps.com
www.sap.com
Snap software: www.mercator.co.uk/
NUD*IST and NVIVO: www.qsr.com.au
Online surveys: www.confirmit.com

Getting data out

The major output of results from computer data processing is in the form of tables, or 'computer tabulation'. The tables will indicate the numbers of respondents in each category of answers and percentages. This is usually done for the sample as a whole and for various subgroups. Figure 10.2 shows an example of a computer table. Cross-tabulation is also used, in which answers to one question are tabulated against answers to another question. For example, answers to questions about home ownership or renting might be cross-tabulated against DIY purchases. Values on one variable are plotted in one direction and the values of the second variable in the other direction, with totals given as the marginal entries. The variables considered might be any two questions on the questionnaire. The major danger in using tabulation and cross-tabulation as a tool of analysis is in asking for too much printout.

Q.11 When do you think you will purchase this/these item(s) you still need?
Base: all with items still to purchase

		SEX		AGE		SOCIAL CLASS			OPINION OF INFORMATION			REGION	
	TOTAL	MALE	FEMALE	15–44	45+	AB	C1	C2DE	GOOD	AVERAGE	POOR	LONDON/ HME CNTY	OTHER
Base	127	56	71	63	64	74	41	12	109	4	4	48	79
Within the next week	2 2%	2 4%	– –	– –	2 3%	1 1%	1 2%	– –	2 2%	– –	– –	1 2%	1 1%
Within the next fortnight	2 2%	– –	2 3%	1 2%	1 2%	2 3%	– –	– –	2 2%	– –	– –	1 2%	5 6%
Within the next month	7 6%	7 13%	– –	3 5%	4 6%	6 8%	1 2%	– –	7 6%	– –	– –	1 2%	6 8%
Within the next two months	13 10%	8 14%	5 7%	10 16%	3 5%	9 12%	3 7%	1 8%	10 9%	1 25%	1 25%	8 17%	5 6%
Within the next three months	21 17%	9 16%	12 17%	9 14%	12 19%	13 18%	8 20%	– –	17 16%	– –	1 25%	8 17%	13 16%
Within the next six months	34 27%	11 20%	23 32%	18 29%	16 25%	20 27%	12 29%	2 17%	28 26%	1 25%	– –	10 21%	24 30%
Longer ahead	41 32%	15 27%	26 37%	21 33%	20 31%	22 30%	13 32%	6 50%	37 34%	2 50%	1 25%	18 38%	23 29%
Don't know	7 6%	4 7%	3 4%	1 2%	6 9%	1 1%	3 7%	3 25%	6 6%	– –	1 25%	1 2%	6 8%

Figure 10.2 Example of computer analysis

Typically, the new research user will ask for everything tabulated against everything else, and this will result in literally hundreds of pages of computer printout which the user finds impossible to handle.

10.3.3 Statistical analysis

There are three main ways in which statistics are used in the analysis of data: to describe data, to measure its significance and to indicate relationships between sets of data. These are described in the following sections.

Describing data

The purpose of descriptive statistics is to give the user an impression of the location of the data and its spread. The statistics used are frequency, percentage, average and dispersion.

Frequency

The simplest kind of statistical description is a straight frequency count of the number of responses in each category.

For example, 13,337,000 adults drink mineral water in Great Britain. These data can also be represented as a frequency distribution, which shows how frequencies (i.e. numbers in the category) are distributed across a number of categories (in this case, frequency of drinking mineral water). This is shown as a histogram in Figure 10.3.

Percentage

While straight frequency counts are useful to give an idea of the absolute values involved, percentages will indicate what shares of particular markets are concerned, and are useful for making comparisons. In the example in Figure 10.3, the 13.4 million mineral water drinkers in Great Britain were 29.5 per cent of all adults. This is of interest to those involved in the business, particularly when compared with other percentage statistics, such as 47 per cent of buyers bought mineral water because it was natural, and 38 per cent because it was good for them. Information like this can help to frame all kinds of business decisions, from new product development to advertising and promotional messages.

Averages

Averages are a useful device for indicating with just one number roughly where the data as a whole is located.

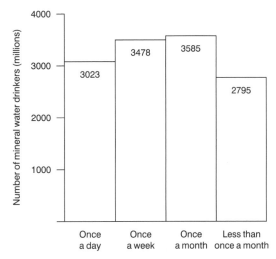

Figure 10.3 Frequency of drinking mineral water. *Source:* Mintel/TGI

> For example, in October 2001 about 77 per cent of homes bought lamb and the average household consumption of lamb was 4.3 kg a year. Multiplying average consumption by the number of households buying lamb will give the total retail market size for lamb in the UK.

The average used in this example is the *arithmetic mean*, which is the most commonly used and colloquially understood measure of average.

Another useful measure of average is called the *mode*. This refers to the most frequently occurring figure. The mode is useful in market studies concerning brand usage, or when it is important to know the most frequently mentioned brand in a brand recall survey.

A less frequently used average is the *median*. This is the middle value when all responses are arranged in order. In considering income, the mean average is likely to be a higher value than the median. This is because the mean will be drawn upwards by very high salaries at the top end of the range, whereas the median will indicate what the middle earner is earning.

Dispersion

Measures of dispersion give more information about the mean because they indicate the range of values around it. In the example above, the mean consumption of lamb was 4.3 kg a year. A measure of dispersion would give an idea of how much variation exists around this figure.

The simplest measure of dispersion is called the *range* and is simply the highest minus the lowest value in the data.

> In the case of lamb consumption, the range was from 0 to 25 kg per year, i.e. the range value was 25 kg. This indicates that if the mean was only 4.3 kg then most meat eaters are not buying very much lamb since the top end of the range is 25 kg. However, it could be that only one household in the sample actually consumed 25 kg of lamb in a year and the next nearest level of consumption was 15 kg. If this were the case then our interpretation about the variety of consumption behaviour would be inaccurate.

To avoid this problem, where the absolute values at each end of the range may be extremely unrepresentative of the actual spread of the data, a standard measure of spread has been calculated. This measure indicates the values within which large proportions of the data lie, and is called the *standard deviation*. The same measure, when calculated from sample data rather than population data, is called the *standard error*. The usefulness of this measure lies in the fact that once it has been calculated it is known that (roughly) 68 of all values lie within 1 standard deviation/standard error of the mean, 95% of all values lie within 2 standard deviations/standard errors of the mean and 99.7% of all values lie within 3 standard deviation/standard errors of the mean. For most business purposes it is common to work at the level of 2 standard deviations/standard errors of the mean, that is, where 95% of all the values lie. In the lamb consumption example, the standard error was 1 kg. This means that 95% of all households consuming lamb were eating between 2.3 and 6.3 kg per year. This gives a much better feeling for average consumption behaviour than either the mean on its own or the use of the range.

Measuring significance

Although there are many advantages to using samples rather than collecting data from the whole population under review, one of the disadvantages is that sample statistics only give an approximation of the population statistics within a given range, called *confidence limits* (see Section 7.5.3). Often the same measure is taken twice from two different samples. This may be from two different samples at the same time, e.g. a comparison between a sample of men and a sample of women; or between similar samples at two different points in time, e.g. recall of a brand at one point in time and again six months later after an advertising campaign. In these circumstances it is important to know whether the two figures could have arisen from the same underlying population or whether any difference in the two figures represents a real change in the state of the underlying population. Is there a real difference between men and women in their usage of or attitudes towards a brand? Has recall of the brand name changed over the test period which would indicate the need for more, less or improved advertising?

Significance tests

Significance tests measure whether the difference between two percentages is significant or not, or whether the difference between two means from different samples is significant. In each case the calculation will indicate whether the difference is significant at a particular level. A statement of significance will appear in the form, 'This figure is significant at the 5% level, or at the 1% level'. The 5% level of significance means that there is only a 1 in 20 chance that two different values could have arisen from the same underlying population. The 1% level of significance indicates that there is only 1 in 100 chance that two different values could have arisen from the same underlying population.

Significance, then, relates to *sampling error.* Sampling error is not the same thing as mistake. Sampling error is the variation possible between two samples drawn from the same population simply because a sample was taken and not a complete census. When only 1000 respondents are selected to represent the views of 19 million households, then however well the sample has been selected the estimate of the figure for the 19 million households will not be exact. Because of this, two different 1000-respondent samples could produce two slightly different estimates of the population parameter of the same population. Measures of significance test whether two different values could have arisen from the same population or whether their values are too far apart to have arisen from sampling error, and therefore represent an actual difference in values.

An important distinction must be drawn between the significance of a value and its importance or relevance. All that significance tests indicate is whether there is a real difference or no real difference between two values. They do not indicate that the difference or lack of difference is of any great importance or significance to the decision maker.

An insurance company carried out a piece of research to measure awareness of the company's name. They used an unaided recall question followed by an aided recall question showing a list of company names. The unaided recall question gave a figure of 3.5 per cent of respondents who spontaneously recalled the company name. Since the company achieved a much higher figure on aided recall, they decided to carry out an advertising campaign to bring their company's name more into the front of the target population's mind.

Six months later, following a £600,000 brand-awareness advertising campaign, the company repeated the piece of research using a similar research methodology. This time unaided recall for the sample was 2 per cent. Immediately, the individual who had commissioned the research became very concerned about significance testing in order to indicate whether the change in levels of recall represented a real fall in awareness following the advertising campaign, or whether both figures could have arisen from an underlying population in which the level of awareness of the company's brand name had not changed.

The significance test showed there was no significant difference between the two figures, i.e. awareness had not fallen during the period of the campaign. However, the important point here, surely, was that the best possible statistical interpretation of the figures was that there had been no change in awareness, yet this followed an expenditure of £600,000 on a campaign with increased awareness as its sole objective. Even without carrying out the significance test the best possible interpretation of the statistical data might still be considered as a measure of the failure of the advertising programme to achieve its objective. Executives in the company concerned, however, were relieved that the results of the significance test indicated no significant difference. They felt that it exonerated them from the even worse position that recall might have actually dropped following their advertising programme!

It has already been pointed out that significance testing is only theoretically relevant for use on simple random sample data. In practice, statistical tests are applied to more complicated random sample designs and to quota samples for which they are not really appropriate. When significance tests are carried out on data from other than simple random samples a *design factor* of 1.5–2 is applied to the standard error used in carrying out further calculations. This has the effect of increasing possible variation in the data and therefore reflects the fact that these samples are thought to be slightly less accurate than simple random samples in producing statistical estimates.

Chi-square

In the same way that significance tests described in the preceding paragraphs measure the significance of the difference between two means or two percentages, there is a statistical significance test that measures whether differences in cross-tabulated data are statistically significant. This is called the *chi-square test*.

For example, purchase of white bread was analysed by social class to indicate any difference in purchase rates among middle-class and working-class households. Since there were different numbers of buyers and non-buyers in the sample, and different numbers of working-class and middle-class households in the sample, inevitably each cell in the table had different values. The problem for the decision maker was to interpret whether those different values represented a real difference. A chi-square test was applied to the data and indicated that working-class households were statistically significantly higher purchasers of white bread.

Since tables are commonly the output of research surveys, a general-purpose computer program used for obtaining cross-tabulations will normally also indicate significance levels for the data in the table.

Measuring statistical relationships

The importance of statistical tests of relationship between variables is that these measures indicate how various factors operating within a market influence and interact with each other. They can indicate how a market *works* by identifying and quantifying cause-and-effect relationships. These make it possible for a decision maker to predict the outcomes of particular actions that *could* be taken, because they indicate which variables influence the marketplace and by how much. Armed with this kind of information the decision maker becomes a far more informed operator in the market. He or she can measure which of the marketing and non-marketing variables have what effects in the marketplace, for example, how sales are affected by changes in price, advertising or average daily temperature. It is at this point that marketing decision making becomes more of a science than an art. These are compelling reasons why any commissioner and user of marketing research data should attempt to understand what measures of relationship a research agency should be asked to provide following a research survey, and should appreciate the importance of their implications for decision making once they are available. As in the preceding paragraphs, this subsection will attempt to explain the meaning of statistical measures of relationship without explaining the statistical formulae.

Correlation analysis

Correlation analysis is a statistical device which measures the degree of relationship in the movement of two sets of variables. This is expressed as a *correlation coefficient*, which can have a maximum value of +1 and a minimum value of −1. Perfect positive correlation between two sets of variables is indicated by +1. That is, if there is a movement of 10 per cent on one variable it is accompanied by a movement of 10 per cent in the same direction on another variable, e.g. when the advertising budget is increased by 10 per cent then sales in the subsequent period also increase by 10 per cent. If this were the case (regrettably it is never that simple) then the resulting correlation coefficient calculated for the two variables would be +1.

Similarly, if the two variables had a perfect relationship but in opposite directions, say for every 10 per cent increase in price, the sales volumes decreased by 10 per cent (equally unlikely), then the correlation coefficient would be −1. When changes in one variable are not associated with changes in the other variable, then the correlation coefficient will be calculated as zero and this indicates no relationship between the two sets of variables.

The usefulness of correlation analysis lies in the fact that it indicates which variables appear to have common sets of movement in the market and the strength of association between them. The value taken as significant depends on the sample size but, as a rule of thumb, correlation coefficients above +0.7 or below −0.7 are generally thought to indicate an increasing degree of association, and therefore to warrant further investigation of the two variables under consideration, for data derived from large samples.

The usual use of correlation analysis in marketing decision making is to attempt to measure the degree of association between those variables that the marketing manager would like to see associated. Correlation coefficients can be calculated for the relationship between company sales volume and variables such as price, level of advertising expenditure, competitive activity, and various consumer variables such as purchase behaviour, income and attitude. Correlation coefficients can also be calculated for variables which, experience suggests, are relevant to sales volume: seasonal factors, economic factors, competitive activity, and so on.

The simplest form of correlation analysis is *bivariate correlation analysis*, in which only two variables are considered. For most practical marketing applications *multiple correlation analysis* is more useful, since it indicates association between three or more sets of variables.

It is important for the user of correlation analysis to remember that the statistical technique will simply indicate that there is a statistical relationship in the movement of two sets of data. From this, the assumption is made that there is a cause-and-effect relationship. If a high degree of statistical correlation is found between the amount of money spent on advertising and sales volume, then it is assumed that the high level of advertising support is resulting in high levels of sales. But the statistical technique does not indicate cause-and-effect relationships, it simply indicates related movements in the data. Whether it is appropriate to consider cause-and-effect depends entirely on the subjective application of the user: if a cause-and-effect relationship appears to make sense then it is assumed to be so, if it does not make sense then it is assumed that the correlation is irrelevant. Inevitably, there are dangers in subjective interpretation and common sense is at least as important as statistical technique in interpreting the results.

Regression analysis

Where correlation analysis is concerned with association, regression analysis is concerned with dependence. That is, if correlation analysis indicates a number of variables that are associated with sales volume, regression analysis makes it possible to predict sales volumes from knowledge about the other variables. This introduces the concept of *dependent* and *independent* variables. Movement in the dependent variables depends on movement in the independent variables. The most commonly used dependent variable in practice is sales volume. The independent variables, on which this may depend, are any of the marketing decision variables such as price, advertising, level of distribution and product quality, and non-marketing external variables such as level of income, changes in the weather, and a whole host of other social and economic variables that may influence sales volume in a particular market. Typically, then, correlation analysis and regression analysis are both carried out on the same set of data. Correlation analysis indicates which variables have a relevant association with sales volume, for example. Regression analysis can then be used to predict sales volume given a set of decisions about marketing variables and assumptions about probable movements in external variables.

The most common use of regression analysis in marketing research is for sales forecasting. Since sales volume is normally dependent on a number of variables, it is more common to use multiple regression analysis than simple bivariate regression analysis. Multiple regression, as with multiple correlation, makes it possible to deal with the effect of a number of variables at once, and therefore to cope with a more realistic analysis of actual market movements.

Multivariate analysis

Multiple correlation and multiple regression analyses form the basis for further complex statistical methods of analysis that can deal with a number of variables at once. These make it possible to cluster respondents who are similar on a number of univariate attributes or to group similar attributes into a smaller number of factors. These techniques are therefore extremely useful in market segmentation studies. They identify and describe market segments, describe and group product attributes, and measure product similarities. The techniques are only briefly introduced here in a non-statistical way. However, readers wishing to obtain the most from the use of quantitative marketing research data should equip themselves with sufficient statistical background to find out more about the use and application of these methods.

Multivariate analysis of data is a highly specialized area requiring thorough statistical knowledge of the range of techniques and their appropriate application. The growth in use of computers for analysis of marketing research data has resulted in the increased use of multivariate analysis, but sometimes in inappropriate ways and on unsuitable data. The purpose of this section introducing the idea of multivariate analysis is simply to indicate that some very useful statistical analytical techniques exist which, if applied in the right way to the right type of data, can provide worthwhile operating knowledge to the marketing decision maker. Research agencies that carry out quantitative research will have statisticians on their staff with whom the possibilities for multivariate analysis applied to a specific problem can be discussed. Four techniques are mentioned here: factor analysis, cluster analysis, multiple discriminant analysis and multi-dimensional scaling.

Factor analysis

This technique reduces a large number of original variables, such as attitude statements, to a smaller number of *factors*. Each factor consists of a group of related statements that form a broad dimension of attitude. In a research survey on television programme assessment, 750 viewers used 58 rating statements to describe 61 different programmes. Factor analysis reduced the 58 statements to nine factors. One factor was called 'information' and contained attitude statements about the degree of scientific interest in the programme, whether it made the viewer think, whether it contained education/information or whether it was meant to entertain. The value of this exercise lay in the fact that 58 possible comments about television programmes were reduced to nine main dimensions of thought, which allow viewers to give a rating to any programme.

Cluster analysis

This technique analyses responses on a large number of variables, for example attitude statements, from a large number of respondents and groups together, or clusters respondents who are similar in the pattern of their responses. Cluster analysis can therefore be used as the basis for identifying segments in the market that exhibit similarities to each other and differences from other clusters in the market. Identification of market clusters and knowledge of the ways in which they are similar can lead to changes in the product or marketing methods used to reach this group.

Multiple discriminant analysis

The objective of this technique is to classify respondents into two or more groups on the basis of a number of items of information about them. Once respondents have been discriminated into one group or another it may become possible to predict or explain their response to a given marketing situation.

The major discriminating factor between shoppers and non-shoppers in a particular department store was found, through discriminant analysis, to be the perceived price level within the store. Subsequent advertising of lower priced lines resulted in an increase in the number of shoppers.

A variant of this technique is called *automatic interaction detection* (AID), and is commonly used for market segmentation studies.

Multidimensional scaling

This technique is used for producing perceptual maps. Consumers rate brands or products by their attributes, by the degree to which brands are seen as similar or by the degree to which one brand of product is preferred to another. These rating questions usually include a rating for the consumer's 'ideal' brand. Multidimensional scaling is applied to the responses, resulting in perceptual maps. An example is shown in Figure 6.3.

These can be used to change product attributes to be nearer the 'ideal' brand, or to suggest advertising messages that will stress the brand attributes nearest to the ideal brand. They indicate the real competitors in a marketplace from the consumer's point of view and so can be used to determine market positioning strategies.

10.4 Interpretation of quantitative data

Interpretation of quantitative research data is an area in which a systematic method of approaching data and a great deal of common sense are the two most useful attributes. The first step is to go through all the tables one by one looking at the statistics. What do the descriptive statistics indicate about the characteristics of the market?

● Frequencies, percentages, averages, dispersion?
● When a difference is seen between two related statistics, is it a significant difference?
● Do men differ from women?
● Older people from younger?
● Users from non-users?
● When there is no difference, is that significant?
● If it is statistically different, will it matter anyway?
● What relationships exist within the data using techniques of correlation and regression?

The purpose of the analysis is to uncover whatever is relevant and significant in the data; for instance, to isolate trends, tendencies or new factors in such things as competition, market structure, consumer habits or external variables. Interpretation should draw out implications of the data for management policy and action in the present and in the future. It should also highlight indicators based on this survey by which to monitor and assess the results of any action proposed. Interpretation of the data should also identify any weaknesses in the database and point these out if real assistance is to be given to the decision maker.

Within the marketing research industry there are two schools of thought about the interpretation of marketing research data. One school suggests that the role of the marketing researcher is simply to collect, analyse and report on the data without drawing interpretation for management policy or action. Only in this way can the researcher's objectivity be preserved and freedom be left for management to act on data as it sees fit. The other school of thought suggests that the researcher who has been involved in deciding what data is to be collected, with its collection and its subsequent analysis, will have developed ideas about the implications of the data for the decision to be made. Those ideas should be transmitted to the research user as recommendations. It is up to the research buyer to indicate at the outset whether or not he or she is looking for guidance on possible action as part of the interpretative process.

10.5 Reporting

The final stage of the marketing research process, from the researcher's point of view, lies in the report. This can take a number of forms. It may be written, and a written report can be either brief comments on tables or a full report. For research data of sufficient significance to the organization, the report may be given in the form of a personal presentation, often using a variety of sophisticated audiovisual devices.

For the research user the form in which the research report is presented has some significance. First, in terms of cost: a full written report is far more expensive than brief comments on tables, since it involves a considerable amount of senior research executive time. For the same reason, a personal presentation by members of the research agency will normally be charged to the client. Whether these additional costs are justified will depend on the type of research, the sophistication of the client in handling research data and the degree of importance attached to the research survey in question.

Research users unfamiliar with research reports, or who may be presented with raw data from a research survey and have to compile their own report, may find the following brief section on research reports useful. It discusses report objectives and suggests a convention for report writing.

10.5.1 The research report

Objectives

The research report has two equally important objectives. The first is to *communicate* the findings and their *significance* to decision makers. This has implications for the layout, style of writing, content and analysis of the data. The second is to gain *acceptance* of the findings. This has implications for the manner in which the report is presented. A short report is more likely to be read and assimilated than a long one. The key elements in a research report are listed below, although variations may be required for specific reports. A concise communication of the nature and outcome of the research programme is contained in Sections 1–5. Sections 6–10 provide the detailed evidence from which conclusions and recommendations are derived.

The research report

1 *Title page*
Lists the title, client, research organization and date.

2 *Executive summary*
A concise summary of the report in no more than one page.

3 *List of contents*
Gives a detailed numbered guide to report sections, followed by a list of graphs and statistical tables.

4 *Preface*
Outline of the agreed research brief, followed by a statement of objectives, scope and methods of research undertaken.

5 *Summary of conclusions/recommendations*
Summary of main findings, sometimes accompanied by some creative interpretation in the form of recommendations.

6 *Previous related research*
It is sometimes useful to show how previous knowledge may have had a bearing on the research undertaken.

7 *Research method*
Procedures used to collect information. Where, how and from whom, and techniques used in analysis. The characteristics and size of samples should be recorded.

8 *Research findings*
The main body of the report commenting on the findings in detail. Emphasis should be on ease of understanding and logical presentation for the reader.

9 *Conclusions and recommendations*
Even though the findings may speak for themselves, it is helpful to bring them together in a conclusion related to the terms of reference stated in the Preface.

10 *Appendices*
Any detailed or technical matter that is essential to a full understanding of the research report, e.g. a copy of the questionnaire.

Whether the findings of a research report are read, noted and acted upon should properly be a concern of the individual commissioning the research.

If the findings are of such significance that the power to implement any recommendations lies outside that individual's area of authority, then it is a useful device to call a meeting of appropriate personnel to receive and consider the main findings of a research study. This ensures that the findings can be effectively communicated, and that they will be considered and action decided upon as part of the agenda of the meeting.

If report findings are not noted and acted upon, then the whole research procedure represents an area of wasted resources for the organization and the position of research expenditure within the organization must be questioned.

10.6 Summary

Analysis and interpretation of qualitative data are subjective and impressionistic. They are usually carried out by the individual who conducted the fieldwork, and the report contains direct quotes from respondents. Analysis of quantitative data involves the process of data preparation, data processing, computer and statistical analysis, and interpretation. Each of these is discussed and statistical procedures for analysis are described. The chapter concludes with a brief section on reporting research findings.

11 How do you buy good research?

11.1 Introduction

'Good' research is research which produces findings that are directly useful to the manager and contribute to better decision making. The research answers the questions it was designed to answer and those questions were directly relevant to the problem. The research design was appropriate and it was well conducted, analysed and reported.

The art of buying good research is very much like buying anything else. The buyer who knows why research is needed, what is needed, what it will be used for, when it is needed by and what cost represents value for money is more likely to make a good buy. It also makes sense to shop around to find a good supplier, and having found one to check that they are doing a good job. After the event one can learn from experience and so get better still at buying good research in the future. This chapter suggests a systematic approach to buying research, which should increase the chances of making a good buy when commissioning an agency to carry out 'made-to-measure' research surveys. It also looks briefly at buying 'off-the-peg' syndicated services, and at judging how good, and therefore reliable, a piece of research is when one is presented with the report without having been involved in commissioning the survey.

11.2 Getting the research requirement right

It is very easy to waste money on research that is interesting rather than necessary. The difference lies in having a clear idea of why the research is needed, what research is required, what it will be used for, when it is needed by and how much should be spent on it. Working out the answers to these questions will clarify the research requirement and form the basis for a good research brief.

11.2.1 Is research really necessary?

It is just as important to know when not to use research as to know when it should be used. Almost all research is of some value to an organization, even if only at the level of general interest. It is all too easy for the manager facing a decision to decide that research will help in making a better decision without really thinking it through. 'What would happen if the research were not carried out?' is the most basic, yet most challenging and most often overlooked question. It involves analysing the action alternatives available, and may highlight the fact that with or without research the options are so limited that research cannot materially influence any subsequent action by the organization. It is also possible that the manager will discover that the organization is already fairly heavily committed to what it wants to do and the moment for decision-making research has effectively already passed. In that case, it would be more efficient to decide not to carry out a research programme, however desirable it may seem. Research may also be unnecessary if the costs or risk involved in taking action are small. The only research that should survive this question is that which can be clearly identified as being essential for the organization because it is relevant to an important, costly or high-risk decision and has the power to influence its outcome.

11.2.2 What type of research is needed?

As with a lamp-post to a drunken man, research can be used in two ways: for illumination or for support. The type of research needed will be affected by the purpose for which it is used. A decision maker may want research in order to generate new ideas or to help in understanding a situation better. In this case, research is being used for illumination and qualitative research would be most appropriate, often before undertaking a quantitative study. Using research for support implies the need for some factual base on which to rest a decision, and usually indicates quantitative research.

It may be that the organization is considering entering a new field of operation in which it is unfamiliar, or dealing with a new group of customers whose requirements are unknown. In these examples the most appropriate research approach is an exploratory study. More commonly, an organization may wish to make decisions in an area in which it is already familiar, but where some market data is necessary to direct the decision to be made. For this purpose descriptive information will be most useful: a descriptive profile of customers in terms of age, gender, social group, geographical location, and so on. A third possibility is the organization that has been operating in its market for some years and now wishes to understand more about cause-and-effect relationships in its markets. In this case the requirement will be for causal research, using experimental approaches to uncover the relevant variables in the marketplace and measure the ways in which they influence it. Analysing the purpose for which the research is required will suggest the type of research needed: qualitative or quantitative, exploratory, descriptive or causal.

11.2.3 What will the research be used for?

The particular reason for which research will be used and who will be using it, are also relevant in deciding the type of research required. A manager deciding which new products to introduce may be at the early stage of the new product-development process looking for possible new product ideas. In this case, qualitative research methods will be useful. When the new product idea is farther along the development process, the decision to be made is a quantitative one about production and distribution levels. This will require a large-scale research survey producing hard, quantitative data.

For the creative team deciding what message to use in a new advertising campaign there are also two possibilities. A range of ideas for them to work on may be generated by group discussions, and the same method could be used to test the initial response to creative ideas. A decision about what kind of background to use in advertisement illustrations, or what kind of activities to show individuals in an advertisement being engaged in, could come from quantitative research. Large-scale surveys would show the kinds of activity in which members of the target audience are most likely to be involved, and these can be used in advertising.

11.2.4 When is the research needed by?

Most business decisions have deadlines and this should be taken into account before any research is undertaken, to allow for the fact that some research methods take longer to complete than others. However good a piece of research may be, if its findings are produced after the deadline for the decision, then the whole exercise has been a waste of time and money. The decision deadline may mean that the most appropriate research method cannot be completed in the time available. If so, a choice must be made between delaying the decision until the research findings are available, carrying out no research at all, or deciding that a less than ideal method of search can be used within the time-scale and still be valid for the purposes of the decision. The most common mistake made in this situation is to carry out rushed research and then not allow for this in using the findings.

11.2.5 How much is the research information worth?

Gathering information is a costly procedure and so some attempt at evaluating the worth of the information needs to be carried out before deciding on the level of research expenditure. Common sense indicates that there is no point in spending more money on marketing research than the costs of making a wrong decision and so an attempt must be made to estimate the costs of the decision.

Sometimes this is easy. If a new product is to be launched then the costs of this include all the development costs associated with the product plus the marketing costs associated with its launch. This generally indicates a large cost and is therefore a rationale for considering an expensive research programme. It is more difficult when a decision concerns whether to use one message or another in an advertising campaign. In this case the costs of a wrong decision are extremely hard to quantify, as are the costs of making a right decision.

One approach for deciding how much research information is worth is simply to take a subjective view which attempts to relate the overall amount involved in the project costs to the amount to be set aside for research.

Marketing research expenditure can be looked upon rather like insurance, in that its aim is to reduce risk. Its value is therefore related to the level of risk likely to be incurred: the higher the level of risk then the higher the level of research expenditure appropriate to guard against that risk. In assessing the value of research information most people operate at this subjective and intuitive level. However, some more formal devices offer a framework for putting a monetary value on information costs.

One technique uses theoretical calculations of expected profit from the project with and without availability of prior research information. The basic assumption of the technique is that research information increases the certainty of a particular outcome being achieved and the outcome can be evaluated in terms of expected profit. Expected profit without the benefits of research information is likely to be less than the expected profit after buying research information. The difference in the two calculations puts a monetary value on the reduction of uncertainty produced by the research findings. The implication is that research is worth the difference in monetary values and therefore a research project costing up to that amount would represent a worthwhile investment for the organization.

This technique requires the decision maker to quantify subjective assessments of possible outcome, i.e. to quantify factors that might otherwise be called 'hunches' or 'intuition', or simply 'experience'. This is an advantage because it allows other members of the organization to evaluate and perhaps challenge what might otherwise remain as implicit decision-making processes. The disadvantage of this technique is that it gives a superficial air of elegance and sophistication to what is, in effect, guesswork. However, it does form a useful framework for those who would simply like to work out the numbers as just one way of estimating how much to spend on research. A simplified version of the calculation is shown below.

A manufacturer wishes to decide whether to improve the quality of its product. The improved product will cost more, but it is likely that sales and profitability will increase. If sales increase by 25 per cent, then the product's contribution to profit will increase by £100,000. The manufacturer therefore needs to assess the chances of achieving that 25 per cent sales increase. In a meeting, the experienced senior management team is asked to assess subjectively the probability of achieving the sales increase, i.e. to make a joint 'guesstimate'. The outcome of the meeting is that the management team assesses the probability of achieving the sales increase at 0.4. Expected profit can therefore be calculated at: £100,000 (profit estimate) × 0.4 (chance of making it) = £40,000. However, the company has used research in the past to assist in making sales forecasts, and in its experience has found that, if a particular value is forecast by research then there is a 75 per cent probability of the value being achieved. In this case, then, if the research forecasts a sales increase of 25 per cent, then the probability of its being achieved would be 0.75. Expected profit following the research can therefore be calculated at: £100,000 (profit estimate) × 0.75 (chance of making it, following research) = £75,000.

This calculation indicates that expected profit after research is £35,000 greater than expected profit before research and assumes (oversimplistically) that the sales increase would be maintained for only one year. A research programme costing less than £35,000 would therefore be a worthwhile undertaking, i.e. what this reduction in uncertainty is 'worth'. The two factors in the equation are the value of the decision outcome (in this case profit) and the degree of certainty with which that outcome can be anticipated without conducting research. The higher the outcome value and the higher the level of uncertainty within the organization about achieving it, then the greater the need for, and worth of, research.

11.3 Preparing the brief

Armed with answers to the question posed in the previous section, the decision maker must produce a specific written definition of the research requirements. This forms the basis for briefing the research agency, so the clearer and the more specific it is, the better able the agency will be to meet the needs identified.

Preparing the brief will involve a consideration of the environment in which the decision is to be made and the resources available. It is usually helpful at this stage to involve other managers within the organization. The aim should be to agree the objectives for the research programme, and these should be distinguished from marketing objectives. An adhesives manufacturer with the marketing objective of attracting new users to a product set the research objective 'to identify groups who might have a use for the product and the attributes which appeal to them most'.

The second point to agree internally is the limitations of the research programme. What is it reasonable to expect the research to accomplish? Research does not make decisions for managers, it gives them more information to enable them to make better decisions. For example, research cannot directly predict the sales of a new product. What it can do is to measure the new product's acceptability, performance in blind trials against competitive products, and so on. Increasing use of research in mathematical market modelling is, however, improving predictive ability and is a major area of current development.

A third point for internal agreement is the action standards required of the research programme. Research prior to the launch of a new product may measure factors such as rate of trial, intent to purchase or preference. In these cases it is necessary to decide beforehand what figures will be acceptable for the launch to go ahead. A chocolate manufacturer sets a minimum score of 40 per cent preference for the launch decision to be taken. The reason for deciding action standards prior to the research programme is that if these are left until later it is always possible to persuade oneself that the results are good enough, whereas before the research is carried out a greater degree of objectivity is possible in determining what requirements must be met for the project to go ahead.

Internal agreement on all these points in the course of preparing the brief will ensure that the eventual research programme takes account of all essential information needs. This is generally better decided by a group than by an individual. The other reason for obtaining internal agreement at this stage is that organizations that hold their first meeting about proposed research projects with would-be research agencies in attendance may find themselves disagreeing about what exactly is required. Apart from presenting a poor view of the organization to the research agency before any working relationship has been established, this will probably result in a very poor brief being given.

Confusion and lack of clarity in the brief tend to produce confusing and unclear research. Adequate time and thought must be given to this process of preparing the brief before any research agencies are approached. The outcome of the process should be a clear definition of the research requirement committed to paper and approved by all appropriate people within the organization.

11.4 Choosing the right agency

11.4.1 Drawing up the shortlist

The first step in buying research from an outside agency is to draw up a shortlist of agencies that might be appropriate. A set of guidelines for doing this is outlined in Section 9.6.1. The same rules apply here.

A good starting point is to obtain the Market Research Society's booklet *The Research Buyer's Guide*. The details given in this make it possible to match the agency to the job: large job, large agency; small job, small agency; industrial job, industrial agency, etc. The booklet also identifies agencies with appropriate specialist services, e.g. in travel and tourism, motoring research, industrial research and financial research. Another useful source is to ask colleagues, friends and business acquaintances to recommend agencies with whom they have had good experience. From this selection procedure a shortlist of two or three agencies should be drawn up and a meeting arranged to discuss the research.

11.4.2 Briefing the agencies

The purpose of a briefing is to enable the research organization that will carry out the research to know exactly what it is required to do. The brief should contain all that is necessary to accomplish this. The following suggestions come 'straight from the horse's mouth', having been made by the managing director of one of the largest and most successful research agencies in the UK. He suggests that the research brief should contain the following.

Background and objectives of the research

This section should indicate to the agency why the research is being carried out, the competitive situation of the product concerned, any preconceptions that the organization may have about possible outcomes of the research and as much relevant information about the history of the product as it is possible to provide. The research organization can draw more useful conclusions from their interpretation of the research material if they have a thorough understanding of the background to the product situation.

Data on the relevant population group

If the population group of interest is entirely male it makes sense to tell the agency, because that will prevent them wasting research money on collecting data from females. The same thing holds for age, occupation, interest, industry, service or any other specific group. It is also helpful to give an indication of the probable rate of occurrence of the population group of interest, as this will affect the sampling method used.

A car component manufacturer wanted to learn more about the growing phenomenon of motorists who have their cars serviced at home by someone else. In particular, the component manufacturer wanted to know where these individuals who service other people's cars obtain the spare parts they need. It was known that some of the people carrying on this trade did so openly, but many more did this kind of work on an 'unofficial' basis. The manufacturer suspected that they accounted for something like one-tenth of all servicing done. If so, they would represent a useful source of business if some method of distributing parts into this unofficial trade could be devised. The first step was to undertake a research survey to confirm the number of people who had their cars serviced in this way and learn more about it. By indicating to the research agency their suspicion that this represented approximately 1 in 10 of all motor car owners, the agency knew that to generate a sample of 500 relevant respondents it would be necessary to contact 5000 motorists. This would mean a more time-consuming and expensive

> sample identification procedure than would be necessary, say, for the manufacturer of a food product used by 80 per cent of all households. In this case, to generate a sample of 500 respondents only 625 would need to be contacted in the first place.

Receiving as much information as is available about the characteristics and occurrence of the target group will enable the agency to suggest the most appropriate method for contacting the sample, and to be more precise in estimating the cost of doing so.

The type of research envisaged

The agency should be informed about the thinking that has gone into suggesting the kind of research that might be required. If it is felt internally that the most appropriate kind of data would be qualitative, perhaps involving group discussions, then the agency should be told this. If a quantitative decision, based on hard data, is to be made then a quantitative survey will be needed and the agency should be informed. This will guide them in deciding on an appropriate sample size. It is likely that the research buyer is looking for the agency's advice on the most appropriate type of research for the problem and it is perfectly reasonable to expect this. Any agency worth its salt will tell a client if they believe an inappropriate type of research is being suggested. However, it also makes sense to give the agency clues as to the sort of work that is being expected from them. This will avoid the aggravation of receiving a detailed proposal from the research agency for a major survey when all the client really wanted was a few group discussions.

The question areas to be covered

The agency will do a better job the more specific the client is about exactly what is required. This can be accomplished by indicating in some detail the question areas to be covered. This does not mean writing a questionnaire, because that is part of the expertise for which the agency is needed. A detailed list of question areas identifies for the agency exactly what it is required to find out about. It is their responsibility to obtain answers to the questions in as technically correct a manner as they can. It is the commissioner's responsibility to ensure that the agency is adequately briefed about the areas of questioning to be used.

A realistic timetable

In briefing a research agency it is essential to indicate the date by which answers are required. This has implications for the type of method that can be used and for the factors that the agency will need to take into account in planning its fieldwork programme. The first date to be included in the timetable will be an indication of by when the research proposal is required. This will be followed by the amount of time available for research from the date on which the research is commissioned. Research agency experience shows that clients are at least as likely as agencies to create delays in the research timetable, either by taking too long to decide to commission the survey or by taking too long to agree the questionnaire. Any such delays reduce the time available for carrying out the research. Giving an agency an impossible deadline by which to complete a research survey is bound to produce poor work. As in any other area, rushed work is likely to suffer from lack of attention to detail and general inaccuracy. The commissioning organization should be sure that it is able to meet any obligations required by the timetable; for example, if a product test is under consideration it must be able to produce the product for test in the quantities required and by the dates specified.

An invitation to discuss the research

A research brief, particularly for a new, important, unusual or complicated survey, should always include an invitation to the research agency to discuss the research. During these discussions the research agency will ask questions to clarify all the points they need to know to carry out a good job. The discussion will be useful in identifying different, and perhaps more effective or cheaper ways of undertaking the research than those which occurred to the client. Discussions with research agencies will be especially helpful to those organizations who have not used a great deal of research in the past. They will learn whether their original written brief has proved adequate in communicating to the research agency exactly what is required. From the questions asked by the agency personnel, the client will learn more about technical problems that may arise and more about what the research will be able to produce in the way of answers to questions. During these discussions the original brief will probably be improved upon. A revised brief should be written, including any changes that have taken place.

The less familiar the client is with research, the more time should be devoted personally to enabling the agency to brief itself through comprehensive discussions with the client. At the conclusion of these discussions it is important for both parties to agree in writing exactly what it is the agency is being asked to do. Client–agency discussions are useful not only in producing a good final brief, but also in giving the client an extended opportunity to assess the ability of the personnel from the research agency to understand the requirements. These discussions are the basis for any subsequent working relationship and from them it should be possible to determine whether the client and the agency personnel are on each other's wavelength. It is important to ensure that good two-way communication can be established at this stage. If the client does not feel that the agency has a clear idea of what is expected of it, then it is quite probable that the work produced will give only approximate answers to the questions set.

In discussions with agency personnel the overriding principles, particularly for the new research user, should be to provide as much relevant marketing information as is available and to be as technically specific about the survey as possible.

The budget

There is some disagreement about whether or not the budget available for the research programme should be disclosed to the research agency at the briefing stage. The argument for disclosing the budget available is that the type and scale of research that can be carried out is clearly limited by its size. If the agency does not know what this working limit is, then it may well produce a proposal that is rejected simply because it cannot be carried out within the budget available. This is a waste of time for both parties to the exercise. The argument against disclosing the size of the research budget is that if the agency knows how much money there is to be spent then they will find a way of spending it.

On balance, the authors believe that the weight of the arguments lies in favour of giving some indication of the funds available to the research agency before a proposal is received from them. This avoids the time-wasting exercise of the agency producing an inappropriate scale of research to that envisaged. Sufficient protection is available from an agency being tempted to do an unnecessarily large and expensive survey by the fact that three agencies will be invited to submit proposals. If the agencies know of this competitive element in the situation then they are not likely to produce a proposal that is certain to lose them the job on cost grounds.

11.4.3 The research proposal

Having briefed three research agencies, what can be expected from them by way of a research proposal? In the first instance, the proposal should arrive by the agreed deadline. The proposal should be in writing, so that it is absolutely clear both to the client and to the agency what is being promised. It should demonstrate that the quoting agency has a good understanding of the problem. Most importantly, the research proposal should be a detailed specification of exactly what the agency is planning to do for the money it is asking.

In general, it is unreasonable to expect that the research agency will have done a great deal of work on the problem at this stage, because they do not know whether or not they are going to get the job. However, if the agency is worth its salt (and the client's money) it should have put in enough work to demonstrate in the proposal that it is quite clear about what is expected and is competent to deliver that efficiently.

It is not usual for agencies to charge clients for producing research proposals, but members of the British Market Research Association (BMRA) have a policy of asking clients how many agencies are being asked to write proposals. If it is more than three agencies then BMRA members may charge the offending organizations for each proposal produced. This is an attempt to control the activities of client companies who waste time and money by asking for an unreasonably large number of research proposals as a means of obtaining free research advice.

What points should be looked for in a research agency's proposal?

Statement of objectives

The first thing to look for is a clearly defined statement of the objectives for the survey. They should reflect those agreed as a result of the briefing procedure and be no more and no less than required by the client. The objectives should be checked for their relevance to the needs of the problem.

Description of how the research will be done

The sample

The proposal should contain a precise and relevant definition of the sample to be selected. It should explain the method to be used in selecting the sample and indicate the size of sample to be used, with reasons for this.

The fieldwork

The proposal should indicate clearly the research method to be used: group discussions, personal interviews, telephone research, postal research, and so on. It should indicate how the fieldwork is to be organized, and how the quality of the fieldwork is to be controlled and checked. This section will also be used to indicate whether the agency is a member of the Interviewer Quality Control Scheme (IQCS). If so, this can be taken as an indicator of the quality standards maintained by the company concerned. If not, this does not necessarily indicate poor quality of fieldwork, but the client must make a personal judgement of this.

The questionnaire

It would be unreasonable to expect to see a final questionnaire included in the research proposal. What should be shown are comments indicating what the agency believes should be included in the questionnaire. This will be partly as a result of the briefing they received and partly as a result of their own analysis of the requirements of the problem. There will be suggestions from the agency as to what topics might be included and what type of question might be used. There should also be an indication of the expected length of the questionnaire and its composition.

Data handling

For a quantitative survey, the proposals should contain details of the work to be undertaken in editing, coding and processing the data produced. If tables are to be produced then the proposal should indicate how many tables there will be and whether any cross-tabulation is to be produced. For a qualitative survey, an indication should be given of how the data produced will be handled. Will the tapes be transcribed, or will analysis be conducted straight from the original tapes by the moderator?

Reporting

Proposals should make it clear whether or not a written report is included in the costs. This is particularly important nowadays, since, for a large report on an important survey written by a senior research executive, it is not unusual for a substantial charge to be made. Often a full report is not required, particularly by a client who is a regular user of research and perfectly able to write the report personally. If a report is included in the cost then the number of copies to be provided should be shown. This may seem a trivial point, but faced with a large report it can be very irritating and time-consuming to have to run off additional copies. It is as well to have these matters clearly specified from the outset.

The proposal should also show whether a verbal presentation of the results will be made. If a personal presentation is required this will be costed to cover the time and preparation for presentation required of agency personnel.

Research timetable

The proposal should contain a detailed schedule of start dates for each phase of the research procedure. From the date of commissioning, when will the draft questionnaire be produced? When will fieldwork begin and end? When will data processing begin? When will top-line results be available? When will the final report and verbal presentation, if these are included, be available?

The timetable should be one that the research agency can reasonably be expected to meet and that the commissioning organization can also meet for its input into the research procedure. If the timetable allows one week for approval of the questionnaire, then is the client company able to involve all those who need to be involved and reach agreement within five working days? If the product is required in special packaging for testing, is it feasible that the amount required in the test packaging can be produced by the date indicated?

Costs

The proposal should give a clear indication of the cost of the research being proposed and of how those costs are derived. When comparing costs of a number of different proposals against each other, the cost-related assumptions should be checked. Is the length suggested for the questionnaire reasonable for the data required of it? If a 10-minute questionnaire is indicated in the research proposal and the questionnaire finally approved turns out to be 20 minutes long, then additional costs will be incurred. If the number of tabulations indicated in the proposal turns out to have been unrealistic and further tabulations are required, then once again additional costs will be incurred.

Are the costs all-inclusive? Check whether or not a report with the number of copies required and a verbal presentation are included in or excluded from the cost quoted. Is VAT included or an extra? For how long is the proposal cost valid? It is unusual for a research agency to offer open-ended cost proposals. Like all other businesses, research agencies' costs rise, so it is unreasonable to expect the price to remain the same for a research proposal quoted in one year and commissioned in the next.

Justification

As shown in the foregoing sections, the research proposal is a detailed specification of exactly what the research agency proposes should be done to solve the research problem. This specification of the research method should be accompanied by an explanation and discussion of what is proposed and why.

Questions that should be answered in the agency's proposal include:

- Why the sample selection procedure indicated?
- Why the size of sample indicated?
- Why the personal interview technique rather than group discussion?
- Why a 20-minute questionnaire and not a 30-minute questionnaire?
- Why are open-ended questions requiring expensive coding and analysis being included in a large-scale quantitative survey?
- Why is a written report or verbal presentation included, or why not?
- Why the timetable indicated?
- Why the cost indicated?

At each stage of the research proposal, the agency should make clear why they are proposing what they are proposing, and the client should find their arguments convincing.

Supporting evidence

It is sometimes useful to be aware of any evidence the agency may have in support of their particular qualifications to undertake the research. For example, they may have particular experience in this marketing area. The problem may be to do with new product development and the agency is particularly well known for the quality of its new product development studies. It could be an advertising problem and the agency is particularly well known for its expertise in the area of advertising research, and so on.

The agency may have particular experience of the kind of techniques involved. Perhaps the research problem demands the application of complicated scaling exercises. It would be reassuring to know that the agency, or more particularly its interviewers, are well practised in the use of these techniques and will not be experimenting with a new and complicated system on this survey.

It is sometimes helpful to read brief and relevant curriculum vitae of the personnel who will be working on the research project and involved in the day-to-day matters of organizing and controlling it. This is particularly so when agency personnel have relevant industry experience. A point to note here, as with most service agencies, is which personnel will actually be working on the job, as opposed to those who have been involved in selling it. A good job is more likely to be done if the people involved in the day-to-day running of the research have also been involved in the briefings and proposals.

Points to watch

In assessing the research proposal it is wisest to assume that anything not specified will not be provided or will have to be paid for in addition. For example, if no mention is made of a report or a verbal presentation, then assume that these will have to be paid for, if required. Check every point of assumption about what will be provided and ask the agency quite specifically whether or not it is included in the costing.

Beware of vagueness in a research proposal. If the proposal does not make it quite clear exactly what is going to be done, why it is going to be done, who is going to do it, and when they are going to do it by, then assume that the agency itself is not perfectly clear on these points, otherwise they would have communicated the information. Beware, too, of research mumbo-jumbo. The point of a research proposal is to explain to clients what they are getting for their money. Research jargon and techniques can be used to confuse and impress clients rather than to explain and reassure them of the agency's ability to answer their questions. Suspect that the agency will be no more concerned to make the findings clear than it is to make its proposals clear. So, if the proposals are not given straightforward explanations where necessary, another agency should be selected.

11.4.4 Selecting the research agency

It will be clear from the preceding section of this chapter that a fair amount of contact with all the research agencies invited to produce proposals will already have taken place. Also, if research proposals are produced in the form suggested in Section 11.4.3, then there should be a good basis for comparison, although not necessarily a straightforward one. There are several points to take into account when deciding which agency should be given the job. As with buying most things, the cheapest is not necessarily the best. Five criteria for determining which agency to award the job to are considered.

Approach

An assessment should be made of the agencies' approaches to solving the problem:

- Have they been imaginative or creative?
- Have they followed precisely the brief given to them?
- Have they improved on it?
- Is the approach the one that the agencies were instructed to take and, if not, have they given convincing reasons for changing it?
- If three different agencies have been asked to quote and three different approaches to solving the problems have turned up in the proposals, then which approach seems most likely to produce a good and cost-effective answer to the problem?

Perceived quality

As in buying any service, it is impossible to test the quality, measure the length or feel the width before agreeing to purchase. However, some clues as to the potential quality of the services to be offered are provided by the proposal and by contact with the agency personnel:

- Do the agency personnel seem to know what they are talking about?
- How many interviews are you being offered for your money?
- Does the organization's fieldwork impress you with its adequacy and efficiency?
- Is the company a member of the IQCS?
- What proportion of quality checkbacks is done on the fieldwork?
- Does the procedure for handling the data appear to be efficient and well-organized?
- Was the proposal itself a good-quality piece of work?

Relevant expertise

- Did the agency produce any convincing evidence to support their particular suitability for the work?
- Do they have relevant expertise?
- How many years of appropriate research or marketing experience do they have?
- Have their fieldworkers used the sampling and questionnaire techniques before?
- Have their data processors used the statistical techniques before?

Communication

This is a most important aspect of determining which agency to select. If the proposal is well explained then it is likely that the final report will be. If the agency personnel have clearly demonstrated their understanding of the problem, then it is likely that they will produce a sensible answer to it. The client should feel 'on the same wavelength' as the agency personnel. If the client and the agency personnel have communicated easily over briefing and proposals then it is likely that they will work effectively together in handling any problems that may arise during the research. Feeling that a particular group will be the right people for the job should not be underestimated as a criterion for awarding the job to them.

Cost

Now to tackle this most important criterion in deciding from which agency to buy the research. How useful is cost as an indicator of good value? As will be seen from the foregoing points it is important to check any differences in the cost-associated variables, such as sample definition, size of sample, number of interviewing points, length of interview, composition of questionnaire, number of open-ended questions included, data processing techniques to be applied, and provision of a written or verbal report. Differences in these variables will naturally lead to differences in cost. What then has to be decided is the extent to which differences in the variables are justified by the quality of research required. That depends on the importance of the problem and can only be judged by the individual commissioning the research.

There are two circumstances in which it may make good sense to go for the cheapest research proposal. The first is when the research brief is tight, i.e. when the research agency has no discretion over the cost-associated variables. All agencies are quoting to exactly the same specification and hence the only variation will be in cost. The second case is when the research agencies are in a competitive business situation. There are times of the year, and some years, when research work is comparatively scarce. Since the major area of cost for research agencies is their personnel, if these are relatively underemployed they represent a very high level of fixed cost. This can best be defrayed by offering research 'bargains' when the agency is short of work. If a comparison of cost-associated variables indicates no real reason for variations in cost, and yet variations exist, then suspect that one agency is pricing high. It probably already has sufficient work and additional work will impose an extra burden of cost. The agency therefore feels that the client adding to their costs should pay for them. A research agency pricing low is signalling that it wants the job, and providing all the other criteria are satisfied, then it makes sense to respond to that signal.

The commissioning letter

Using the criteria outlined in this section, one of the agencies invited to submit a research proposal will be judged as most capable of producing research of an acceptably high standard at an acceptable cost. When the selection has been made, the research buyer should write a commissioning letter, authorizing the agency to begin the work, and restating all the points of agreement. This letter then provides the basic specification for the work and its costs, by which both parties to the agreement are bound. The importance of ensuring that a detailed commissioning letter is written occurs when the actual research design and costs agreed on differ from both the original research brief and the agency's original research proposal. At some stage an agreed set of rules for the conduct of the research must be laid down to govern the content of the research programme, and to avoid the possibility of later disagreement over exactly what the rules were.

11.5 Checking that the agency does a good job

Having agreed to buy the research, the buyer will want to achieve good value for the organization's money. There are two stages to checking the quality of research bought. The first is monitoring during the progress of the research programme, and the second is evaluation when the final results are delivered. It should be emphasized that, if the research has been bought in the manner suggested in this chapter, then the evaluation of its quality should be straightforward and the risk of poor-quality research low. Choosing the right agency in the first place is the best way to get a good job done.

11.5.1 Monitoring while in progress

Questionnaire and fieldwork

Once the research is in progress it becomes the responsibility of the research agency. However, the wise buyer will keep informed. The first opportunity occurs when the questionnaire arrives for approval.

- Does it arrive in the time allowed for this in the research timetable?
- Has it been piloted?
- How satisfactory does it seem to be generally?

Arrival of the draft questionnaire for approval is also the first opportunity the agency has for working with its new client.

- Do they introduce delays by taking too long to approve the questionnaire?
- Do they suddenly decide to introduce different topics from those agreed in the final brief?

For an effective working relationship to develop, both parties to the research should keep to the agreements laid down in the commissioning letter.

A second opportunity to monitor the research in progress arises at the fieldwork stage. The buyer should ask to spend the day with one of the interviewers, and should personally suggest the day and area to be used, rather than allow the agency to select its best interviewer. Particularly for the new research user, this experience gives great insight to and understanding of the real situation in which the questionnaire is applied and how consumers respond to it. This greatly enhances the client's understanding of the final research report when it is presented, and the insights gained are likely to influence the quality of the client's interpretation of the data and use of the findings.

Data preparation and processing

It is useful to discuss data preparation and processing with the agency after the fieldwork has been completed and before data preparation and processing begin. This will ensure that any modification that it would be sensible to implement as a result of discoveries made during the fieldwork can be applied and agreed. It can also be helpful from the agency's point of view. A discussion at this stage can be useful in deciding code frames and will focus on what might be useful in terms of analysis and emphasis in the final report. This will lead to a more useful report being presented to the client.

Timing

A simple way of monitoring research in progress is to check that timings agreed are adhered to. This will indicate whether the agency has been able to meet the objectives that it set for itself in its proposal, in the time-scales that it designed for itself in the same document. If nothing else, it indicates something about the agency's realism and efficiency.

11.5.2 Evaluating the final results

Once the final results have been delivered, there are several indicators as to the quality of the research.

Was the research to specification?

The importance of a detailed research proposal being agreed and confirmed in writing in the commissioning letter has already been emphasized. Since this commissioning letter contained the agreed specification for the research, it can be used to check that the research was to specification. The technical aspects of the survey should be checked: sample, definition, method of selection, size, interviewing method, organization, questionnaires, data handling procedures, and so on. Are the tabulations as agreed, with the correct number of tables and the correct cross-tabulations? Is the report as agreed, with the number of copies required?

Fieldwork quality checks

If a quantitative survey has been undertaken then the research agency will have indicated in its specification the percentage of backchecks to be done. 'Backchecks' is the term used by researchers to refer to the fieldwork quality-control checks described in Section 9.5.1. The client could ask to see the backcheck results of the survey. This will give an indication of the quality of the fieldwork undertaken.

Tabulations

Nowadays, tabulations are likely to be copies of computer printouts and this can create problems. Check that the tabulations are legible, simply from the point of view of print quality. Check that they are comprehensible. Original tabulations are likely to have abbreviated headings which may not be immediately understandable. It is important that either a key to the headings is provided or the headings are shown typed in full. If a large number of computer tabulations is included with the report it is helpful if these are indexed. Reams of computer printout with no clear means of identifying the answers to one question from the answers to another are of little help to the report user.

The report

A written report provides an important indicator of the quality of the research, since it gives clues to the clarity of the researcher's mind. The first thing to check is whether the findings have been presented in a logical order, i.e. not necessarily in the order that questions come off the questionnaire. A logical order is one in which the report either presents relevant data and draws conclusions from it, or draws conclusions and offers supporting data for them. Topics will be sequenced in such a way that the report draws the reader along a well-structured argument to the point of conviction. A jumble of ill-organized facts is not an indicator of good-quality research. The report should be clear and readable and written in good English. It should include a meaningful summary, and should reach sensible and well-argued conclusions, if appropriate.

The research buyer must be convinced that something sensible was specifically asked for, that the result represents good value for money and that it is of good quality. This will give them more confidence in relying on and using the results.

11.6 Learning from experience

Even research that has been done to specification, and in which the agency did all that could be reasonably expected of it, may not turn out to be good research. Good research is that which influences a decision to be better than it would have been without research. This can only be judged after the event. To become an intelligent and informed research user, taking the time to learn from experience is very worthwhile. The following questions can help the user to do this.

11.6.1 Were the objectives right?

A common fault of research is that the objectives were not defined with sufficient precision. This results in a research report which, although interesting, turns out to have no real practical value. The more precisely the objectives can be defined, the more specific the research can be to meet the requirements made of it. Responsibility for getting the objectives right must lie largely with the research buyer. The buyer has most to learn if he or she fell down in this area, but the agency input should also be questioned.

11.6.2 Was the research programme right?

An assessment should be made of whether the research programme was adequate for meeting the research objectives. It may well be felt on reflection that the research programme went astray from the objectives set for it, resulting in information not suited to the decision maker's real need. Responsibility for adequate translation of the research objectives into an appropriate research design must lie largely with the research agency.

11.6.3 Was too much or too little information produced?

The most common fault at the end of research programmes is that they produce more information than the decision maker can deal with. This is probably a fault in research since it means that the research buyer has paid for more information than can be used, and the information not used represents waste. Although the defence can be made that information is always useful, in practice it does not turn out to be so. When someone actually comes to make the decision for which that information might be useful, it is probably out of date.

The problem of having too little information from a research programme is also of concern since it also means that money has been unwisely spent. In this case, better value might have been achieved through spending a little more money.

11.6.4 Did it help to provide a solution?

The 'acid test' for research results must be whether the findings assisted in solving the original problem. If they did, then that is fine and indicates an appropriate use of research. A similar approach might be used in the future. If the results did not help in solving the original problem then this may indicate a poor use of research or inappropriate research design. An attempt should be made to assess why the research failed, so that the same mistakes will not be made again.

11.6.5 Using feedback

As the items discussed so far indicate, both the research buyer and the researcher have something to learn from their joint experience. It is therefore a wise move to feed back to the research agency any points that they could learn from the outcome of the research programme. A client may be genuinely satisfied with the quality of research received from the agency, but still feel that lessons could be learned from it. It makes sense to share these with the agency, as in working together on a second project both parties are likely to produce a better result.

11.6.6 What action resulted from the research?

The point of conducting research is to change or influence some action to be taken or decision to be made. This holds true even when the results indicate no certain outcome or perhaps that the right decision is to do nothing. If nothing occurs as a result of the research then this must be considered bad research. It was either unnecessary or undertaken for the wrong reasons. The individual responsible for buying this piece of research needs to question why it influenced nothing. Was it a fault of the buying, commissioning or conduct of the research programme?

If some decision or action resulted from the research, then the outcome of the decision or action needs to be analysed for its correctness. If it turns out that a wrong decision or wrong action was taken as a result of the research programme, then the research buyer must assess why this was so.

Was the research poorly applied or poorly conducted? If so, what can be learned from that?

The value of learning from experience cannot be underestimated. It involves thoughtful and intelligent analysis so that good experience may be learned from and built upon, and bad experience may be used as the basis for future improvement.

11.7 Buying syndicated services

Buying syndicated services is 'the same as, but different' from buying made-to-measure research surveys. The difference is that the results or the design of the service already exist, and this makes buying easier. The similarity is that it is still necessary to ensure that the service is specifically appropriate to the real information need, and that it is of good quality and offers good value for money. The buying procedure is therefore as follows.

11.7.1 Defining the requirement

First, identify exactly what information is needed. This is an essential first step in all research buying.

11.7.2 Does the service meet the requirement?

It is important to judge the service offered specifically against the research requirement. The danger in buying syndicated services lies in bending the information requirement to meet the service provided, and therefore buying inappropriate data.

11.7.3 Does the service provide adequate flexibility?

Are the timing and frequency of reporting appropriate, or can they be varied? Can relevant groups and subgroups be analysed from the data provided? Is it possible to add supplementary questions to the existing format, or to influence the wording of existing questions to make them more appropriate?

11.7.4 Is the money worth spending?

Most syndicated services produce good-quality data and represent good value for money. The key question for the buyer is whether the money is worth spending from the organization's point of view, i.e. will the information influence decision making in a cost-effective way? The prospective buyer should be able to produce specific instances to support the answer 'yes' to that question.

11.8 Evaluating other research reports

It will often be the case that a manager is presented with a research report and asked to apply its findings when he or she was not personally responsible for commissioning the research programme. In this case, the research must be assessed for its quality before its findings can be used with confidence. The following checklist can be used to judge research quality when only the report is available for assessment.

11.8.1 A scheme for judging research quality

1 What were the objectives of the research?
   Are they appropriate to the problem to which the findings are now to be applied?
2 What method was used to collect the information?
   Is it appropriate to the information need?
3 Who was asked the questions?
   Is the sample definition appropriate?
4 How many people were asked?
   Is the sample size adequate?

5 What were the actual questions?
Check the copy of the questionnaire in the technical appendix. Do they seem to be good questions, well framed and appropriate to the objectives?
6 Who did the fieldwork?
Is there a basis for judging the quality of the fieldwork?
Were professional interviewers used?
What checking procedures were used?
7 When was the fieldwork carried out?
Was the timing sufficiently recent for the results still to hold?
Was the time of year/time of day appropriate?
8 Are the tabulations comprehensible?
Are they legible, with clear headings, and indexed?
9 Would further cross-tabulations produce useful information?
Are these possible?
10 Is the report in a logical order and readable?
Does it make sense?
11 Is there a meaningful summary?
Is it easy to grasp the main points being made?
12 Are there conclusions? (if appropriate)
Are they supported by the data?
13 Did the research meet its objectives, and if not, why not?
Does this invalidate the research?

A satisfactory answer to all these questions should reassure the decision maker that the report to be used is of real relevance to the current problem, and is of sufficiently good quality for its findings to be applied with some confidence. An unsatisfactory answer to some or all of the questions would indicate the use of appropriate caution in applying the findings of such research.

11.9 Summary

Most organizations requiring research, commission it to be carried out by research agencies. A systematic approach for buying 'made-to-measure' research is suggested covering five stages: getting the research requirement right, preparing the brief, choosing the right agency, checking that the agency does a good job and learning from experience. Buying and evaluating syndicated services is also discussed. A checklist for judging research quality is suggested.

12 Using research in experiments

12.1 Introduction

Experiments are used when some decision is under consideration and the results cannot be predicted from the existing experience either of the organization itself, or of the activity of other organizations within the marketplace. Experiments attempt to measure change under, as far as possible, normal marketplace conditions. The problem is that they are expensive and can disclose plans to competitors. It may also be difficult to achieve normal marketplace conditions on a sufficiently small scale for the exercise to be considered an experiment rather than a 'suck-it-and-see' trial. In addition, retailers are often unwilling to co-operate with a test in one area alone. Experiments should normally be confined to situations where the expense and effort involved are calculated to be more than compensated for by the outcome of the experiment. This should be estimated beforehand. It should also be determined that the information could not be gained any other way; for example, by monitoring similar approaches by other companies, comparison with other markets, or reanalysing existing data from past or syndicated surveys. Given that experiments are thought to be worthwhile, several approaches are possible.

Two types of market experiment can be used before new product launching: *experimental launching* or *pilot launching*. For existing products, market tests may be either *specific* or *exploratory*. If an experiment is to be carried out, then the type of experimental design to be used must be decided, and this may be *ex post facto*, *split-run*, *before-and-after with or without control*, or a *formal experimental design* based on statistical theory. Some factors to be considered in setting up research experiments are discussed, and syndicated research services available for testing purposes are described. Further reading, for those wishing for more guidance in particular areas, is given in Chapter 17. Most major research texts also contain sections on experimentation and test marketing; amongst the best is Raymond Kent's text *Market Research in Action*. For contemporary cases on market testing and experiments the *Journal of the Market Research Society* is a useful source.

12.2 Types of research experiment

12.2.1 Experimental launching

This can also be called the 'projectable test launch'. It represents the most demanding type of market experiment because it is used to project the results from those achieved in the test area to what might be expected following national launch. For such projections to be made with any degree of accuracy it is necessary that the experimental procedure be statistically designed and rigorously controlled. Validity of the test procedure and accuracy in measurement are essential if usable projections are to be achieved. The difficulty and expense involved in carrying out a projectable test launch have led to a situation in which this kind of major test launch procedure is used less commonly than it was. Its main objective was to produce a sales projection with sufficient accuracy for a go/no go decision to be made for the product, based on sales probability forecasts. In practice, inadequacies in procedure, or simply changes in the marketplace, made statistical calculations very difficult. An absolute measure of the product's likely success in the marketplace cannot necessarily be achieved.

12.2.2 Pilot launching

This has a less demanding, and therefore more easily achievable, objective than experimental launching. In this case, the decision to launch a new product has already been made. The aim of the pilot launch is to introduce the product into a limited area to test various aspects of the marketing approach, such as the price, the advertising, the distribution method, and so on. A pilot launch is often the first stage in a 'rolling launch'. In this case, the new product is launched into one area, measurements are taken about its performance in that area, and the marketing strategy is modified accordingly. The product is then launched into a neighbouring area, and so on, rolling out to cover the whole country. Decisions about whether this product form is better than that, whether this package is more successful than that, whether this price commands higher sales volume than that, can quite reasonably be made as the launch is under way.

12.2.3 Specific market test

This is used for market testing of some aspect of an existing product's marketing mix. Some specific decision is to be made, and the experiment is required to predict the outcome of that decision. Once again, when prediction is involved, the need for rigorous control of the experimental situation, experimental validity and accurate measurement, is demanded.

12.2.4 Exploratory market test

This type of market test is more exploratory. It involves testing a number of possible variations in the mix to discover which alternatives might produce better results. This kind of comparative testing is more amenable to experiment than the predictive type.

12.3 Types of experimental design

12.3.1 Informal experimental designs

These designs are termed 'informal' because no statistical control is exercised over the variables under test, and no calculation can be made of experimental error.

Ex post facto (after-the-event) measurement

This approach can hardly be called an experimental design since it involves the measurement of a situation only after a decision has been made and implemented. For example, awareness might be measured using omnibus survey questions following an advertising campaign. The difficulty with this approach is that although the level of awareness at the end of the campaign is known, the prior level of awareness is not known, and therefore the results of the advertising campaign cannot be assessed. This is not the case when some new activity has been undertaken and an 'after-the-event' measure of awareness is, in itself, indicative of the results of the action. A measure of the awareness of the product name after its launch will evaluate the success of the product in penetrating the market consciousness. It will not indicate what aspect of the marketing plan has been successful in doing this, for example, whether it was through the advertising or distribution or sales activity.

Split-run (side-by-side) measurement

In this approach half the sample gets one treatment and the other half another, perhaps different prices, or different advertising messages. At the end of the experiment, measurement is taken of both halves of the sample and any differences between them are assumed to be the result of differences in treatment. Difficulties can arise in interpreting data from this type of experiment when, for example, sales increases are observed of a similar order yet the price levels being tested were different. This is usually because some other, more relevant, factor in the marketplace has changed over the period of the test. It might be a change in the weather, or a change in the general economic circumstances of consumers.

Before-and-after without control

This involves commencing the experiment with a 'benchmark' measurement survey. The test treatment is then applied, for example, an advertising campaign or a change in distribution. The measurement survey is repeated at the end of the period. The advantage of the before-and-after measurement is that change during the period of the test is measured. However, the same difficulty as in the last example exists, that the change could be due to the operation of variables that are not part of the test.

After only with control

In marketing experiments the difficulty always exists that variables not under the control of the marketing manager will often affect the results of any marketing activity. The use of control areas in marketing experiments will give an indication of the effect of these other, or exogenous, variables. The test is applied in only one area, but measurements are taken in two areas. The assumption then is that any difference between results in the control and experimental areas is due to the effect of the experiment. The problem remains that no baseline measurement is available.

Before-and-after with control

This is the most sophisticated of the informal experimental designs. It measures change only during the period of the test and takes into account both test variables and exogenous variables by the use of a control area.

12.3.2 Formal experimental designs

These designs are research methods based on statistical principles. This means that in analysing the results not only the result of the experiment can be calculated, but also an estimate can be made of the degree of experimental error in the procedure. Formal experimental designs therefore do for market experimentation what random probability sampling does for sample selection. They allow the experimenter to calculate not only the results of the experiments, but also the probability that the results are good within specified limits of accuracy, at a given confidence level. Since the declared aim of this book is to explain marketing research procedures without going into statistical detail, it would not be appropriate to explain how formal experimental designs are constructed. The non-statistical research user should simply take note of the fact that the use of appropriate statistical techniques in the design of market experiments can increase the number of variables that can be tested in one experiment, allow for calculation of experimental error and assess the interaction effects. The price that must be paid for these benefits is increased design complexity and cost. Four designs are introduced.

Completely randomized design

This allows experimental error to be calculated for the treatment effect only.

Randomized blocks

This technique allows for experimental error to be calculated for the treatment effect and one other variable.

Latin square design

Conducting an experiment using this system allows two different treatment effects to be measured at the same time.

Factorial design

This is the most complex of the formal experimental design methods. It allows the effect of a number of different treatment factors to be measured, and it also measures the interaction effects between them. Since there is considerable interaction in the marketplace between marketing variables and exogenous variables, this type of research design comes closest to representing the real-life situation that the product will face in the marketplace.

12.4 Setting up research experiments

12.4.1 Selecting the experimental design

Three factors must be taken into account in selecting the appropriate experimental design. First, there is the need to measure the change generated by the test; second, the need to assess the reliability of the results; and third, the need to be able to project results with sufficient accuracy to meet the experimental objective. The greater the need for each of these to be achieved, the more complex the experimental design must be.

12.4.2 The scale of the experiment

In determining how big the experiment must be, there is a trade-off between smallness, which equates with cheapness, and largeness, which equates with increasing reliability. Whether cost or reliability of data is the more compelling criterion will be decided by the nature of the experiment and its significance to the organization.

> The scale of the experiment may also be influenced by the size necessary to produce a representative experimental area. Sometimes this can be done by simply using a group of shops or outlets for the product, or by using test towns. On a large scale, ITV areas are used for experimenting with consumer products, and sales districts may be used for experiments with industrial products.

The size of the test area will also be influenced by its need to be representative in ways appropriate to the experiment. This may mean representative of characteristics of users (whether they be consumer or industrial), distribution channels, sales of the product group or sales force capacity, or representative in terms of media coverage.

12.4.3 Choosing the test area

Area selection is influenced by most of the considerations discussed in Section 12.4.2. The area selected should be of sufficient size to achieve the test objectives and should be representative in appropriate ways. It is helpful if the test area is not too popular as a test market, since this can result in unrepresentative behaviour in the marketplace. In general, test areas must be selected in such a way as to give a reasonable representation of what might be expected of the product from a national launch.

If control areas are to be used, these should match the test areas as closely as possible. The same measurements are taken in both areas, and this makes it possible to isolate effects of the test from the general effect due to market change in both areas during the period of the test. Multi-area testing is more efficient than single-area testing in detecting change due to the experiment, but has the disadvantage of increasing cost.

12.4.4 Timing

The longer a market experiment is continued, then the greater the probability that it will give a correct prediction of results. Set against this is the fact that the longer a product is in the test market the greater the risk of disclosure to competitors. This raises the possibility that they may copy the product and launch it nationally either before, or not very long after, its originator. In addition, the longer the product is in test, the greater the cost of the experiment. The question must be asked whether the additional information generated by increasing the length of test is worth the additional cost. It is usually necessary to stay in test for long enough to be able to calculate initial penetration data for the brand and repeat purchasing rates. The length of time will therefore be indicated by the normal pattern of repeat purchase of the product under test. Both items of data are necessary for an ultimate brand share to be estimated.

12.4.5 Test conditions

One of the difficulties in marketing experimentation is being able to scale down all aspects of the marketing plan. There may be a particular problem in replicating the advertising support that a brand would receive on national launch, particularly if a mini-test procedure is being used. Some allowance therefore needs to be made for what difference this would make in acceptance of the product. When company, and particularly sales, personnel are involved in market tests there is sometimes a problem in persuading them of the need to conduct a test under normal conditions. There is a human tendency to give extra effort to support the product under test, particularly when it is known that the results of those efforts are being carefully monitored. There is also rarely such a thing as a 'fully representative test market'. To the extent that the test does not replicate the normal marketing conditions for the product, allowance must be made for differences between test performance and what would actually happen in the marketplace. This area of subjectivity in extrapolating potential market outcome from experimental procedures has led to a growth in smaller testing procedures, rather than the large-scale, expensive and often unreliable projectable test launches.

12.4.6 Test variables

In any research experiment there are three types of variable: independent, dependent and exogenous.

Independent variables

These are the subject of the experiment. They must be held at known levels so that the response to them can be measured. Examples are price, advertising and distribution level.

Dependent variables

These are the factors that are measured in assessing the outcome of the experiment. Commonly they are sales measures such as factory shipments, retail store audit data, consumer panel data, levels of awareness, trial, repeat purchase and distribution levels. It is helpful to collect more than one type of data in evaluating the outcome of the experiment, since this will increase confidence in the measures and may also prove diagnostic.

For example, if both product penetration and advertising awareness are collected it may be that a high level of awareness is associated with a low level of penetration. This would indicate that the advertising is not communicating a desirable message. Alternatively, a low level of awareness may be accompanied by a low level of penetration and here the problem may simply be insufficient advertising. If repeat purchasing levels are also taken, this adds further insight into performance. High levels of penetration accompanied by low levels of repeat purchase suggest the advertising is communicating desirable messages, raising expectations that the product is not delivering. Alternatively, low levels of penetration accompanied by high levels of repeat purchase would indicate that the advertising is probably insufficient, but that once individuals are persuaded to try the product they like it sufficiently to buy it again.

Data is likely to come from one of three sources. The first source is sales data, such as factory shipments and retail audits. In general, factory shipments are not a very satisfactory measure of sales response since they are separated from actual market behaviour by the length of the distribution chain and this can mask market movements. Retail audits are a better indicator of consumer take-up of the product.

The second source of data comprises consumer panel data and repeat purchasing rates. From these two measures an estimate of ultimate brand share can be calculated.

The third type of data is that from 'usage and attitude' studies. These are consumer surveys that measure awareness of the product and its advertising, the extent of trial purchase and usage of the product, repeat purchase, frequency of purchase, amounts purchased, and opinion and attitudes towards the product.

Exogenous variables

Exogenous or 'outside' variables are the factors that affect the experiment but are not part of it. For example, the effects of competitive activity during the period of the experiment are bound to affect sales, as will changes in the economic environment, the weather and other exogenous variables. In most markets the exogenous variables are more influential on sales than are the variables that can be controlled by the marketer. For this reason control areas are used in market testing to allow an estimate to be made of the influence of exogenous variables.

12.4.7 Cost

In calculating the cost of marketing experiments an estimate must be made not only of the research costs involved but also of the costs of preparing appropriate product samples or samples of other test material. A possibly more important factor involved in calculating the cost of marketing experiments, and one that is often overlooked, is the opportunity cost of delay while the product or change is under test. The point of experimenting is to minimize losses if the experiment turns out to be a failure. The larger costs that would be incurred on a national scale are reduced. However, if the experiment turns out to be successful and the new product or product change is subsequently introduced to the market, there will be an opportunity cost in the sales that have been foregone on a national scale for the period for which the product has been under test. This opportunity cost may also be reflected in the fact that competitors may hear of the test and be in a good position to copy a successful product before its national launch.

12.4.8 Syndicated test procedures

In the fast-moving consumer goods market, a range of sophisticated modelling services can help the process of predicting trial, adoption and repeat purchase of new products. These modelling techniques take advantage of computer-based analysis, which has extended the role of the mini-test market.

Mini-tests generally comprise a consumer panel of 1000 housewives split between two areas of the country, and selected to be representative of households in the north and the south of the UK. Panel members agree to do their regular weekly shopping in a mobile van carrying some 1500 lines representative of supermarket stock and priced accordingly. Members of the panel are sent a monthly catalogue featuring the items that are available and an order form is completed each week with items delivered from stock held in the van. This system can be used to test any aspect of the marketing mix proposed for the launch of a new product, together with some measurement of likely penetration and repeat usage of the product.

Other techniques for testing consumer response to new products are based around questionnaires. An example of this is MicroTest from Research International (Tel: 020 7656 5500, Fax: 020 7201 0701, E-mail: info@research-int.com).

MicroTest is based on key factors that influence consumer behaviour in the trial and adoption phase:

Trial

- Concept acceptability
- Attitude to price
- Propensity to buy
- Propensity to experiment
- Distribution
- Advertising
- Brand heritage

Adoption

- Product acceptability
- Post-trial response
- Fulfilment of expectation
    - Pre-trial
    - Post-trial
- Fidelity/loyalty
- Frequency and weight of purchase

The MicroTest model can be applied to concepts and extended to laboratory techniques. In addition, MicroTest market applies the core MicroTest model to a purchasing panel operating for a minimum of 12 weeks. This allows the analysis of frequency of purchase and long-term adoption in the marketplace.

Other research companies also operate test marketing services, and these can be identified in the Market Research Society's *Research Buyer's Guide*.

12.5 Summary

Research experiments can be used to predict the outcome of marketing decisions, or to test the effects of changes made in a product or its marketing mix. Four types of research experiment are described. Informal experimental designs are not statistically based, and a range of approaches from simple to more complex is discussed, with brief mention being made of the statistically based formal experimental designs. The chapter concludes with a discussion of factors to be considered in setting up research experiments.

13 Using research in business-to-business and industrial markets

13.1 Introduction

The use of research in industrial markets differs from its use in consumer markets mainly in application and degree, rather than in technique. This is because industrial organizations have tended to lag behind consumer organizations in the sophistication of their approach to marketing generally. However, the nature of industrial markets, where the buying decision process is often complex and the product may be spread across several international market-places, means that effective research is at least as important in these markets. Recent years have seen considerable growth in the use of marketing research techniques in industrial markets, and the full range of research techniques and applications discussed in this book is increasingly being applied. In this chapter differences of emphasis in industrial marketing research are considered for each of the chapter topics in the book.

13.2 Getting started

An industrial organization will need to answer the same questions as those presented in Chapter 2. There must be an organizational commitment to the need for marketing research and an allocation of resources to carry it out. In the first instance, this may mean recruiting an individual with the title of 'marketing manager' with market research awareness and allowing that person to build up an in-house marketing department, or giving the responsibility to a senior executive already within the organization. Which of these, or other possible strategies, is most appropriate will depend on the size of the organization and its level of marketing sophistication.

13.3 Marketing research begins at home

This is certainly true for industrial marketing research. Industrial organizations are likely to put far more reliance on the use of internal staff and internal records and the database as a major source of research information. Market intelligence will also form a more significant aspect of the marketing information system than in consumer organizations. This is because industrial organizations, by their very nature, are more directly in touch with their market than is usual in consumer markets, where the nature of the distribution system creates physical separation between the manufacturer and consumers. It is therefore both more feasible and more productive for an industrial organization to organize a market intelligence system using feedback from the sales force or other customer contacts as a mechanism for reporting customer views.

13.4 'Off-the-peg' research

Desk research generally is again of far greater significance in industrial marketing than in consumer marketing. Government publications, trade information, published sources, and so on, form a very important part of the data input for marketing decision making and planning. Setting up an in-house information service to handle the relevant information in such a way that it is collected, classified and retrievable is well worthwhile. This may be concerned mainly with abstracting relevant statistics on a regular basis from appropriate secondary sources, or with generating an original cuttings or abstracting service from appropriate publications. Most of these functions can be handled online and the marketing database will allow remote access. A well-organized marketing intelligence executive may be expected to provide these services for the company, its markets and industry. Advice on searching for secondary sources is largely the same as indicated in Chapter 4. The main difference will be the types of publication or online services found to be useful. Where the consumer researcher is interested in the census of population, for example, the industrial researcher is more likely to be interested in the census of production.

As far as syndicated and omnibus research services are concerned these are unlikely to be available in a meaningful fashion in any but the largest and most sophisticated industrial markets. Some off-the-peg information is available, e.g. the Business Readership Survey, and specialist research services as discussed in Section 4.5.1.

13.5 'Made-to-measure' research

In carrying out quantitative surveys, industrial marketing researchers are more likely than their consumer counterparts to make use of postal, online and telephone research. Postal research presents itself as a fairly obvious first step for an organization new to using research. It has the attraction of economy and may be seen as particularly appropriate when address lists of the population to be sampled, such as lists of customers, are readily available. It is also particularly suitable for gathering basic market data and very often in industrial marketing research this is what is required. Its limitations as to representativeness of respondents when response rates are low must, however, be considered. There is some evidence to suggest that as industrial organizations become more regular users of research they are less likely to be users of postal research methods.

In the business-to-business sector, online research has a good chance of success. Almost all executives have access to the World Wide Web. In some cases the companies under consideration may be linked via an extranet (i.e. a system that links specific firms to each other externally for the purposes of sharing information). Certainly in the early days of e-mail, response rates were very high. This is levelling off with the increase in spam (electronic junk mail) and the number of e-mails busy executives have to process. It may be that the novelty value of a letter may now elicit a better response. Most executives today work on computer and the convenience of dealing with e-mail or online questionnaires means that they should be considered in this sector.

Telephone research has traditionally been an important technique for industrial marketing research. Its major advantage over the use of personal interviewing in industrial marketing research is that a geographically dispersed sample can be contacted more economically. It can produce better response rates than postal research, and many industrial respondents will give a brief telephone interview, but would be unwilling to see a personal interviewer.

The most frequently used technique of qualitative research in industrial marketing research is depth interviews, rather than group discussions. This is a result of the simple practical difficulty involved in bringing together eight industrialists in the same room at the same time for the purpose of research group discussion. This is not to say that group discussions in industrial marketing research are not used or are not useful, but simply that depth interviews are more readily obtained. In industrial marketing research, expert informants in particular fields of industrial marketing are more likely to be of value in providing information than is the case in most consumer markets. For this reason, too, depth interviews at the exploratory stage of research study are of particular significance in industrial marketing.

13.6 How are the data collected?

The previous section indicated that the research techniques more heavily used in industrial markets than in consumer markets are postal research, online research, telephone research and depth interviews. Having said this, the manner in which these and other research techniques are applied in industrial markets is similar to that in consumer markets and is covered in Chapter 6.

13.7 Who provides the information?

The sampling methods discussed in Chapter 7 are also used in industrial marketing. Random probability sampling is only possible when a comprehensive sampling frame (or list of all members of the population to be sampled) exists. In some industrial markets such lists do exist and are used as the basis of random probability sampling. Business directories are often used for this purpose, or internal lists such as customer lists or business mailing lists. Stratification as a sophistication of random sampling and, to some extent, quota sampling are also practised in industrial marketing research. In this case, the allocation of sample segments would be based on appropriate industrial criteria such as Standard Industrial Classification

(SIC) or the size of an organization in terms of turnover, or number of employees. When applied to customer lists, stratification is used in order to ensure appropriate representation of large, medium and small customers.

A difficulty that exists in industrial sampling, which is not apparent in consumer sampling, is who is actually to be asked the questions. The sampling procedure described above may produce the name of the firms to be sampled, but the industrial marketing researcher has also to be concerned with which individual in the firm should be asked the questions or to whom a postal or telephone enquiry should be addressed. It is often a problem in industrial marketing research to know who might be the correct individual for any particular enquiry. This is further complicated by the fact that in different organizations the same functional responsibility may be held by individuals with different job titles. Only experience in a particular market can suggest the most likely prospects. Even so, problems in this area are notoriously difficult to resolve. Some filtering or screening questions at the start of the questionnaire may help to identify the qualifications of the respondent in terms of their appropriateness to complete the interview. If a postal questionnaire is sent to the firm, the covering letter should make it very clear who the ideal respondent in the firm would be.

13.8 How are the questions asked?

Problems of question and questionnaire design discussed in Chapter 8 hold equally for industrial marketing research.

13.9 Who asks the questions?

Here, industrial marketing research differs from consumer research in that it is more likely that the researcher will be a member of the organization's own staff. This is particularly so when the interviews are depth interviews with expert respondents, as in an exploratory market survey. In this case, the company researcher may wish to carry out these interviews personally as a briefing background to acquire greater insight into the market being studied.

Some industrial organizations use sales personnel to carry out research interviews, but there are dangers in doing this. The first is that sales personnel are rarely sufficiently objective to make good researchers. The second is that although the use of sales personnel makes the research appear very cheap, once the opportunity cost of lost selling time has been costed into the procedure, the specialist industrial marketing research interviewers appear to be a more economical and effective means of gathering the required information.

Some research organizations specialize in industrial marketing research, and these carry teams of industrial interviewers who are generally more qualified than consumer research interviewers and better able to obtain co-operation from industrial respondents. For certain technical enquiries it may be necessary for interviewers to have particular specialist background qualifications, and these personnel are often available from specialist industrial research organizations. When this is not the case, a more comprehensive briefing should be given to interviewers than would be usual in consumer research surveys.

13.10 What happens to the answers?

Techniques for analysis of both qualitative and quantitative data are as described in Chapter 10 and hold equally well for the results of industrial marketing research surveys.

13.11 How do you buy good research?

Systematic procedures for identifying, evaluating and selecting a marketing research agency, as described in Chapter 11, are equally applicable in industrial markets. The main differences are that in many technical industrial markets characterized by relatively few and highly specialized potential customers, it may be more likely that the company's own research department will handle any depth interviewing required. It is also more likely that industrial companies will make use of industrial marketing research consultants for guidance on specific 'made-to-measure' projects, rather than establish an in-house research department.

Appropriate industrial researchers can be found via the Business and Industrial Group (BIG) of the Market Research Society. This group is very active and has its own conference. Relevant industry expertise will be found in the *Research Buyer's Guide*. Details of BIG and other research interest groups can be found on the MRS website: www.mrs.org.uk.

13.12 Using research in industrial markets

Most industrial markets are active users of research, and the need for good and timely information to support business decisions in this sector is as great as in consumer markets. Uses to which industrial marketing research is put are, in order of importance:

- sales forecasting
- analysis of market size

- trends in market size
- estimating demand for new products
- competitive position of company products
- determining characteristics of markets
- determining present uses of existing products
- studying economic factors affecting sales volume
- general business forecasting
- evaluating proposed new products and services.

This list indicates the relatively limited range of applications for marketing research in industrial markets compared with consumer markets, and marketers in industrial organizations are perhaps less likely to use marketing research data than their counterparts in consumer product and services industries.

13.13 Summary

The use of marketing research in industrial markets is growing, but there are some differences in emphasis in the way in which techniques outlined in this book are applied. This chapter considers each of the previous chapter topics in turn and indicates ways in which there are similarities or differences for using research in industrial markets.

14 Using research in online markets

14.1 Introduction

The growth of online business over the past decade has been phenomenal. The World Wide Web was developed by Tim Berners Lee as the graphical interface for the Internet. The first commercial website was developed in 1994. Since then the number of sites has multiplied so that almost every area of human interest is covered in some way online. In 2001 the estimates of the online population in the UK ranged from 14.17 to 18.8 million. In August 2002 the estimate was 17.9 million regular users, including work-based access. This is around 40 per cent of the UK adult population. Of online access, 62 per cent is from home computers and the remainder from work. This means that around 40 per cent of households in the UK are connected to the Internet.

These impressive figures are increasing dramatically. Most businesses are integrating online working practices within the day-to-day administration of the office. According to Xerox in 2001, the average UK office worker received 28 e-mails per day; this figure is higher than anywhere else in Europe.

Online advertising is the fastest growing advertising medium ever seen. In the UK, total online advertising spend grew from £154.7 million in 2000 to £165.7 million in 2001, a year-on-year increase of 7.1 per cent: an impressive figure, but only slightly more than 1 per cent of total UK advertising spending. However, according to the same survey Internet advertising overtook cinema advertising for the first time in 2000.

The development of broadband access will enhance the effectiveness of the Internet by increasing its speed and ability to stream moving images and sound, and its potential remains to be fulfilled.

The move to online business has proceeded at a similar pace. Dell, Amazon, Tesco.com, Expedia, Lastminute.com and other online retailers are now producing impressive revenue figures, despite some remaining uncertainty about their prospects. These successes are newsworthy. However, many companies experienced the dot-com boom and bust of the late 1990s. These companies burned through vast amounts of venture capital and failed. At the heart of the fall of many dot-com companies was the failure to ask the simple question, 'where is the customer in all this?' It is this question that marketing research is able to answer. The need for pertinent, reliable, accurate and timely information lies at the heart of good business planning. The need for this type of information is even greater in managing the new high-risk business models developed using the potential of digital media and Internet technologies.

This chapter focuses on the marketing research needs of those businesses that use the Internet as a sales outlet, communications medium or channel of distribution. The online environment provides a compelling environment for all types of marketing research, both quantitative and qualitative; however, it needs careful management and adherence to the methodological principles that underpin all research, online or offline. The chapter reviews each of the principles considered in earlier chapters in the light of the needs of the online business.

There is no reason why more familiar offline techniques may not be used to solve a problem that relates to online business. These techniques are discussed in detail earlier in the book.

14.2 Getting started

An Internet-based organization will need to answer the same questions as those presented in Chapter 2. As with any business, there must be an organizational commitment to the need for marketing research and an allocation of resources to carry it out. A major issue in Internet-based businesses is the conflict between information technology (IT) and marketing departments. The problem emerges because the question of ownership of customer data does not have a clear answer. Much of the information that is generated and held on customers is produced through the work done by IT departments in setting up databases, and tracking and analysis of customer browsing and other online behaviour. Some of this data will be used to drive particular content to the website browser. Much of the data, however, is a by-product of Internet business and is not planned marketing research, in that it may not relate specifically to marketing problems or opportunities. It may at some point be used to drive strategy, but until it is analysed and acted upon it remains data rather than intelligence. In addition, for real meaning to be derived from this data it must be placed in the broader business context. A business may be delighted that the average time spent on the site is 12 minutes; however, if their competitors are keeping customers on their site for longer then clearly the business could be doing something better.

This needs very careful management. The marketing function should determine the extent and scope of any website's design and transactional capability. Indeed, marketing research should have provided information on the nature and extent of demand for the online service and how this service should have been configured to deliver customer satisfaction. In many Internet start-ups, technology drove the business rather than working within the business to deliver profits from satisfied customers. The simplest example of this was the development of technically impressive websites that took too long to load and/or crashed the users' browsers. IT must be part of the total strategic approach to customers and the extent to which sophisticated technical solutions are developed depends on customers' ability to benefit from them.

Despite the amount of customer data held by companies with an online presence, marketing research still needs to be carried out in a planned and professional manner. The database gives some of these companies an advantage in providing them with an existing sample frame of customers, and this can save time and money. However, the broader aspects of marketing research outlined in Chapter 2 still need to be carried out, perhaps more so in the highly uncertain, rapidly changing online business environment. This may be carried out by the marketing department, specialist agencies or a combination of in-house and external experts. New roles such as data planners and software engineering may have some input to the research task in these businesses.

14.3 Marketing research begins at home

The great advantage of online business is the direct contact between the company and the online customer, which will automatically generate a significant amount of information on which to base decisions (see Figure 14.1). This may take the form of web server logs, also known as traffic reports, which report on the amount of traffic into the site, second by second. 'Path analysis' allows companies to track browser behaviour through the site, i.e. which pages are visited in which order and for how long each.

Companies such as Web Trends and Red Sheriff provide systems that allow this type of data to be collected and analysed. There are some issues around this. Server logs generally track the address of the computer (the Internet Protocol or IP address, a unique identifying code for every computer) rather than the individual browsing the site. In addition, the server log will occasionally register the proxy address of an Internet Service Provider (ISP), rather than the address of the browser's own computer.

The database will also generate a significant amount of useful data, presenting the recency, frequency, amount and product category of purchases, and this is known as the transactional database.

Web businesses are usually integrated within a multichannel communications and distribution approach to customers and these other channels will also provide useful data. The call centre or contact centre may generate useful data about customers' complaints or other issues, and a field sales force may also be used to sell the service to customers. Again, these will provide useful sources of information.

The danger here is overreliance on the data generated from customers or potential customers. The data generated is inevitably biased. The sample on which it is based is a sample of customers or browsers who have access to

Most requested pages
Most requested content groups
Least requested pages
Leading entry pages
Leading entry requests
Most common exit pages
Access pages
Most browsed directories
Leading routes through the site
Browsed dynamic pages & forms
Number of users against number of visits
New users
Leading users
Returning users
Most active geographical source
Most active companies
Activity level by week or day of the week
Activity level by hour or minute of the day
Pages & form errors
Client errors
Page not found (404) errors
Server errors
Leading referring sites
Leading referring URLs
Leading search engines
Leading search phrases
Leading search keywords
Most used browsers
Visiting search engine spiders

Figure 14.1 Types of information collected by web server analysis

the Internet; it may not be a sample of the market as a whole. It is therefore vital that the marketing intelligence system includes independent market and competitor research to present the full business picture.

14.4 'Off-the-peg' research

Desk research in Internet marketing is growing in importance as the industry develops greater sophistication and the tools required to report effectively on the online market. A significant number of reports on the online economy is being published. Government publications, trade information, published sources, and so on, now form an important part of the data input for Internet marketing decision making and planning. Much of this is available online and can be integrated easily into the company's marketing intelligence systems. Advice on the best sources for secondary data is also given in Chapter 4 and most of the organizations listed there will produce data on the online economy. The best sources for online research are often American. However, there is a range of other appropriate sources. The following sites are among the best.

http://www.nua.com

A very comprehensive website that offers Internet demographics and trends compiled by other research providers, as well as NUA itself. Information is segmented by geographical location, industry and demographics. The site also has useful links to other sites that have compiled the research. For more detailed information the user needs to subscribe to the site.

http://www.teleconomy.com

A useful site, run by a website effectiveness consultancy. It offers bespoke research services to clients and other Internet research information. This site is focused towards organizations requiring specific research to be undertaken.

http://www.forrester.com

A very comprehensive and informative US-based site that offers a wealth of international information across all areas, and can be filtered down into industry segments for relevant research information. Once the user has subscribed, more detail and information on specific research studies is available.

http://www.siebel.com

A useful site that has several e-commerce-based customer relationship management (CRM) reports generated by Siebel, a system provider, and other organizations. It also offers a book-buying facility related to particular e-commerce theories and case studies.

http://www3.gartner.com

An extremely comprehensive site produced by a consultancy company that covers all areas of e-commerce, including daily news updates of the latest trends and e-commerce stories. This site is the ideal starting point for any research needed on the Internet, its uses and its users.

http://www.broadvision.com

Broadvision's website contains a large amount of information on e-commerce activities. The site can be searched by industry segment for information on e-commerce. It also contains some very extensive discussion papers that are free to download.

http://uk.jupitermmxi.com

Contains Internet market information that can be viewed in terms of the global marketplace or by specific country. Their 'Multi-Country Usage Report' is up to date and very useful as a starting point to understanding the Internet generally. More detailed research is available if you subscribe to the service. An added facility of the site is that they offer multiple language or country sites for international markets.

http://www.accenture.com

Contains some interesting studies on e-commerce activities produced by a leading UK management consultancy. Some client case studies are useful, as are its e-commerce reports and links to key texts and reports.

http://www.pwcglobal.com

Contains some interesting articles on e-commerce, produced by a global accountancy practice, so examples are taken from all over the world. It gives a good starting point for information on the global e-commerce marketplace.

http://www.bcg.com

Boston Consulting Group is an international management consultancy firm and their website has a variety of excellent research papers on e-business, many of which are global case studies. This site also has a BCG publications search engine, which is very useful for research purposes across all areas of online business.

http://www.idc.com

A very detailed site that enables the user to obtain research information on technology intelligence, industry analysis, market data, and strategic and tactical guidance to builders, providers and users of information technology. The majority of the site is run on a pay-to-view basis and covers all areas of e-commerce in either local or global terms. The site also promotes bespoke research activities to its clients.

http://www.bitpipe.com

A portal (a site that offers entry to other sites), which offers huge amounts of information and reporting that has been compiled by various other third-party research firms, including Gartner, Datamonitor and IDC. This site is very comprehensive and detailed as it covers every area of e-communications.

http://www.iabuk.net

The Internet Advertisers' Bureau is a trade association for interactive advertising, e-commerce and online marketing. Its site offers a wealth of information relating to the e-commerce marketplace. Users must register to become members to obtain more detailed information. However, even when not registered, a large amount of valuable information is accessible.

http://www.ovum.com

Offers extensive research into the whole of the new media phenomenon, including mobile networking, e-commerce and mobile marketing case studies. The daily news and critique section of this site is very informative, but the more detailed archive reports have to be purchased.

http://www.it-analysis.com

Offers research and information on computing, new media and IT support systems. It offers some generalist information on these areas, and operates a pay-to-view policy on the majority of its research documentation. This is a good new media news website.

http://www.gigaweb.com

An advisory company that helps companies and institutions to maximize their technology investment to deliver business results through a combination of objective research, advice and continuous technology coaching. It is more specific to software design issues than research on the e-business arena as a whole. To obtain more than abstract information it is necessary to become a member and, in most cases, purchase the required research.

Other good sources include the major suppliers of CRM technology and the management and IT consultancy firms who are selling these systems into organizations

A significant number of syndicated and omnibus surveys is available to the researcher, and these are listed in Chapter 4.

14.5 'Made-to-measure' research

The range of techniques available to the online researcher includes all the offline techniques described in earlier chapters, but doing these online has several advantages. Online research is much faster than offline, so surveys can be administered and reported on very quickly. Online offers a global survey universe and surveys can be conducted domestically or internationally via e-mail or through a website very easily. The same caveats discussed in Chapter 5 apply to international online research as apply to offline research. However, if these are taken into account, online research offers access to a global audience very cheaply. Surveys are increasingly conducted using mobile devices, and the increased use of personal digital assistants (PDAs) and third-generation mobile devices means that this type of delivery is becoming more viable as it reaches a wider audience of users.

Online research overall is likely to be cheaper than administering offline surveys, particularly if they are self-administered. In general, the administration of online surveys is carried out more efficiently than offline. Costs will vary according to the type of research that is to be carried out. If the survey is to be supported with an 'e-mail me' or 'call me' button, in order to support the respondent in the completion of the questionnaire, then the cost will be higher. E-mail surveys usually offer an incentive to respond and the cost of the incentive may be a significant part of the cost of the survey.

Typical costs for an online survey developed in-house, covering 500 respondents including incentives, would be £2000. For an externally developed survey of 2000 respondents the cost would be around £15,000.

The costs of an online focus group would be around £1500 per group, including incentives of £30–50 per respondent. Offline, the costs would be around £3000 with incentives of around £70.

The richness of online media can enhance the execution of research; hypertext mark-up language (HTML), sound and even moving images can be incorporated into research designs and this may boost response and create a richer experience for the interviewee and the researcher. Care has to be taken in using these enhanced online media. Recent estimates are that only 60 per cent of e-mail users can read HTML e-mails.

The online medium is very adaptable, and questionnaires can be targeted at individuals who have viewed a particular page, expressed interest in or bought a particular product, or followed a certain route through a site. This interaction can produce very sensitive systems in which content, including questionnaires, can be delivered according to a developing customer profile. The example in Figure 14.2 shows how interactivity can enhance the interviewing process. In this example, after completing the questionnaire the respondent is given access to a summary of the results to date, showing his responses in the context of the questionnaire as a whole. There are dangers in this approach, but careful management may enhance the quality of responses.

Various issues need to be taken into account when considering the use of online techniques. The major concern for market research is the representativeness of the sample and therefore the overall validity of the results and reliability. The Internet is developing rapidly, but rather like the telephone 40 years earlier, penetration levels mean that the medium is not representative of the population as a whole. The availability of e-mail lists is still not as good as mailing lists and there is complexity in the fact that most people have more than one e-mail address. A recent rented list of e-mails produced 50 per cent bounceback (i.e. addresses were inaccurate) and a response of less than 1 per cent. Some lists are more reliable, e.g. subscriber lists, but the rule is always to pilot any survey to check the list, questionnaire and the likely response rate.

The identity of the online respondent may be hard to verify at times. The use of online panels provided by ACNielsen and TN Sofres, for example, may overcome these issues in specific markets. A full list of providers of online panels is given in Chapter 4. An example of a highly qualified panel is VNU's web panel. This covers 1000 individuals in each of seven European countries, including the UK, France, Germany, Spain, the Netherlands, Belgium and Italy. Questionnaires are delivered in the local language and reports covering 1400 responses cost around £15,000.

The most frequently used technique online is quantitative research based on surveys delivered by e-mail or the website. However, many companies use the Internet to administer qualitative research in terms of both depth interviews and focus groups.

Focus groups use the web tools of chat rooms (where a group of people with the same interest can 'talk' to each other using their computers) and bulletin/message boards (where a group of people can exchange informa-

That concludes the survey. Many thanks for your help and time today.

At the beginning of the questionnaire, we asked you about a number of technologies, and how important you think they will be over the next 12-18 months. We thought you may be interested in seeing a summary of what *everyone* thinks...

Base	Technology	Summary of importance	In %	You said..
[2281]	Security	Very important / Fairly important	77% / 19%	*4 - Very important*
[2281]	Web services	Very important / Fairly important	40% / 41%	*3 - Fairly important*
[2281]	E-commerce	Very important / Fairly important	36% / 32%	*4 - Very important*
[2281]	Remote access systems	Very important / Fairly important	35% / 42%	*4 - Very important*
[2281]	Storage	Very important / Fairly important	33% / 40%	*3 - Fairly important*
[2281]	CRM - Customer Relationship Management	Very important / Fairly important	34% / 31%	*3 - Fairly important*
[2281]	Broadband	Very important / Fairly important	33% / 34%	*3 - Fairly important*
[2281]	Knowledge management	Very important / Fairly important	29% / 43%	*2 - Not very important*
[2281]	SLM - Service Level Management	Very important / Fairly important	25% / 32%	*4 - Very important*
[2281]	Online content management	Very important / Fairly important	20% / 37%	*2 - Not very important*
[2281]	EAI - Enterprise Application Integration	Very important / Fairly important	19% / 29%	*4 - Very important*
[2281]	Thin/Lean Client	Very important / Fairly important	15% / 27%	*3 - Fairly important*
[2281]	Wireless technologies	Very important / Fairly important	14% / 28%	*2 - Not very important*
[2281]	Linux/Open systems	Very important / Fairly important	13% / 25%	*3 - Fairly important*
[2281]	Handheld computing/PDAs	Very important / Fairly important	10% / 28%	*3 - Fairly important*
[2281]	Mobile commerce	Very important / Fairly important	10% / 26%	*3 - Fairly important*
[2281]	Voice-over IP	Very important / Fairly important	9% / 22%	*3 - Fairly important*
[2281]	Itanium-based 64bit systems	Very important / Fairly important	3% / 10%	*2 - Not very important*

You can return to check these results at any time during the fieldwork period of this survey. To do so, please either bookmark this page, or save the following link..

http://websurvey2.nopworld.com/scripts/242453/onexit.pl?id=00114

Should you have any problems or questions about this survey, feel free to contact Matthew Churchill on m.churchill@nopworld.com

Figure 14.2 Interactivity and online questionnaires. *Source*: VNU Business Publications

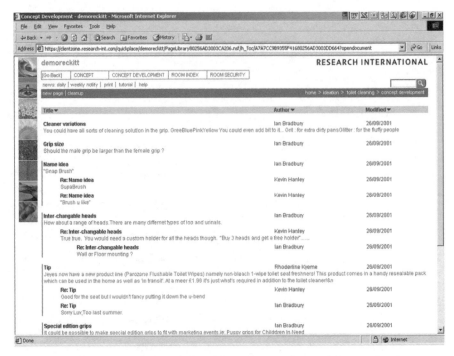

Figure 14.3 Online bulletin board discussions. *Source*: Research International

tion about a specific topic), but create a unique space for the interview or group to take place. Respondents are recruited by e-mail and agree to participate. Each member can read the responses of other members and respond to their comments as if in a group situation (Figure 14.3).

Depth interviewees are recruited in the same way, but the communication takes place simply between the respondent and the interviewer.

The web is not the ideal medium to deliver this type of research. It is often hard to recruit suitable respondents; for example, the technical know-how to interact in a chat room is not universal. However, it does allow geographically dispersed respondents, e.g. IT buyers for multinational companies, to be bought together.

Online groups lack several advantages of offline focus groups. It is hard for an online group to go much beyond 45 minutes (especially if the respondent is paying for the online access), simply because of the demands of looking at and concentrating on the screen for so long. It is, however, possible to reconvene the group at a later date and extend the focus group over time. There are also issues over the reliability of the Internet connection, diverse browsers, etc. Respondents may view screens at different speeds, in different frame sizes and so on.

The valuable and productive multiple interaction between focus group members that occurs offline cannot take place online. It is a less creative environment for responders. It is hard or impossible for respondents to comment on the feel or look of a mail piece or the taste or smell of a new product. Equally, it is hard to moderate the contribution of all respondents in a group discussion online. A dominant respondent may be hard to switch off, while a respondent who is contributing less may be hard to draw in. The personal, physical presence of the moderator in offline groups is important in helping to moderate discussion, and this is missing online. It is very hard to read or interpret body language and tone of voice. A sarcastic comment may be interpreted literally without the verbal intonation. This may be moderated by the use of emoticons or symbols that can be clicked on or dragged to provide extra meaning to the printed word. It is also hard to establish who exactly is sitting at the terminal. This can be moderated by careful recruitment and incentivizing the contribution of participants.

Online qualitative research demands technical skills of the moderator. However, for certain customer groups, particularly those who are interacting online in their business, qualitative online research may be useful (see Figure 14.4).

Other qualitative methodologies include website usability studies. These can be administered through networked personal computers. Some companies offer the use of specialist viewing facilities which record the facial expression of the user and can also record the key strokes that the user makes. In a remote viewing facility the researcher can also see the user's screen. These techniques are designed to ensure that the design and feel of the site are acceptable. Jakob Nielsen's web usability studies are a useful starting point in this area.

Web address: www.useit.com

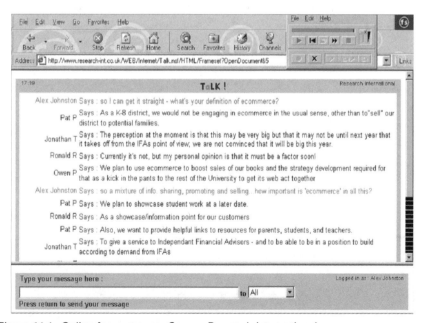

Figure 14.4 Online focus groups. *Source*: Research International

Online depth interviews gain some advantage in business-to-business markets where respondents might be dispersed internationally and are hard to reach via the telephone. The use of online techniques may fit more easily with the respondents' work practices. In general, however, the telephone is a more effective remote medium. Online depth interviews can be sustained effectively for eight to 10 minutes, while the telephone can be used successfully for up to 15 minutes.

14.6 How are the data collected?

There is very little difference in the way in which online and offline data are collected. The usual techniques of survey, depth interviews and focus groups are used online. The key difference is the mechanism by which the data collection instrument is delivered and information returned.

Survey questionnaires may be delivered by e-mail or through a link on a website (Figure 14.5). Cold e-mail questionnaires (i.e. those not expected by the recipient) will almost certainly need to be incentivized to achieve adequate response rates.

This is due to the proliferation of unsolicited e-mails or Spam. 'Warm' surveys, or surveys to existing customers or known individuals will achieve greater levels of response and the incentive may be more appropriate to the nature of the relationship. In delivering surveys by e-mail the researcher must be careful in using rich techniques such as HTML. As mentioned earlier, only around 60 per cent of e-mail users can read HTML e-mail. E-mails may deliver the questionnaire itself, or automatically link through to the Internet site holding the questionnaire via a clickable icon on the screen or a hypertext link. Examples of web-based questionnaires are shown in Figure 14.6.

Questionnaires may also be delivered as pop-ups or interstitials on a website. Dell is a good example of a company that uses ratings scales to judge browser satisfaction with the website. As the browser scrolls over a

---

Dear Attendee

On Wednesday 19th June you attended the IT Week symposium 'Bridging The Corporate Digital Divide'.

We are now interested to hear your reactions to the event organization, content and speakers so that we can incorporate your feedback into the organization of future events. The questionnaire includes 9 questions and should take no longer than 6–8 minutes to complete. All responses will be processed confidentially and anonymously. In addition, as a thank you for your feedback on the event, IT Week will send out via e-mail a summary of a recent survey we carried out on the topic of Service Level Management. Please click on the below link to take you to the survey.

IT Week greatly appreciates your help with this survey.

Figure 14.5 Example of a drive to a questionnaire, delivered via e-mail

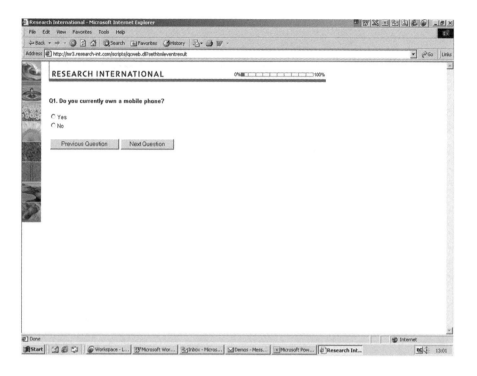

Figure 14.6 Web-based questionnaires. *Source*: Research International

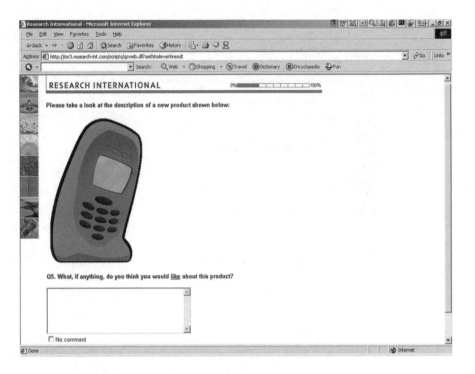

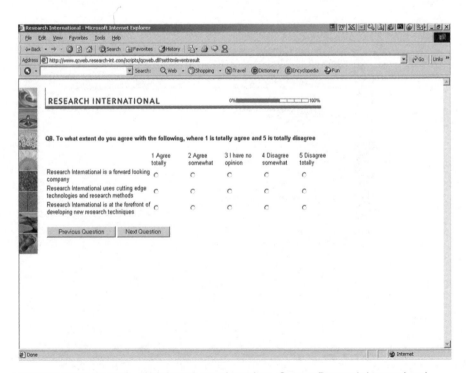

Figure 14.6 (continued) Web-based questionnaires. *Source*: Research International

Figure 14.7 Example of comments and rating scale for web pages from Opinion Labs. *Source*: Dell/Opinion Labs

small icon, a rating scale pops up asking for ratings on a five-point scale. There is also the opportunity to make comments. This system is administered by Opinion Labs (Figure 14.7).

Web address: www.opinionlab.com

Questionnaires are now being delivered in Personal Digital Assistant (PDA) format, using the increasing bandwidth available to mobile networks (Figure 14.8).

Qualitative group work and depth interviews are described above. However, there is one other way in which observation research may be carried out. Non-participant observation may be carried out by joining user groups and chat rooms. These may deliver some very interesting data about the company's goods and services.

14.7 Who provides the information?

Sampling methods discussed in Chapter 7 are also used in Internet marketing research. The major problem in Internet marketing research is the availability of suitable, accurate sampling frames. E-mail lists are very

An I-mode panelist's screen....

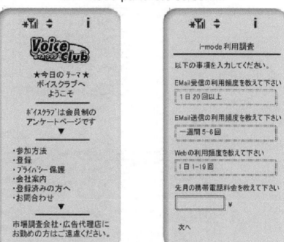

Figure 14.8   Questionnaire delivered to an I Mode Mobile device in Japan. *Source*: Research International

unreliable at present and the proliferation of spam in the marketplace means that many prospective respondents will delete an e-mail that was not expected or of immediate relevance or interest. Random probability sampling is only possible when a comprehensive sampling frame (or list of all members of the population to be sampled) exists. In some markets such lists do exist and are used as the basis of random probability sampling. For Internet marketing internal lists such as customer lists or business mailing lists are the most useful and reliable source.

Stratified and quota sampling are also used in Internet marketing research. The use of online panels can help this process. In business-to-business research, standard industrial classification (SIC) codes, or the size of an organization in terms of turnover or number of employees, would be used. Lists of companies using these criteria are available from Dunn and Bradstreet, whose details are listed in Chapter 4. Further work may have to be done to identify the relevant e-mail address of the individual to be contacted.

14.8 How are the questions asked?

Problems with question and questionnaire design discussed in Chapter 8 hold equally for Internet marketing research. However, there are some specific questionnaire design programs from which online research can benefit. The use of online survey design software, for example Confirm-IT, can produce effective questionnaires very quickly (Figure 14.9). These can deal with questionnaire logic and ensure integrity throughout the design process. As with computer-assisted telephone and personal interviewing (CATI and CAPI), coding and analysis can be built in and results can be downloaded, for example to PowerPoint presentations.

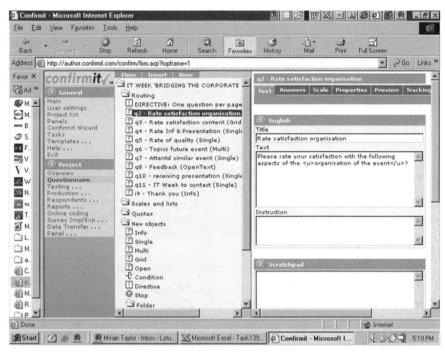

Figure 14.9 Confirm-IT online survey design

Online questionnaires benefit from the richness of the medium, and the use of progress bars and summary tables can help with a sense of involvement and produce better results. Graphical interfaces and emoticons can be used to liven up scale questions, for example temperature gradients or smiley faces.

Filter and skip questions are easier to incorporate, and answers to a particular question can drive the subsequent questions. If the questionnaire is particularly complicated, call me or e-mail me buttons can allow researchers to help with any questions the respondent might have.

14.9 Who asks the questions?

Because of the complexities of online Internet research in terms of both methodology and the technical platforms required to support it, the use of specialist companies indicated in Chapter 4 is recommended. However, if the technical infrastructure and software skills exist in-house then it is easy to set up and deliver an online research project within the company. The ease with which it is possible to carry out simple surveys means that some organizations are failing to co-ordinate the use of research effectively, and this can create fatigue in respondents, inadequate research design and flawed decision making.

14.10 What happens to the answers?

Techniques for analysis of both qualitative and quantitative data are described in Chapter 10 and hold equally well for the results of Internet marketing research surveys. The ease of analysis and data verification online gives online research a distinct advantage in this area.

14.11 How do you buy good research?

Systematic procedures for identifying, evaluating and selecting a marketing research agency, described in Chapter 11, are equally applicable in Internet markets.

Relevant Internet expertise may be identified in the organizations listed in Chapter 4 or through the Market Research Society and ESOMAR websites. The *Research Buyer's Guide* also lists those research companies with expertise in this area.

14.12 Using research in online markets

Most Internet or online businesses require research to support all stages of business planning, and the need for good and timely information to support business decisions in this sector is as great as in any market. Indeed, the absence of research in the sector and the overreliance on data rather than intelligence are major issues. Research in these markets will help in:

● forecasting market trends
● analysis of market size
● trends in market size
● estimating demand for online services
● competitive position of company products
● determining characteristics of markets
● determining present uses of existing products
● studying economic factors affecting sales volume
● generating online/offline pricing strategies
● evaluating proposed new products and services
● evaluating the impact of channel integration
● assessing the impact of online advertising
● evaluating affiliates
● ensuring ongoing customer satisfaction.

14.13 Summary

The use of marketing research in online markets is growing, but there are some differences in emphasis in the way in which techniques outlined in this book are applied. This chapter considers each of the previous chapter topics in turn and indicates ways in which there are similarities or differences for using research in online markets.

15 Using research in international markets

15.1 Introduction

Globalization has become a business buzz word and the market research industry, in common with marketing services companies across other sectors, has expanded its role to take into account the international ambitions of key clients and to exploit market opportunities in the growth areas of the world.

An increasing amount of the research now undertaken by organizations has an overseas' dimension. The business environment for British-based organizations has become increasingly international. Even the smallest organizations are subject to international influences through either direct international competition, European legislation or the need to explore the perceived opportunity in international markets for British products or services. The most recent balance of payments figures indicate that Britain is in a unique position within Europe to exploit international markets and that many companies are already doing so with some success. However, some companies are put off international marketing research by the perceived difficulty of 'getting started'.

The broad methodology and research plan used to develop international marketing research are, however, little different from those used in the home market. The complexity of the task lies in the number of markets to be considered and the different levels of support available within them. Other difficulties in international marketing research include:

- socioeconomic differences in national markets, e.g. the UK is used to using the social class definition described in Chapter 4, but this is unlikely to be relevant in international markets
- differences in the level of support for marketing, the marketing and market research infrastructure, e.g. access to key statistical data varies substantially from country to country
- lack of familiarity with data sources
- cost, payment and economic instability
- doubts about the competence of overseas' research agencies, and differences in research procedures
- problems of communication between client and agency, and agency and respondents
- differences in the levels of market development
- differences in legislation, which affect the ability to carry out research and store data
- the longer time taken to complete international research studies
- differences in language, the use and meaning of words
- other cultural differences, including levels of technical infrastructure, religious differences, attitudes to privacy and information dissemination.

> The idea that international data has to be comparable is relevant only if the marketing strategy demands immediately comparable data, for example owing to the development of a pan-national advertising campaign, or the creation of a regional pricing policy. Of utmost importance, as in the domestic market, is that the data collected must be accurate, valid and relevant to the user's research objectives.

15.2 Who monitors the quality of international research?

The European Society for Opinion and Market Research (ESOMAR) provides a similar service to the Market Research Society (MRS) in Europe. It represents market research specialists and sets standards for the industry. It runs an annual conference and publishes papers and a useful journal, *Marketing and Research Today*. ESOMAR can be contacted in Amsterdam (Tel: +31 20 664 21 41, Fax: +31 20 664 29 22, E-mail: email@esomar.nl). The World Association for Public Opinion Research (WAPOR) is a similar organization based in the USA (Tel: +1 919 962 1204, Fax: +1 919 962 0620). Other countries have their own organizations representing the market research industry; a list of these is contained in the MRS *Research Buyer's Guide*.

15.3 Who are the users?

- Global companies
- multinational companies
- exporting companies
- governments
- charities
- international organizations
- advertising agencies
- marketing consultancies
- any commercially aware organization.

The last point is probably the most significant: no company can afford to ignore the international dimension of their business. Even organizations not yet involved in international markets or not foreseeing the need to become internationally active can be sure that somewhere in the world an organization is eyeing their market with interest.

15.4 Who undertakes the research?

- The organization itself
- home-country research agencies
- foreign, locally based agencies
- international agencies
- governments.

15.5 International market research begins at home

The amount of data obtainable through the internal information system will depend on the level of international involvement of the company. For the large global or multinational company, resources and exposure to the international marketplace will be greater.

> Carlsberg, for example, has a substantial, computer-based, international marketing information system at its headquarters in Copenhagen. This provides managers with up-to-the-minute marketing information on activity world-wide. It also means that these companies should be in a stronger position to carry out research using internal data sources.

For the small company or the company with little or no overseas' exposure, things can be far more difficult. The traditional sources of internal data will not contain the same amount or quality of information about overseas' markets and in some cases there will be no information at all. This can be an extremely daunting prospect for budding international researchers.

Research, however, does not happen in a vacuum and in many businesses the move towards international activity will be signposted as part of the strategic plan. The information needed to support this decision should be gathered in a systematic fashion and be available to the researcher.

For those companies that are looking to develop an existing international presence, the types of data outlined in Chapter 3 should exist.

The major difference is that in international research the importance of market intelligence cannot be overstated. In the home market the manager has the substantial advantage of familiarity with the market and its environment. Day-to-day business experience will to some extent familiarize him or her with the issues being researched. When researching overseas' markets, this input is not available and it becomes necessary to seek out what might seem even the most commonplace information about a market. The use of contacts in the trade, and the other methods of drawing on market intelligence and secondary information sources, are therefore important in informing overall research planning and essential in the first exploratory phase of any project.

15.6 'Off-the-peg' research

Many researchers will be approaching the international arena as first timers. It is important to realize that many of the resources available in the home market are also available for overseas' research. It is possible to gain much of the information needed to solve international market research problems by using secondary or desk research, syndicated research and the increasing number of international omnibus surveys (see Chapter 4).

15.7 Secondary desk research

The international dimension of secondary desk research does not necessarily have to create insurmountable problems for the researcher. The problems of sourcing secondary data on international markets should be no greater than for the home market, and these are discussed in Section 4.2.1. Nevertheless, some additional factors need to be recognized.

- *Cost*: Where a charge is made, the research will tend to be more expensive. This reflects the additional costs of collating data from international sources.
- *Language*: Material prepared for an English language audience will generally be prepared in English. In international research, there may be problems with mistranslation, especially of technical terms.
- *Comparability*: Any secondary data on international markets needs to be assessed for its relevance and comparability. It is necessary to ensure that the data being used is precisely relevant to the area of interest. Problems with secondary data include different definitions of markets and the environmental factors that affect them. For example, definitions of educational attainment and what constitutes the urban population of a country will inevitably vary.

Market definitions also vary from country to country. In some south-east Asian markets, for example, candied fruits are included within the sugar confectionery market. Many of the differences in definitions reflect key market variables, and awareness of these variables is crucial to success in international markets.

It is often tempting to force data into our preconceptions of how markets should be structured and this can be important if adopting a standard approach to international marketing. Often, however, it is crucial to appreciate differences. For example, in the south-east Asian confectionery market, medicated sweets are popular because of their strong flavours rather than for cold relief.

Even simple measures that might appear straightforward to compare meaningfully need careful thought.

For example, measures of gross domestic product (GDP) per capita are useful only to a degree. Measures of disposable income that take into account tax regimes, etc., may be harder to obtain, but more useful. Per capita GDP measures do not reflect the distribution of wealth within a country. Brunei, for example, has one of the highest GDP per capita in the world, but this is unevenly distributed and does not affect general levels of spending power.

- *Grey areas*: Certain sectors may not be included in the data. For example, in the food market the data may exclude the catering sector. In certain markets the informal trade from street markets may be important and this may not be included in official statistics. In other countries there may be a substantial black market operating, for example that operating currently in dutiable goods between France and the UK. If in any doubt the precise definition should be checked with the publisher of the information.
- *Timeliness*: Data on certain international markets will be out of date, especially in fast-moving markets such as the newly industrialized countries of south-east Asia and in fast-moving sectors such as computer hardware and software. In certain developing countries the statistical data from which much secondary data will be drawn is subject to lags of three to five years.
- *Sophistication*: In certain countries the level of data gathered and disseminated by governments will be very general, perhaps only comprising a four-figure customs classification code. This, for example, will look only generally at sweet biscuits as opposed to chocolate biscuits in particular (see Figure 15.1).

The way to deal with these problems is as for domestic research. Where possible, the researcher should cross-check data from a number of different sources. In any case, a degree of healthy scepticism is needed in dealing with all secondary data. Above all, one should keep fully informed about the market of interest, both at home and abroad, by keeping up to date with current affairs through relevant journals and conferences, and by developing a network of relevant business contacts.

15.8 Sources

As for domestic research, the hardest part of a desk research survey is actually beginning. Chapter 4 gives a comprehensive list of sources for international desk research. Once the research project has commenced, one source will lead on to another.

S.I.T.C. (R3)	Commodity Code No	Trade descriptions
		Bread, pastry, cakes, biscuits and other bakers' wares, whether or not containing cocoa in any proportion; communion wafers, empty cachets of a kind suitable for pharmaceutical use, sealing wafers, rice paper and similar products
048.41		Crispbread, rusks, toasted bread and similar products
	190510 00 0	Crispbread
	190540 00 0	Rusks, toasted bread and similar toasted products
048.42		Sweet biscuits, waffles and wafers, gingerbread and the like
		Gingerbread and the like
	190520 10 0	Containing by weight of sucrose less than 30% (including invert sugar expressed as sucrose)
	190520 30 0	Containing by weight of sucrose 30% or more but less than 50% (including invert sugar expressed as sucrose)
	190520 80 0	Containing by weight of sucrose 50% or more (including invert sugar expressed as sucrose)
		Sweet biscuits: waffles and wafers
		Completely, or partially coated or covered with chocolate or other preparations containing cocoa
		In immediate packings of a fat content not exceeding 85 g
	190530 11 1	Sweet biscuits
	190530 11 9	*Waffles and wafers*
		Other
	190530 19 1	Sweet biscuits
	190530 19 9	*Waffles and wafers*
		Other
		Sweet biscuits
	190530 30 0	Containing 8% or more by weight of milkfats
		Other
	190530 51 0	Sandwich biscuits
	190530 58 0	Other
		Waffles and wafers
	190530 91 0	Salted, whether or not filled
	190530 99 0	Other
048.43		Other
	190590 10 0	Matzos
	190590 20 0	Communion wafers, empty cachets of a kind suitable for pharmaceutical use, sealing wafers, rice paper and similar products
		Other
	190590 30 0	Bread, not containing added honey, eggs, cheese or fruit, and containing by weight in the dry matter state not more than 5% of sugar and not more than 6% of fat
	190590 40 0	Waffles and wafers with a water content exceeding 10% by weight
		Biscuits; extruded or expanded products, savoury or salted
	190590 50 1	Extruded or expanded (snack) products, savoury or salted
	190590 50 9	Other
		Other
		With added sweetening matter
	190590 60 1	Cakes
	190590 50 9	Other
		Other
	190590 90 1	Cakes
	190590 90 9	Other

Figure 15.1 The customs classification relating to biscuits. Some countries' data will only give data under the four figure code

15.8.1 Government published data

For the UK-based company researching overseas' markets the starting point will almost certainly be the Department of Trade and Industry (DTI). The services provided by the DTI are comprehensive and vary in sophistication and depth. The service is a useful springboard and even if the information required is not available a number of new leads may be created.

The DTI maintains a library of publications for marketing at Trade Partners. Information sources include the following:

Foreign statistics

These cover trade and production data, prices, employment, population and transport. An online service is available which can be used to search selected trade statistics. The use of this information can be extremely rewarding. Trade and production data can give a useful guide to consumption levels in a country. It is possible to arrive at apparent consumption by using the simple calculation of production plus imports less exports, which should equal that which remains in the country for consumption. This is only a broad guide, but it can be quite accurate, especially in fast-moving consumer goods (FMCG) markets in which there is high turnover of stock. When this information is combined with population figures, per capita consumption figures can be calculated. Often this data is presented in volume and value terms, and will give an indication of the market value at manufacturers' prices. If distributor mark-ups are known, then a retail value for the market can be estimated. United Nations (UN) data on exchange rates can then be used to estimate the sterling value.

In concentrated industrial markets data on source of supply by country could identify which competitor is supplying the target market.

For the services sector, international trade data is not readily available and is generally less useful. However, the DTI also covers invisibles and again a visit to Trade Partners is often a requirement for researchers in this area.

Trade Partners UK Information Centre, Kingsgate House, 66–74 Victoria Street, London SW1E 6SW (Tel: 020 7215 5444, Fax: 020 7215 4231).

Web address: www.tradepartners.gov.uk

Trade Partners UK Information Centre can be visited between 9.30 am and 5.30 pm on Mondays to Fridays. Staff are available to help with enquiries. Short enquiries can be dealt with by telephone or by e-mail. The centre holds a list of independent consultants who may be able to undertake research commissions. A full list of DTI services is given in Chapter 4.

Commodity codes

All product sectors are given a code for the purpose of classifying trade data. This is known as the harmonized commodity description system number or commodity code. To use the trade statistics service effectively it is important to identify this number. Codes are contained in the *Integrated Tariff of the United Kingdom*, which is available at some libraries as well as at some Customs and Excise establishments. Advice on the correct classification can be obtained from local Customs and Excise classification liaison officers, by telephone for an opinion or in writing for a firm ruling.
Web address: www.hmce.gov.uk

The Trade Partners website has links to relevant services in this area. Trade statistics are available from Customs and Excise. Statistics are available on CD-ROM, microfiche or floppy disk. The website has links to other useful sites, including the *Tariff*.

The *Tariff* may be ordered from The Stationery Office, publications centre (Tel: 0870 600 5522, Fax: 0870 6005533,
E-mail: book.enquiries@theso.co.uk)

Directories

Directories can be extremely useful in identifying target companies, both for the purposes of research and for selling. The best known directory is *Kompass* (see Chapter 4), which lists companies by product type and by country. Trade Partners holds a number of directories.

Development plans

These provide a useful guide to the current state of overseas' markets and can be useful in the early stages of assessing a country's attractiveness.

Mail-order catalogues

These are useful to identify competitors in consumer markets.

Market research reports

The DTI keeps a number of published research reports. These include its own reports compiled by commercial attachés in overseas' markets and the reports of commercial organizations. The MRS also has reports on different countries, as does the Economist Research Unit.

The DTI is not the only source of government data. The European Union and the UN also publish statistical information on member countries (see Chapter 4). Other national governments provide information services and the commercial information section should be contacted at embassies in London, or for more comprehensive information the commercial information section can be asked for contact details in the country being researched. Other countries may also hold more comprehensive information on those countries with which they have close historical ties, such as the Dutch in Indonesia. In many of these countries a language facility is not vital, for example, the Danish Confederation of Industry provides an excellent information service, and US government departments are also very useful in certain sectors. Foreign governments are important sources of data on markets in their own countries, but they are also looking at overseas' markets for their own exporters, and this can be useful.

Other important secondary data sources are listed in Chapter 4, along with omnibus and specialist research services.

15.9 'Made-to-measure' research

The principles guiding made-to-measure research in overseas' markets are the same as those underpinning market research in the domestic market, and these are outlined in previous chapters. There are, however, significant differences when conducting research in international markets.

15.9.1 Sampling

It must be stressed that in many markets of interest to UK companies, a full range of techniques and research services will be available. These will enable the overseas researcher to carry out market research to the same levels of sophistication as in the home market.

In most cases many of the methods outlined in Chapter 7 are available in international markets. However, in some underdeveloped markets the information required for both random and quota sampling may not be available or may be of dubious quality.

For example, the estimates of overall population in Nigeria range from 80 to 120 million. When a difference of this magnitude is registered on what would normally be considered a fairly straightforward measure, it is clear that measurements relating to socioeconomic status or household numbers may not be totally reliable. Certain methods of constructing sample frames may not be adequate in some countries; for example, the use of telephone directories in countries in which household penetration of telephone ownership is low. Russia boasts 100 per cent penetration of telephones, but it should be noted that the basis for this is buildings, not households. In online research access to the World Wide Web is limited in certain markets.

Identifying street names and house location is very difficult in some countries, while in others physical accessibility is a major problem. Experienced researchers should be able to suggest innovative ways of addressing these problems, although not all of them can be overcome entirely. The answer is to try to allow for the variability that local conditions introduce into sampling procedures. Local research agencies will be aware of methodologies that can be used to address what may seem insurmountable obstacles, and will advise on their impact on the reliability of results achieved from a less-than-perfect sampling technique.

Even in Europe differences in approach can be seen. In France quota sampling is the norm, and when working in France it is probably wise to be guided by a local agency or to delegate control of the project to a UK-based agency with representation in France. Use of a preferred methodology need not compromise research objectives and will lead to greater understanding and less room for misinterpretation. This, in turn, will make the research more cost-effective and hopefully more reliable.

15.10 Data collection methods

Normally, the most appropriate data collection method will be determined by the requirements of the research problem. However, in international research a number of other factors will influence the choice of data collection method.

- *Telephone interviewing*: In the USA the level of telephone penetration means that telephone research is more common than elsewhere. In other markets the use of the telephone is possible in business-to-business or industrial research, and the development of the international telephone network means that this research can be carried out from the UK. Evidence suggests many respondents are flattered that someone from the UK should be interested in their work, and response rates are good. Telephone contact can also be supported by faxed questionnaires for self-completion. The development of the Internet is also raising some interest among researchers. However, the use of the telephone for consumer research in many markets is not practical or will lead to unrepresentative data being collected.
- *Personal interviewing*: This may cause problems in certain countries where strangers asking questions are viewed with suspicion. In other countries, the gender of the interviewer is important. In certain cultures women will not be suitable interviewers and vice versa. In some countries a lack of trained personnel may be a problem. However, in many countries the use of personal interviewing, as in the UK, is standard practice.
- *Online interviewing*: There are advantages in using online technologies to carry out interviews in international markets. However, the issues of reliability, representativeness, sample availability and language persist in this environment. Online international business-to-business research

tends to be more developed than consumer research, although online research of e-commerce customers and Internet users is feasible.

> Although personal interviewing might be expensive, its use in certain 'difficult' markets is advisable. In general, the price of personal interviews in these markets is significantly lower than in the UK, and so more effort can be expended in ensuring quality of data. The ESOMAR prices study compares the prices of certain standard research projects world-wide. For a usage and attitude survey on a dairy product with a quota sample size of 750 the average price in western Europe was 40,800 Swiss francs. The US price was double, in Indonesia it was just over half and in India under one-fifth of the price of the European study. The same applies to other data gathering techniques.

In certain countries, group discussions may be difficult to arrange and it may be impossible to construct groups of mixed gender or social status.

The use of postal survey techniques depends on the postal infrastructure available and also on the literacy levels of potential respondents. International postal surveys can be cost-effective but response rates tend to be low. They can be useful for gathering information that may be of a sensitive or embarrassing nature.

15.11 How do you ask the questions?

Questionnaire design in international markets is a difficult process. Problems occur when one set of cultural values is used to interrogate another. Language is the most obvious problem; questionnaires should be translated, and checked through the use of back-translation. Understanding of a basic questionnaire can be enhanced through the increased use of show cards or other stimuli. However, even when this is done problems still occur. The view that the USA and the UK are divided by a common language reveals the importance of other cultural factors.

> For example, in the USA to 'wash up' means to wash one's hands. In the UK it means to wash the dishes.

The problem of differences in cultural references, symbols and associations is very difficult to resolve without an understanding of the cultural construct of the country concerned.

> For example, in Japan or China respondents may not wish to offend interviewers by giving negative responses to questions.

Attitudes towards ideas of time, material culture, the role of women, religion and sexual behaviour will differ. This can be solved through the use of local research agencies and a desire to be locally sensitive to customer needs so that questionnaires are designed for the market under consideration rather than for the sponsor of the research.

> Where strategy dictates a uniform approach to multicountry marketing, adequate briefing and control of the agency or agencies concerned are crucial. Research International has several approaches to international research that have been shown to be useful. Paramount among these is the creation of a multicultural team of internationally trained and developed researchers, who can think in the 'Research International way' but maintain sensitivity to cultural differences.

General advice on questionnaire design is given in Chapter 8. For international research it is particularly important that the questionnaire should be clearly worded and well set out, with country-specific questions at the end. Pilot testing by local researchers will allow informed discussion of the questionnaire and question design and content, to ensure that valid and relevant questions are asked. For qualitative research it is helpful if country nationals can be found with the relevant skills and experience. The nature of qualitative work makes it less likely that the non-national would have the range of language or the cultural awareness to be able to use these techniques satisfactorily.

15.12 How do you buy good research?

15.12.1 Preparing the brief

The most important aspect for the international research commissioner to concentrate on is to prepare a very clear statement of what information is wanted and why, how, when and in what circumstances it will be used. This will form a key framework to check that the right questions are asked of the right groups of people with a suitable methodology and an appropriate sample size to give reliable and, most importantly, comparable information for the purposes specified.

For example, a French leisure developer is currently considering investing in building a development on a piece of land available on one of the Caribbean islands. He knows that the British have a particularly strong reputation for market research, and has commissioned a research company in London to guide his decisions. He wants to know what kind of facility to build to give him the best return on his investment. The information he needs is:

● Which countries are already the major tourist markets for this island?
● Which other countries have good access, where a market could be developed? What do travellers from these countries want from their leisure time?
  – Active leisure, e.g. scuba diving, sailing, golf, excursions?
  – Passive leisure: sunbathing, reading, films, television, shows and entertainment?
  – Special interest leisure, e.g. talks, lectures, guided sightseeing, 'leisure learning'?
● What standard and type of accommodation should be provided, e.g. fully serviced hotel, budget hotel, self-catering apartments or individual villas?
● What standard and type of cuisine will be needed, e.g. haute cuisine, 'international' cuisine, silver service or buffet style?

And so the questions go on. The answers will probably need analysis to produce a balanced mix of business that will attract visitors from a number of countries, wanting different styles of leisure pursuit, accommodation and cuisine. The aim of the research will be to guide practical decision making about the style and operation of the facility, so that it is successful in satisfying the requirements of an appropriate mix of customers who will coexist successfully. The greatest danger for a mixed leisure facility is that one set of customers drives away another set. The greatest risk is to aim for only a single set of customers whose preferences may change, or who for reasons relevant to their home country simply stop arriving.

15.12.2 Selecting the agency

General advice given in Sections 9.6.1 and 11.4 continues to apply in the selection of an agency for international research. In short, it is 'horses for courses'. *The Research Buyer's Guide* indicates which companies specialize in international research, and within that one should look for a company that has experience of the industry, sphere of interest and countries under consideration.

15.12.3 Government assistance for overseas research

> If an organization is undertaking overseas research for the first time, then using the DTI's Export Marketing Research scheme will offer not only free professional advice, but also the possibility of financial assistance. This scheme is focused on the small to medium size business sector. Under the provisions of the scheme the DTI will fund up to 50 per cent of the cost of approved market research in overseas' markets up to a maximum grant of £20,000. Research proposals are assessed by three advisors at the Association of British Chambers of Commerce (Tel: 01203 694 484, Fax: 01203 694 690). Companies can apply to the scheme up to 10 times or to a maximum total grant of £60,000. Up to three studies can be made in Europe and North America. The scheme will also fund one-third of any published research, syndicated work or multiclient studies.
>
> The DTI also runs a Market Information Enquiry Service, which will provide basic research carried out by the commercial departments of overseas' embassies and high commissions. Using this scheme, basic information can be provided at very low rates. Details are available through the Trade Partner's website.
> www.tradepartners.gov.uk

Foreign agency selection is a particular problem, mainly because of a lack of knowledge of the research business in the overseas country concerned, and often compounded by a lack of adequate and relevant language skills. It therefore most often makes sense for the intending research user to work with a home-country research agency that it judges to be competent and trustworthy, which has existing established links with foreign agencies in the relevant countries. Previous experience of multicountry research is of special relevance in selecting an agency. There are so many potential pitfalls that it is preferable to use an agency that has learned by experience at some other company's expense.

15.12.4 Commissioning the research

The first step is to work on the brief discussed in Section 15.12.1 with the home-country agency, to ensure that it is as clear and specific as possible about exactly what research information is wanted and why, and from which countries. A brief in writing is essential for the continuing goodwill of all concerned, through to the end of the project. Maintaining goodwill and good co-operation is essential to producing good and reliable research data, especially under the difficult and complex constraints of multicountry research. All of the issues to be covered by the research project must be specified in detail, all potential ambiguities clarified, and all roles and tasks allocated.

Good communication is vitally important to good international research. Links between the user in the home country, the home-country research agency and the foreign agency or agencies must be established early on. The research objectives and brief need to be understood and agreed by all parties. This requires either the home-country user or the agency to have bilingual staff, or the foreign-agency staff to speak good English. This is one of the main reasons why the briefing process in multicountry research can be difficult. Frequently, misunderstandings occur about the objectives of the study and the information required between the user and foreign agency, particularly when a user company decides to brief an overseas agency directly. Time spent at the briefing stage, in ensuring that all parties to the research share a common understanding of what is wanted, is time well spent.

Two key aspects of research, price and quality, will also vary across countries.

If research is being undertaken in more than one foreign country at the same time, then an attempt must be made before the research takes place to ensure comparability of quality and to check value for money. The timing, as well as the cost, of the research is important. These factors will vary by country depending on transportation problems and other delays, legal issues, taxation, inflation, exchange rates and currency convertibility. This last factor, although not a major European issue, can be of significance for research in developing nations. Consideration of all these factors should be undertaken and agreed before the decision to commission the research is made.

15.13 Implementing the research

This may require close supervision by the personnel of both the home-country organization and the home-country agency, if one is used. Time and costs for this should be allocated in the research budget. At the briefing stage, standardization of research techniques and of reporting styles must be established and agreed. Where standardization is not appropriate, then comparability, particularly of techniques and questions, must be determined.

15.14 Summary

The world continues to 'shrink' through the effects of improved communication, data links and travel. The term 'global village' is not new. It is, however, becoming more relevant in marketing practice, and therefore in the practice of marketing research. This chapter considers the special implications relevant to carrying out marketing research in different countries.

16 Using research in marketing decision making

16.1 Introduction

This chapter consists of a set of guides for research users. The purpose of these guides is to introduce the new research user to some of the common marketing problems to which research is applied, and in each case to suggest a data requirement and data sources. To use the guide, read down the following list and if one of the problems shown is close to your needs then look up the data requirement suggested. If this also meets your needs, then the problem could be tackled using the research approaches suggested under 'data sources'. Each data source mentioned is referenced back to its description elsewhere in the book. Some specific terms and techniques used in this section are explained in notes which follow the guides at the end of the chapter.

Research users' guides

Guide 1: Using research for market analysis (Section 16.2)
- Where do our products/services stand in the market?
- Should we enter a market?
- Should we withdraw from a market?
- What different market segments exist and how do they differ?
- What different needs, motives and satisfaction could my product/ service gratify?

Guide 2: Using research to develop new products and services (Section 16.3)
- Generating ideas for possible new products or services
- Selecting the most promising ideas for further development
- Identifying target market segments and appropriate appeals
- Developing product attributes, design and formulation
- Testing the marketing plan
- Testing different marketing strategies
- Predicting market sales.

Guide 3: Using research to select brand names and pack designs (Section 16.4)
- Which name to choose for a new product or service?
- Which pack and pack design to use for a product?

Guide 4: Using research for pricing decisions (Section 16.5)
- What price to charge for a new product or service?
- What is the actual selling price for our product in retail outlets?
- What is the actual selling price for competitive products in retail outlets?

Guide 5: Using research for decisions about advertising (Section 16.6)

Before an advertising campaign:

- Who would the advertising be aimed at?
- What should the advertising be saying?
- How much should we spend on advertising?
- Which media should advertisements go in?
- How much should we spend in the media?
- How much space and time should be bought?
- How much should we spend on each medium?
- Which advertisements to use?

After an advertising campaign:

- Were our advertisements seen?
- Has the advertising worked?

Notes for Guides 1–5 appear at the end of Chapter 16.

16.2 Guide 1: Using research for market analysis

Problem

- Where do our products/services stand in the market?
- Should we enter a market?
- Should we withdraw from a market?

Data requirement (market size and structure)

- How big is the market?
- How profitable is the market generally?
- Is the market growing or declining?
- What are the main products in the market?
- Who are the major competing firms in the market?
- What is the distribution pattern?
- What marketing strategies are used in the market?

Data sources

- Secondary desk research: government and other published statistics, information services (see Section 4.2).
- Syndicated research services: if available for this market. Consult index in Section 4.3.2 and the Market Research Society (MRS) (see Section 4.3).
- Omnibus survey: to collect basic market data. Only possible for markets in which this service operates. Consult index and MRS (see Section 4.4).

Problem

- What different market segments exist and how do they differ?

Data requirement

- Market characteristics.

Data sources

- Secondary desk research: see Section 4.2.3 for sources, e.g. Mintel, Euromonitor.
- Syndicated research services: TGI, ACNielsen and TN Sofres retail audits, etc. (Section 4.3).
- Omnibus survey: for basic data on market characteristics related to product attributes. Only possible if this service operates in the market.
- Consult index and MRS (see Section 4.4).

Problem

- What differing needs, motives and satisfaction could my product/service gratify?

Data requirement

- Characteristics and attributes of users and potential users.

Data source

- Made-to-measure: market segmentation study (see Notes for Guide 1, Section 16.7), psychographic market analysis (see Notes for Guide 1, Section 16.7).

16.3 Guide 2: Using research to develop new products and services

Problem

- Generating ideas for possible new products and services.

Data requirement

- New and creative ideas and suggestions.
- Identify areas of unfilled customer need.
- Brand mapping to identify possible market gaps (gap analysis).

Data sources

- Synectics (see Section 6.2.4).
- Group discussions (see Section 6.2.4).
- Depth interviews (see Section 6.2.1).
- Made-to-measure market survey: usage and attribute study (see Notes for Guide 2, Section 16.8).

Problem

- Selecting the most promising ideas for further development.

Data requirement

- Need to identify big, growing, profitable, not-too-competitive, relatively easy-to-enter markets, i.e. market size, structure, characteristics, trends, profitability, competitors, basic market facts.

Data sources

- (See Guide 1: Using research for market analysis.)
- Secondary desk research (Section 4.2).
- Syndicated research services (Section 4.3).
- Omnibus survey (Section 4.4).

Problem

- Identifying target market segments and appropriate appeals.

Data requirement

- Reaction of different consumer groups to product appeals.
- General consumer response and characteristics.
- Identification of market segments.

Data sources

- Made-to-measure research surveys.
- Concept tests (see Notes for Guide 2, Section 16.8).
- Group discussions (see Section 6.2.4).
- Quantitative attitude survey using factor and cluster analysis (see 'Psychographic market analysis' in Notes for Guide 1, Section 16.7).

Problem

- Developing product attributes, design and formulation.

Data requirement

- Consumer response to product attributes.
- Data on product quality and attributes in use.
- Product performance tests.
- Comparative product performance.

Data sources

- Specialist research services for product testing (see Section 4.5).
- Made-to-measure research surveys for product testing.
- Test centres, hall tests or mobile vans, using monadic tests, paired comparisons or blind testing (see Notes for Guide 2, Section 16.8).
- In-home placement tests (see Notes for Guide 2, Section 16.8).
- Test panels (see Notes for Guide 2, Section 16.8).

Problem

- Testing marketing plan.
- Testing different marketing strategies.
- Predicting market sales.

Data requirement

- Consumer reactions to elements of marketing mix: product, price, promotion.
- Rate of purchase of product (penetration level).
- Pattern of purchase of product.
- Pattern of retail sales.
- Consumer reactions to different marketing strategies.

Data sources

Research experiments using:

- Specialist research services for market testing (see Sections 4.5 and 12.4.8).
- Consumer panels (see Sections 4.3 and 6.4).
- Mobile shop/van purchasing panels (see Notes for Guide 2, Section 16.8, and Section 12.4.8).
- Matched area/town tests (see Notes for Guide 2, Section 16.8).
- Retail outlet test stores (see Section 4.5).
- Made-to-measure research surveys with users/buyers (see Chapter 5).

16.4 Guide 3: Using research to select brand names and pack designs

Problem

- Which name to choose for a new product or service.

Data requirement

- Is the name easy to pronounce?
- Does the name suggest any associations or expectations?
- Does the name carry any, and/or appropriate, imagery?
- Is the name easily recognized?
- Does the name work online
- Is the name easily recalled?

Data sources

- Specialist research services (see Section 4.5.1).
- Made-to-measure research surveys, usually small scale, using pronunciation, word association, name imagery, recognition and recall tests (see Notes for Guide 3, Section 16.9).

Problem

- Which pack and pack design to use for a product.

Data requirement

- Does the pack stand out in a display?
- Is the pack easily recognized?
- Is the pack easy to open, use and close if necessary?
- Does the pack design communicate positive messages?

Data sources

- Specialist research services (see Section 4.5.1).
- Consumer surveys to measure:
  - Attention value (see Notes for Guide 3, Section 16.9).
  - Identification score (see Notes for Guide 3, Section 16.9).
- Test centres, hall tests or mobile van tests: for functional performance, e.g. ease of opening, understanding of pack instructions (see Notes for Guide 3, Section 16.9).
- In-home placement tests: for performance in normal use (see Notes for Guides 1 and 2, Sections 16.8 and 16.9).
- Group discussions and depth interviews: for package concept association tests.
- Consumer survey using attitude rating scales for pack designs (see Notes for Guide 3, Section 16.9).
- Pseudo product test: to uncover pack communication value (see Notes for Guide 3, Section 16.9).

16.5 Guide 4: Using research for pricing decisions

Problem

- What price to charge for a new product or service?

Data requirement

- What prices are competing products selling for?
- What price would consumers expect to pay?
- What price would consumers be prepared to pay?
- What quantities are likely to be sold at different price levels?

Data sources

- Secondary desk research: recent market reports, or trade sources, may provide information on the price structure of the market (see Section 4.2).
- Observation research: a simple DIY exercise on price range and ruling prices (see Notes for Guide 4, Section 16.10).
- Syndicated research services: retail audits provide price and quantity of sales in the markets they cover (see Section 4.3, Notes for Guide 4, Section 16.10).
- Specialist research services: pricing is offered as a research specialism by some agencies (see Section 4.5.1).
- Made-to-measure research surveys: using buy–response method and/or propensity to purchase (see Notes for Guide 4, Section 16.10).

Problem

- What is the actual price for our products in retail outlets?
- What is the actual selling price for competitive products in retail outlets?

Data requirement

- Prices charged for our product in different retail outlets.
- Prices charged for competitive products in different retail outlets.

Data sources

- Observation research: a simple, but limited, DIY exercise in local retail outlets (see Notes for Guide 4, Section 16.10).
- Syndicated research services: retail audit data for markets covered by this service (see Section 4.3).

16.6 Guide 5: Using research for decisions about advertising

1 Using research before an advertising campaign

Problem

- Who should the advertising be aimed at?
- What should the advertising be saying?
- How much should we spend on advertising?

Data requirement

- How big is the market/potential market?
- What are the demographic characteristics of users/potential users?
- What are the demographic profiles of different market segments?
- What are the behaviour and attitudes of different market segments?
- What language do consumers use in talking about the product field?
- Are we underrepresented in particular market segments or geographic areas compared with our competitors?

Data sources

- Secondary desk research: especially online market reports and trade press data (see Section 4.2).
- Syndicated research services, e.g. Nielsen (see below); consult index in Section 4.3.2 and MRS (see Section 4.3).
- Omnibus research: for basic market data (see Section 4.4).
- Made-to-measure research surveys: group discussions (Section 6.2.4); quantitative usage and attitude surveys (see Notes for Guide 2, Section 16.8).

Problem

- Which media should the advertisements go in?
- How much space and time should be bought?
- How much should we spend in the media?

Data requirement

- How big are the media audiences?
- What are the demographic characteristics of the media audiences?
- Which media do our market targets use?
- How much do advertisements cost to place?
- Which media do our competitors use?
- How much are our competitors spending?

Data sources

- Secondary desk research: BRAD (British Rate and Data) (Tel: 020 7505 8031, E-mail william.fox@brad.co.uk). Publishes data on line covering 13,000 media entries with data on circulation target audiences, etc. Web address: www.intellagencia.com/default.asp.BRADInfo=true
- Syndicated research services: BARB, JICNARS, POSTAR, RAJAR, Radio Audience Board, CAVIAR, Superpanel, TGI (see Section 4.3), National Readership Survey (www.nrs.co.uk), Business Readership Survey and European Business Readership Survey (from Ipsos-RSL, www.ipsos-uk.com)
- ACNielsen Co. Ltd, Oxford (Tel: 01865 742 742, Fax: 01865 742 222, E-mail: marketing@acnielsen.co.uk). Through its ACNielsen MMS subsidiary it can also provide data on advertising spend and media spend, including continuous information on advertising expenditure (at rate card costs) for individual brands. Includes national advertising in press, magazines, terrestrial and satellite television, posters, cinema and regional and trade newspapers. Nielsen net ratings give information on online advertising audiences.

Problem

- Which advertisement to use?

Data requirement

- Consumer response to advertisement ideas/roughs:
- Do they understand the advertisement correctly?
- Can they recognize it easily?
- Can they remember it easily?
- Do they like the advertisement?
- Does it give positive associations and imagery to the product?
- Does it make them want to buy the product?

Data sources

- Specialist research services: some research agencies specialize in advertisement testing (see Section 4.5.1).
- Made-to-measure research surveys: usually small-scale qualitative research using recall tests, recognition tests (see Notes for Guide 5, Section 16.11), group discussions or depth interviews for comprehension, liking, positive associations and imagery. Projective techniques may be used (see Sections 6.2.3 and 6.2.4, and Notes for Guide 5, Section 16.11).
- Hardware techniques occasionally used for advertisement testing are the eye-camera, tachistoscope and psychogalvanometer (see Notes for Guide 5, Section 16.11); area testing using quantitative techniques (see Chapter 12).

2 Using research after an advertising campaign

Problem

- Were our advertisements seen?
- Has the advertising worked?

Data requirement

- Did the media chosen reach the target audience?
- Did we get good value for our media expenditure?
- Are more of our target audience aware of the brand name?
- Can more of the target audience remember the brand name?
- Does the target audience have more favourable attitudes towards the brand?
- Do more of the target audience intend to buy the product?
- Have more of the target audience bought the product?
- Have more of the target audience used the product?

Data sources

- Syndicated research services: see under 'advertising' and 'media' (see Section 4.3) for relevant syndicated services: advertising measurement services, e.g. product panel data, retail audits; media measurement services, e.g. BARB, JICNARS.
- Omnibus research surveys: for advertising tracking studies (see Notes for Guide 5, Section 16.11). Repeated measurement of brand recognition, recall.
- Specialist research services: for measuring advertising effectiveness (see Section 4.5.1).
- Made-to-measure research surveys: measuring recall, recognition, attitude, pre- and post-advertising to detect shifts (see Notes for Guide 5, Section 16.11), coupon enquiry counts from keyed advertisements, sales enquiry counts post-advertising, point-of-purchase research to measure intent-to-buy and area testing (see Chapter 12).

16.7 Notes for Guide 1

Market segmentation studies

These are research surveys designed to discriminate between consumers and identify different market patterns or segments. Segmentation criteria should predict or explain market differences and be exploitable in practice. The traditional segmentation criteria are geographic (north/south), demographic (gender, age, social grade, income, marital status, number and ages of children) and product usage (heavy versus light buyers). In each case, collecting data using the criteria listed will increase understanding of the relevant characteristics of buyers.

A more complex, but very revealing type of segmentation analysis is termed psychographics. This term distinguishes the approach from demographics, which uses general 'people' characteristics. Psychographics is concerned with people's subjective attitudes towards, and feeling about, specific products or services. It produces multidimensional groupings that are often highly explanatory of actual market behaviour.

Psychographic market analysis

Background

To carry out this type of study, some background knowledge of the market is needed, including purchasing profiles and ways in which the brands are used. From this, a topic guide can be developed for use in qualitative research.

Qualitative research

Group discussions or depth interviews are used to develop ideas about different market groupings, to indicate the language that consumers use about the market and brands in it, and to suggest attitude statements for developing measuring instruments.

Developing measuring instruments

To quantify market segments large-scale questionnaire surveys are necessary. The long list of attitude statements from qualitative research must be reduced to those that are most discriminatory. A quantitative survey with factor analysis of the results will reduce the list of specific attitude statements to more general factors relevant in the marketplace. Alternatively, the list may be reduced through piloting and subjective analysis.

Identifying customer groupings

The developed questionnaire containing the final shortlist of relevant attitude statements is administered to a statistically significant representative sample. The statistical technique of cluster analysis is then applied to the results, and this will identify subgroups of consumers with shared attitudes in the marketplace. Psychographic analysis indicates target groups in the market, and may suggest new products that would appeal to them. Alternatively, it can suggest which appeals would be most attractive to different groups in the market.

16.8 Notes for Guide 2

Decisions about products and services

Major decisions about the nature of products or services to be offered by an organization are normally taken before development. After the product has been launched on to the market, modifications may be made to the product/ service attribute mix to appeal to different market segments or for different applications. Guide 2 concentrates on the uses of research in new product development, but the techniques suggested are also used to test product modifications during its market life. The scheme outlined suggests a theoretically ideal approach to the process of new product development. Not all products or services do, or should, go through all stages using the research techniques suggested in the guide. This format is intended to offer an outline approach, which may be of value to the new research user, and should certainly be adapted to meet any specific requirements of the product, service or market under consideration. Notes explaining some of the specific techniques referred to in the guide follow.

Usage and attitude study

The typical usage and attitude (U & A) study is a quantitative survey involving around 1500 respondents to allow for analysis of subgroups of the sample. The questionnaire will include general questions on use of brands in the product group, attitudes towards the product group and one or two brands within it, usually the brand leader and the brand being researched.

Test centres

These are used for product testing when the product is too large, too expensive or too complicated to be taken to consumers for testing. One or more test centres will be set up and a representative sample of consumers brought to the test centre for exposure to the product and questioning about their reaction to it.

Hall tests

These are commonly used for product testing or testing other aspects of the marketing mix such as advertising, price, name and package testing. A representative sample of target consumers is recruited, usually in a shopping centre, and brought into a conveniently located hall. Here they are exposed to the test material and asked questions about it.

Mobile shops

These are used for similar purposes to hall tests, but employ a motorized caravan which can be parked in a shopping centre.

Monadic tests

The respondents are given only one product to try, and asked their opinion of it. This is the normal situation in real life when a consumer tries a new product and draws on recent experience with the product they usually use, to judge the test product. The method is not very sensitive in comparing the test brand with other brands because of this.

Paired comparisons

A respondent is asked to try two or more products in pairs and asked, with each pair, to say which they prefer. This is less real in terms of the way consumers normally use products, but does allow products to be deliberately tested against each other.

Blind testing

Refers to testing products in plain packages and without brand names. The package and brand name heavily influence product perceptions. Blind testing is used when factors such as taste, smell, texture and preference are to be measured comparatively without this brand influence, e.g. in testing a new brand against the brand leader. However, a 'dressed' test must be made at some stage since this will be an important factor in the marketplace.

In-home placement tests

These are used to gain an impression of how the product performs in normal use. The product (or products if a comparative test is being carried out) are placed with respondents who are asked to use the product in the normal way and complete a questionnaire about it, which is collected or posted back after the test. Products may be tested comparatively, i.e. two or more products are left at the same time, and the respondents asked to compare them; or sequentially, where first one product is left and after testing replaced with another.

Test panels

Representative panels are recruited (see Section 6.4) and used for product testing. Many companies who carry out a lot of new product development and testing use panels for this purpose. Once the panel is recruited, test materials and questionnaires can be sent through the post, which cuts down the cost of conducting in-home placement tests. Industrial and service firms may also have test panels of customers or intermediaries with whom new product or service ideas or prototypes can be tested.

Concept tests

Qualitative techniques, especially group discussions, are used to obtain target customer reactions to a new idea or product. Question areas would cover: understanding and believability of the concept, ideas about what it would be like, how it might be used, when and by whom. This would suggest the most promising features of the new product, and groups to whom it might appeal.

Matched area/town tests

The marketing strategy or tactic under test is applied in two or more areas or towns. The areas or town are selected to be representative of the target market and similar to each other. Differences in test treatment can then be applied and the results measured, e.g. different advertising, price and pack. Area/town test facilities may be offered by media owners or by specialist research services (see Section 4.5.1).

16.9 Notes for Guide 3

Decisions about name and packaging: name testing

Debate continues in the marketing world about just how important the 'right' name is in contributing to the success of a product or service. Both sides can point to names that have been a help or hindrance to marketing appeal. Some argue that with sufficient advertising support any name can be made to work for the product or service; others, that if a name is to be given advertising support, then it surely makes sense to ensure that the name has at least no readily uncovered negative associations. This debate has particular resonance in international marketing, with numerous examples of inappropriate or unexportable brand names having been used. Out of this debate, some generalizations about choosing the name for a product or service can be made.

- The name should be consistent with the overall marketing strategy for the product. This implies that any research about names should start with a clear statement of the marketing objective for the brand.
- The name should be easy for its target market to read and pronounce in a consistent way. (How do you pronounce 'Noilly Prat' or 'Meux' in Friary Meux?)
- The name should project desirable associations for the product, and have no negative associations.
- Any imagery associated with the name should be appropriate for the product, its use and its target users.

- The design and execution of the brand need to be acceptable in an online environment:
  – Does the domain name exist already?
  – Are the colours 'web safe'?
  – Are the font and design acceptable on screen?
- It helps if the name is easily recognized and recalled. These aspects of naming are amenable to research testing, as listed in Guide 3, and explained in the following notes.

Ease and consistency of pronunciation

A shortlist of possible names is produced, which respondents read aloud, often onto a tape recorder. Ease of, and variations in pronunciation can be observed.

Name associations

Following the use of a few practice words, the respondent is required to associate freely with the test name by giving all the thoughts and ideas that occur after hearing the name. Time for response and verbatim response are both recorded. The length of time taken to respond is thought to indicate blocking or emotional response to the name. Content analysis of verbatim responses indicates positive or negative associations, related or unrelated imagery, and any spontaneous expectations about the product, arising from the use of a particular name.

Further product expectations that might be associated with the name can be generated by reading the test names and asking respondents to suggest what kind of products they might be names for.

Name imagery

Respondents are given a card listing the test brand names. The interviewer reads out a series of attribute statements (e.g. 'would be a luxury product') and respondents say to which names on the list they feel the statement most applies.

Name recognition and recall

The extent to which a brand name is easily recognized in a pack display, and its name recalled, is best tested as part of the overall packaging for the product, since that is how it will be seen by consumers. Package testing is considered in the next section.

Package testing

Package design has grown in importance with the growth of self-service shopping. Increasingly, the pack has to do the job the sales assistant used to do in terms of drawing attention to the product, communicating its salient features and presenting it in its most favourable light to the target buyer and user. In addition to these new functions, the package has to fulfil its traditional role of containing, protecting and sometimes storing the product, yet allowing it to be extracted by the user with the minimum of frustration.

The need for all these functions to be performed effectively in more and more markets has increased as the self-service concept has extended from consumer-goods supermarkets to consumer durables, builders' merchants, cash-and-carry wholesalers, office suppliers, travel agents and many other market areas. The three aspects of package design described above are tested in the following ways.

Attention value

The degree to which a pack is able to draw attention to itself and communicate its salient features when surrounded by competing packs is tested on two factors: 'stand-out' and 'identification'.

Stand-out is defined as the attention-getting value or impact of the pack when seen in a competing display, and is measured by 'find time'. Respondents are shown usually six realistic-looking product displays with the test pack present and three in which it is absent, the order of presentation and test item being varied for different respondents. Minimum average time in seconds taken to identify the test item is used as the criterion for stand-out or attention value.

Identification is related to the respondents' ability to recognize the brand and the readiness with which salient messages on the product are absorbed. This is measured using a *tachistoscope*, a device that displays a picture for a specific length of time, which can be varied. The respondent is shown a picture of the pack for periods of, say, one-hundredth of a second up to two seconds. After each exposure the respondent reports what has been seen. This indicates the readiness with which various aspects of the pack, including the brand name, are identified. The technique can be used to test different pack designs, colours, brand names, messages and so on.

Functional performance

The ability of the packaging to contain, protect and store the product is testable without the need for consumer research. Where consumers' views are relevant in pack design is in ease of opening, convenience in use, and suitability for closing and reopening if the product is used in that way. For this reason functional performance tests must attempt to replicate in-use conditions.

Products that are opened and consumed only once can be tested in the *test centres*, *hall tests* or *mobile vans*. Ring-pull cans were tested against tear-off tag cans by inviting consumers into mobile vans to try the two opening devices. Film cameras recorded the manner in which respondents handled and opened cans. A similar approach might be used to test whether package instructions are read, and how readily they are followed.

Products that are used over time must be tested by *in-home placement tests*. The packaging is usually plain or blind to eliminate symbolic interference from brand name or pack design. The now familiar flip-top packaging of cigarettes was developed in this way. The product is left with the respondent to use under normal conditions. Often two packs will be tested: either two test-pack variants, or the test-pack against the current pack or a competitor's pack. At the end of the period the respondent is asked which pack is preferred, and why.

Communication value

The introduction to this section on package testing pointed out that an important function for packaging, particularly if sold in a self-service context, is to communicate positive messages about the product to the buyer or user. This is measured in two ways: package concept association tests and pseudo product tests.

Package concept associations are generated using small-scale qualitative research procedures such as group discussions or depth interviews. Respondents are shown the packet and asked what thoughts come to mind as they look at it, what kind of product might be in it, who might use the product, and how, and what type of shop they would expect such a product to be sold in. This exploratory research may be used to generate a range of attitude statements about the product, its attributes and its appeal to users. These statements could then form the basis of rating scales to be applied in a quantitative questionnaire survey, with the respondents being asked their degree of agreement with each statement related to a particular pack design.

The pseudo product-test procedure measures the degree to which the communication value of the package affects the respondents' perceptions of the product it contains. A representative sample, often 200–400 consumers, will be given two packs of the product to use, either side-by-side or one after the other. Respondents are asked to compare the products inside and rate them for various attributes, e.g. taste, quality and strength. In fact, the only difference lies in the packaging. In a beverage test 75 per cent of respondents reported one version of the 'product' to be more acceptable than the other on taste, when the only difference lay in the packaging.

Both these types of communication value tests demonstrate the high level of influence that packaging may exert over the physical perception of contents. In the first case, consumers form quite well-developed expectations about the product and its attributes from looking at packaging, and this must be expected to have an influence on their decision to purchase. The second method goes one stage further in demonstrating that liking or disliking the product in use may be modified by the pack it comes in.

16.10 Notes for Guide 4

Decisions about price

Research is only one input into a company's decision about the price of its products. Other important factors will relate to the cost of production, profit objectives set by the organization for its products, and perhaps the overall financial health of the organization. However, price is an important determinant of whether, and how much of, a product can be sold. For this reason most organizations will want information on the price of products in the marketplace and on consumers' response to different price levels.

Observation research

Market price can be determined using desk research or straightforward observation. This will indicate the highest and lowest market prices at which the product is sold and the range of pricing in between. The ruling price for a market is not necessarily calculated by a straight arithmetic average of the prices available. It is usual to take into account the fact that the ruling price in a market may be determined by the brand leader, particularly when the brand leader has a high level of market dominance. Ruling price may be calculated by multiplying market share by price, to produce a weighted average.

Syndicated research services

Another source of information about price, including different pricing for different packs in different outlets, is by buying syndicated data. Most retail audits provide information of this type. These sources of data will give a clear indication about competitive pricing in the marketplace and will therefore suggest guidelines appropriate to pursuing different marketing tactics. It will indicate the price levels relevant to pursuing a premium policy or a cut-price strategy.

Consumer price responsiveness

This is useful when attempting to estimate a sales forecast, or to indicate the effect on sales volume of a possible change in price. Two techniques can be applied in attempting to determine consumer propensity to purchase products at different prices.

Buy–response research: The buy–response method embodies the idea of price as an indicator of quality. It recognizes that there is a price below which consumers would not be prepared to buy the product, because they would distrust its quality, and that there is a price above which consumers would not be prepared to buy a product, because they would believe it to be too expensive for its worth. This results in buy–response curves, which map the probability that respondents will buy the product in the range of prices between the minimum and maximum. This is discovered using a quantitative survey in which the respondents are asked whether they would buy the product at up to 10 different prices, which cover the range between the minimum and the maximum. A curve is then drawn of probability of purchase against price. For products entering into existing markets, respondents could also be asked the 'price last paid' and this too would be charted. Analysis of the charts produced from this procedure is thought to indicate optimum price levels.

Propensity-to-purchase research: Attempts to calculate consumers' propensity to purchase a product at different price levels have used mock selling situations. At the end of the product tests, and sometimes at the end of concept tests, the interviewer may offer to sell a pack of the product to the respondent. The frequency with which they agree to buy at different price levels is recorded and this is thought to give some indication of the product's worth to relevant consumers.

16.11 Notes for Guide 5

Research about advertising may be used before, during or after an advertising campaign, and if the campaign is of sufficient significance it may be worthwhile using all three time-points.

Pre-campaign research

This is useful to assist in defining the problem that the advertising campaign may seek to solve, to guide creative strategy development and indicate the type and level of advertising that may be required. The objectives for research before a campaign are to increase the effectiveness of the campaign when it does run, to screen out any negatives in ideas being considered, and to select the best ideas. Those who argue against pre-campaign research do so on the grounds that it is generally artificial and limited in nature.

Research during the campaign

This is most likely to be carried out for a long-running and important campaign in which specific objectives for levels of awareness have been set. The use of tracking studies during the campaign monitors performance and allows fine-tuning if, say, objectives are being achieved in one area and not in another. Resources can be reallocated to compensate for this.

Post-campaign research

This measures the degree to which advertising objectives set for the campaign have been achieved. The argument for post-campaign research is that feedback from one campaign becomes input for improving the next. The argument against is that spending research money after the media money has been spent is futile. Research money is more constructively spent on guiding decision making before advertising campaigns than on assessing performance afterwards.

Factors to consider

Which research technique will be appropriate for any particular advertising problem will depend on the objective and significance of the campaign under consideration, the amount of uncertainty about the brand and the market segment, and the possible outcomes of advertising expenditure. Also relevant will be the purpose for which the research is being used. Research for creative development is typically small scale. It uses qualitative methods that are relatively quick and inexpensive, but rich in insight, ideas and depth. For targeting, media planning and campaign evaluation, large-scale quantitative surveys or syndicated data are more commonly used.

At a more sophisticated level, when attempts to measure or predict the effects of particular advertising approaches are required, some form of research experiment is normally indicated.

Experimentation in research may use any of the data-collection methods discussed. The key feature lies in the approach, structure and design of the research procedure. Experiments are normally used when the decision maker has more than one option open, and requires data on the possible outcomes of alternative strategies. The implication of this is that the research design must be sufficiently rigorous to ensure that valid comparisons can be made. Using research in experiments was discussed more fully in Chapter 12.

Recall tests

Respondents are exposed to test or actual advertisements for a specific period and then asked what they remember from the advertisement. Recall test are used in both pre- and post-testing of advertising.

Unaided recall

The respondent spontaneously recalls advertisements and their content from a test selection, or from memory of actual advertising or product classes. This is thought to measure levels of awareness and brand salience of advertising.

Aided recall

The respondent is shown a selection of advertisements or cards with brand names on (usually after a campaign has been run) and asked which advertisements they have seen. This is thought to measure campaign penetration.

Problems exist in using recall as a measure of advertising effectiveness because brand leaders have higher levels of recall, advertising seen in one medium may be reported as having been seen in another, and effects of earlier advertising campaigns may be difficult to distinguish from effects of current campaigns. Respondent variability in memory may also influence results. In general, recall is best used as a comparative measure, i.e. repeating the same test on different occasions and measuring differences.

Recognition

Recognition is mainly used in post-testing advertising. For print media, respondents are taken through a current issue of a magazine or newspaper they report having read and asked to say which articles and advertisements they looked at. Items are scored for their degree of readership: 'noted', 'seen–associated' (saw advertisement and associated it with correct brand name), 'read most' (read advertisement in some detail). These are called Starch scores, after the man who invented the method, now used as the basis for the Gallup Field Readership Index. For television, respondents are shown pictures from television commercials that may or may not have been shown in their areas, and are asked whether they saw the commercials. Recognition scores are thought to measure campaign penetration.

Comprehension

Respondents are asked what they feel are the main points that an advertisement was trying to make.

Advertising hardware tests

A few experimental measuring devices have been applied in communications or advertising research. The method involves connecting the respondent to the appropriate piece of hardware, which measures the degree of reaction. Inevitably, such experiments can only be conducted on a small scale, and the artificiality of the laboratory type of situation under which the experiment is conducted gives rise to the concern that the results cannot be validly generalized to the real-world situation under which advertisements are normally seen. However, given the very high levels of media expenditure necessary for mass-advertised products, it seems reasonable to attempt any possible experiments to ensure that the layout and content of the advertisement selected should be as effective as possible. These techniques are most useful in a minor diagnostic way, and are generally applied on a very small scale, if at all.

Eye camera

This device records the passage of the eye as it looks at a test advertisement. It indicates where the eye falls first, the path it takes around the advertisement, where it lingers and what it misses altogether. The combination of this technique with subsequent recall questioning indicates how effective parts of the advertisement have been in communicating with the respondent.

Tachistoscope

This device exposes test material such as the advertisement logo, brand name or pack design to the respondent for a period of time measured in one-hundredths of a second. The amount of time for which the respondent can observe the test material is gradually increased, and after each exposure the respondent is asked to report what has been seen. It is assumed that the most effective advertisements are those in which the respondent most quickly reports perceiving the name of the product, the pack in a competing display, and so on. This is a useful technique for improving advertisement and display design if its basic assumption is accepted. There is some evidence that advertisements that are not rapidly perceived but are studied in detail can also be effective, so the decision maker must decide whether this device is relevant to the objectives of any particular communication.

Psychogalvanometer

This device is also used as a lie detector. It is attached to the hand and measures electrical skin resistance. Skin resistance varies with the amount of moisture (sweat) present on the skin, and this varies with the degree of emotional arousal in the individual. When used to test advertisements, the psychogalvanometer is therefore measuring the degree to which the advertisement affects the individual emotionally. Since an important objective of some advertisements is to create the emotion of liking for the product, this can be a useful test, particularly when combined with the individual's self-report of whether or not the advertisement was liked.

Advertising tracking studies

Measurements of awareness, penetration or liking are taken regularly using a quantitative survey to track changes over time. A special syndicated service may be used (see Chapter 4). Alternatively, the same questions may be regularly added to an omnibus survey. If sufficiently important, an organization may decide to commission a regular made-to-measure survey to track advertising performance. This would normally be combined with research into other aspects of the product.

16.12 Summary

Research applications in marketing decision making are considered by identifying marketing problems and suggesting data requirements and sources used in providing research data to help to solve them. Five areas are covered: market analysis, developing new products and services, selecting brand names and pack designs, pricing decisions and advertising decisions. The research approaches suggested are referenced back to explanations given earlier in the book, or to the notes that accompany each guide, and appear at the end of the chapter.

17 Where do you go from here?

17.1 Introduction

This book introduces marketing research:

	Chapter
What marketing research is	1
Why an organization needs it	2
What research can be carried out within an organization	3
What research data is already available	4
How research surveys are carried out	5–10
How research services are bought	11
How research is used	12–16

Where you go from here depends on your answers to the questions below.

17.2 Who are you and in which direction do you want to go?

17.2.1 Who are you?

You may be a manager in some specialist area of marketing, or a manager in some other functional area working for a consumer organization, a service organization, an industrial organization, or local or central government. Your motivation for buying *Marketing Research for Managers* is your desire to use marketing research techniques appropriately and intelligently in improving your decision making.

A second possibility is that you are a junior manager or an aspiring junior manager, perhaps a management trainee. You have been assigned some responsibility in the research area in your organization and feel that you would like to do some marketing research yourself on behalf of your organization.

A third possibility is that you are pursuing studies in the business area and wish to know more about marketing research, either because of its value as a managerial tool, or because you wish to pass the marketing research component of your examination system.

17.2.2 In which direction do you want to go?

A title like *Marketing Research for Managers* implies the first step in the development of your knowledge and expertise in this area. There are two directions in which that development may go. Either you may concentrate on developing your use of marketing research techniques for decision making in whatever area you may operate managerially (i.e. develop as a research user), or you may wish to concentrate on marketing research and become a specialist in that area of management (i.e. develop as a research practitioner). The implications of both possibilities are shown in Figure 17.1 and discussed in the following sections.

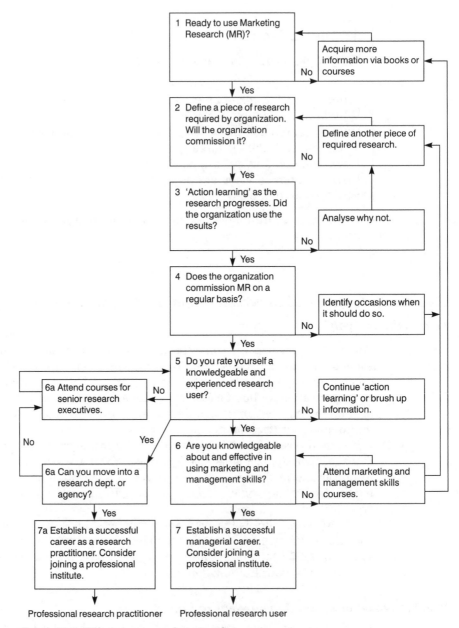

Figure 17.1   Where do you go from here?

17.3 Developing skills as a research user

Step 1

Decide whether you already have sufficient background information and experience to use market research intelligently. If the answer is 'no', then you need more information or experience, or both. More information can be gained about the subject by going on to read books that deal with the topics introduced in this one, in more detail and in more depth.

Further reading

Using books as a basis for acquiring more information is cheap and time-efficient, in the sense that you can acquire the information at your convenience. However, books suffer from being only a one-way source of communication and impose the self-discipline and lack of interaction of learning alone. The book list shown at the end of this chapter suggests further reading which follows on from this introduction to the subject.

Courses

A second possibility for acquiring more information is to attend a course on marketing research. Business training courses provide a more effective 'hot-house' learning situation than is possible when acquiring information from books. They are also two-way communication systems, in which it is possible to tailor the information to meet precise requirements by the simple expedient of asking questions of the lecturer. Another advantage of attending courses is the enormous amount of learning that goes on from interactions with other delegates to the course.

The Chartered Institute of Marketing and the Market Research Society (MRS) both run courses and seminars on aspects of marketing research. The MRS runs an advanced certificate and diploma course in marketing research and there is also a National Vocational Qualification (NVQ) in marketing research. In addition, the MRS runs an extensive training programme covering many different aspects of the discipline. The MRS also accredits a number of Masters degrees in Marketing Research. An enquiry to these organizations or a search of their websites will provide descriptions of their courses and seminar programmes. Keep an eye on the business and marketing press for details of other management training organizations and institutions, and the courses they offer.

Step 2

If and when the answer to Step 1 is 'yes', then the next stage is to define a piece of research required by your organization that will be of indisputable value to it. Chapter 2 should assist in this process. Identify an important decision that has to be made by the organization and indicate in writing exactly how the use of marketing research will improve the decision-making situation. Use this as a basis for lobbying the pursestring holders above you, in favour of commissioning a marketing research survey. Repeat the process on appropriate occasions, as suitable decisions arise within the organization for which you believe marketing research could provide a valuable input, until you are successful.

Step 3

Once your organization has approved the commissioning of a marketing research survey you are in a position to design an 'action learning' programme for yourself. This is done by using Chapter 11 to ensure that a good research organization is commissioned for the survey. As each stage of the survey in action unfolds, practise your new-found research skills by making 'shadow' decisions and comparing them with those advocated by the research agency. For example, set out in writing your research objectives and survey objectives drawn from these. In commissioning the research programme from two or three agencies, discussions with research professionals may cause you to revise your list of objectives. As you do so, take note of your reasons for the revision and what you can learn from them.

The next stage will be the choice of research method. Prepare a research design plan independently from the agency and, when they return with the research proposals, compare them with your own. Did you suggest the same research design as the professionals are suggesting to you? If not, why not? Whose are more likely to achieve the stated research objectives most effectively and most efficiently? You may decide that the research agency's suggestions are better than your own, in which case you will have learnt why in analysing the basis for your decision. The possibility exists, however, that you may believe your own suggestions would improve upon the research design suggested by the agency. In this case, you have the basis for an extremely constructive discussion with the research agency.

The next stage is questionnaire design: repeat the process. In either case you win. Either the agency's questionnaire is better than yours and you can learn from that, or you have suggestions that would improve the questionnaire produced by the agency, and your company gains better research from that.

When it comes to fieldwork, spend a day or two in the field with interviewers to get the feel of the raw data gathering process. You will learn something about interviewing techniques, but you will learn even more in terms of insight and understanding which will be of great value to you in interpreting findings at the end of the research survey. At the data analysis stage visit the agency and discuss their systems for data preparation, processing, editing, coding, tabulating and statistical analysis. Talk through with the researcher what tables and statistical analysis will be most appropriate and most helpful in dealing with the data they have generated.

Finally, sketch out for yourself how you would write the report on the research and, before the actual report is written, discuss with the research agency executive his or her own approach to report writing. Once again, you will either learn from the agency's experience or be in the position to improve what the research agency is about to do for you.

Step 4

If you took enough care at the outset to ensure that the research being conducted was going to be of real value to decision making in the organization, then the outcome will be that your organization will find that research has a positive, constructive and cost-effective role to play in its decision-making procedures. Once this idea is accepted within an organization, then commissioning a research survey the next time around becomes normal operating procedure.

Step 5

By repeating the same action learning programme suggested above on subsequent surveys, you will eventually reach the point where you are coming up with either the same recommendations that research professionals would make, or better ones. At this point you are ready to bring in other individuals to work for you and to establish a research department in your own organization, simply by buying in fieldwork, data processing and other research commodities as you require them.

Step 6

Once you are a confident, experienced and knowledgeable research user, the next step is to develop and improve your analytical and decision-making skills by attending senior management courses dealing with any of the particular problems you may have or skills you may wish to acquire; for example, new product decision making, advertising and pricing. As your analytical and decision-making business skills improve, so will your confidence and career prospects.

Step 7

As a last stage in being a marketing professional you may decide to join a professional institute such as the Chartered Institute of Marketing. Information about the costs and benefits of this organization can be obtained from them.

17.4 Developing skills as a research practitioner

Follow Steps 1–5 as in Section 17.3.

Step 6a

Develop and improve your research skills by attending courses for senior researchers on techniques and applications. The more sophisticated your professional development as a researcher becomes, the more likely it is that you will be interested in building up and heading your own research department within an organization. Alternatively, you may wish to move into a research agency and become a professional researcher.

Step 7a

The professional institute for marketing researchers is the Market Research Society. You should consider joining this organization to pursue your interests in this area.

17.5 Passing examinations

This book has been approved by both the Chartered Institute of Marketing and the Communications, Advertising and Marketing (CAM) Foundation as being appropriate for students of their examinations. It has been recommended as a course text for students following degree courses, BTEC courses or other general courses in business or management. For students taking a specific marketing research examination, it is unlikely that, from the technical point of view, reading this book alone will prove sufficient preparation. In particular, the subjects of sampling and data analysis have not been treated in the statistical manner required for most examination courses. Marketing research students are therefore strongly advised to do more specific statistical studying in these areas, using the recommendations given in the book list in Section 17.6.

17.6 Further reading

Biased towards research in consumer markets

Aaker, D. and Day, G. (2000) *Marketing Research* (7th edition), John Wiley.

Aaker, D. and Kumar, V. (2002) *Essentials of Marketing Research* (2nd edition), John Wiley.

Chisnall, P. (2001) *Marketing Research* (6th edition), McGraw-Hill.

Crimp, M. and Wright, L. (2000) *Marketing Research Process* (5th edition), Prentice Hall.

Hague, P. (1992) *Marketing Research in Practice*, Kogan Page.

Kent, R. (1999) *Marketing research: measurement, method and application*, International Thomson Business.

Worcester, R. M. and Downham, J. (eds) (1988) *Consumer Market Research Handbook*, McGraw-Hill.

International marketing research

Douglas, S. and Craig, S. (2000) *International marketing research* (2nd edition), John Wiley.

European Society for Opinion and Market Research (ESOMAR) (2002) *Handbook of Market and Opinion Research*.

Lewis, K. and Housden, M. (1998) *International Marketing in Action*, Kogan Page.

Secondary research

Jackson, P. (1994) *Desk Research*, Kogan Page.

Marketing management

Jobber, D. (2001) *Principles and Practice of Marketing* (3rd edition), McGraw-Hill.

Kotler, P. (1997) *Marketing Management* (9th edition), Prentice Hall.

Thomas B. and Housden M. (2001) *Direct Marketing in Practice.* Butterworth-Heinemann.

Wilson, R., Gilligan, C. and Pearson, D. (1998) *Strategic Marketing Management* (2nd edition), Butterworth-Heinemann.

Statistical background

Birn, R. (1992) *The Effective Use of Market Research* (3rd edition), Kogan Page.

Diamantopoulos, A. and Schlegelmilch, B. B. (1997) *Taking the Fear out of Data Analysis*, Dryden Press.

Sekaran, U. (2000) *Research Methods for Business* (3rd edition), John Wiley.

Qualitative research

Carson, D. (2001) *Qualitative Marketing Research*, Sage.

Daymon, C. and Holloway, I. (2002) *Qualitative Research Methods in Public Relations and Marketing Communications*, Routledge.

Mariampolski, H. (2001) *Qualitative Market Research: A Comprehensive Guide*, Sage.

Questionnaire design

Hague, P. (1993) *Questionnaire Design*, Kogan Page.

Industrial markets

Sutherland, K. (ed.) (1991) *Researching Business Markets*, Kogan Page.

Experimental research

Kent, R. (1993) *Marketing Research in Action*, Routledge.

Tull, D. S. and Hawkins, D. (1993) *Marketing Research. Measurement & Method* (6th edition), Macmillan.

Journals

Admap: www.warc.com

Harvard Business Review: www.harvardbusinessonline.hbsp.harvard.edu/b02/en/hbr/hbr_home.jhtml

Journal of Advertising Research: www.arfsite.org/Webpages/JAR_pages/jarhome.htm

Journal of Consumer Research: www.journals.uchicago.edu/JCR/home.html
Journal of the Market Research Society: www.mrs.org.uk
Qualitative Market Research: www.emeraldinsight.com/qmr.htm

Periodicals and trade press

Campaign: www.brandrepublic.com/magazines/marketing/
Marketing: www.brandrepublic.com/magazines/marketing/
Marketing Week: www.mad.co.uk
Precision Marketing: www.mad.co.uk
Research: www.mrs.org.uk

Index